VESSELS OF RAGE, ENGINES OF POWER

Also by James Graham:

CANCER SELECTION: The New Theory of Evolution

VESSELS OF RAGE, ENGINES OF POWER

The Secret History of Alcoholism

James Graham

Aculeus Press Inc.

Lexington 1994

Published by Aculeus Press Inc.
Post Office Box 142, Lexington, Virginia 24450, USA

Printed in the United States of America

Publisher's Cataloging in Publication
(Prepared by Quality Books Inc.)

Graham, James, 1929-
    Vessels of rage, engines of power : the secret history of
alcoholism / James Graham.
    p. cm.
    Includes bibliographical references and index.
    ISBN 0-9630242-2-1 (Cloth)
    ISBN 0-9630242-4-8 (Paper)

    1. Alcoholism--Psychological effects. 2. Alcoholics. 3. Stalin,
Joseph, 1879-1953--Alcohol use.   I. Title. II. Title: Secret history
of alcoholism.

HV5045.G73 1993   616.861
                                          QBI93-593

Library of Congress Catalog Number : 93-70831

MAY   1996

To Rosemary and Ellen

PREFACE

Who should read this book?

Although it is, I suppose, natural for authors to proclaim, "Everyone!" there are good reasons for seeking the widest possible audience for this book. Although I have kept a number of different prospective audiences in mind as I wrote it, the book is aimed squarely at people living under the gross misconception that alcoholism is a problem that affects others -- but not themselves.

In order to convince such readers that they are wildly and dangerously in error, I have assumed that the typical reader has no prior knowledge of alcoholism. I then strive to convince him or her of a single truth, the fact that makes alcoholism everyone's business: alcoholics inflict great harm on other people, in ways least suspected by the average victim. With this objective in mind, I deliberately avoid aspects of alcoholism that have already been adequately covered elsewhere. There is, for example, nothing in the book about alcoholics driving while intoxicated. This is not because I don't think they are responsible for most drunk driving fatalities (they are, and I do), but because that fact has already entered the public's consciousness.

As for the already informed, the professional specialists, and those thousands of Alcoholics Anonymous and Al-Anon members who are self-made experts, I think they will find my approach to the subject original. They should, at the very least, find my identification of history's "missing" alcoholics enlightening.

Although the book is intended to be instructive rather than therapeutic, it may nonetheless benefit both recovering alcoholics and those who have survived the alcoholism of others. Because I am emphasizing the destructive behavior of active alcoholics, those

already in recovery may find their intent to remain sober rein-
forced. As for the survivors of life with alcoholics, they will find
that my explanations shed some light on the behavior they have
witnessed and endured. Improved understanding may help to ease
their pain.

Now who, exactly, am I to claim special knowledge of alcoholism?
What are my credentials?

I can't resist paraphrasing that heavily-armed bandit in the film
The Treasure of Sierra Madre, the swarthy fellow on horseback who,
with his equally-menacing underlings in tow, preposterously claimed
(to the American prospectors they had every intention of robbing)
that they were all really Mexican police officers. When asked by
a terrified Gringo why they weren't wearing badges, the boss-bandit
looked down from his saddle at his unarmed victim and snarled,
"We don't need no *stinking* badges!"

When it comes to writing a book on alcoholism, I don't need no
stinking credentials. For one thing, there aren't any. No university issues doctorates in the disease. Anyone knowledgeable in
alcoholism has acquired that knowledge on his or her own. This
includes physicians. Their training in the subject is notoriously
deficient.

But in fairness to readers, since I do claim to be heavily-armed
with alcoholism knowledge and understanding, I will explain how
I came to know what I know.

There are two great human resources in alcoholism, two large
groups of people with "front-line" experience. The first group
consists of recovered alcoholics, those men and women, now sober,
who can look back with clarity and honesty at their own behavior
during their drinking years. Some of the most insightful books on
alcoholism have come from among their ranks. The second group
of "combat veterans" consists of people who have experienced --
first-hand -- alcoholism in others, those who were exposed to active
(drinking) alcoholics at close quarters -- for long periods of time.
Persons who have spent hundreds or even thousands of hours in
the company of those afflicted with this frightening disorder can
accumulate an enormous store of knowledge. And because the
disease causes heavily-patterned behavior, experience with even a
single alcoholic has the potential to teach volumes about all of

them.

That's how I learned about alcoholic behavior -- by observing alcoholism in others.

For obvious reasons, I cannot identify the alcoholics whose behavior "taught" me much of what I now know about the disease, but I can say that I was not exposed to it as a child. Not having an alcoholic parent undoubtedly spared me much emotional pain and, perhaps, permanent psychological damage, but I suspect it also enabled me to be more emotionally detached when I began to realize that the monster had sneaked into my life.

For my luck surely did change as an adult; I have lost count of the number of alcoholics I have known. In addition to several in my domestic life, I've worked with scores of them. Working for a number of large organizations for decades, moving to different assignments in this country and abroad, I probably worked closely with thousands of people. For more than twenty-five of those years my knowledge and awareness of the disease was keen. This asset enabled me to identify as active alcoholics many close colleagues, including some of my bosses, and to watch, warily, as they acted out the patterns I describe in the text.

My amateur status actually enhanced my observation ability, for there is in alcoholism, as in physics, a Heisenberg Effect. Werner Heisenberg discovered the principle that the act of observing physical phenomena influences the target of observation. So it is with alcoholics. Professional observers cause changes in the behavior of alcoholics to such an extent that valid *in vivo* observation is virtually impossible -- for them. If, for example, investigators were to place a dozen active alcoholics in a residential facility, provide them with lots of booze and then watch their daily activities, they would probably not see much of the behavior I describe in the following pages -- and they might not see any of it. The reason for this is that alcoholics modify their behavior when they suspect scrutiny. Most of the alcoholics I observed in the workplace and other situations didn't know I had any special interest in or knowledge of the subject, so they did not greatly modify their behavior in my presence. A few of them learned of my suspicions, however, and when they did they severely altered their behavior patterns. (I describe one example in Chapter Three.) But in most cases, and for most of the time, I was able to observe alcoholics from a concealed vantage point, one not available to professionals.

Even with the advantage of my "covert" scrutiny, direct observation of alcoholism-in-action would have done me no good if I had not also learned something about the disease. I could not have known when I was encountering alcoholism-influenced behavior unless I had done some homework.

I acquired lots of information by attending meetings. I went to Alcoholics Anonymous (AA) meetings (the "open" meetings which welcome nonalcoholics) and to Al-Anon meetings. Most of these were in large metropolitan areas and at several of them well-known alcoholism authorities were invited to lecture. Some of those specialists were especially enlightening. At one New York City meeting in the late 1960s, for example, I first heard the blasphemous assertion (by a practicing psychiatrist) that alcoholics had no more "underlying" emotional problems than nonalcoholics.

I also talked informally to AAs and to Al-Anon members, many of whom are extraordinarily well-informed about this complex problem. AAs were especially helpful in answering my questions about such strange phenomena as denial, blackouts, and the difference between "dry" and "sober." Veteran Al-Anon members helped in many areas, including the matter of alcoholism's invisibility.

And I read books on alcoholism -- a lot of them. I remember telling someone in the early 1970s that I had read at least 100 books on the disease. I also studied scores of pamphlets published by AA, Al-Anon, the National Council on Alcoholism, the Smithers Foundation and others. The bibliography doesn't begin to suggest the breadth of my reading in the field.

I also *thought* about alcoholism. I especially reflected upon the contrast between my book knowledge and my personal experience. The standard works had little to say about what I found most disturbing and baffling about this complex problem: the great and distinct damage alcoholics deliberately inflict on others. Published works on alcoholism in industry, for example, claim it causes absenteeism. Perhaps it does among blue collar workers, but the alcoholic executives I worked with seldom took a day off. The problems they created (including the arbitrary firing of competent subordinates) were far more serious than frequent absences, but this abusiveness was not even mentioned in the books I read.

It occurred to me that if guides on industrial alcoholism ignored the devastation caused by alcoholic executives, perhaps our historians have closed their eyes to alcoholics who abused political power. Of course, some well-known alcoholics do appear with regularity in the literature, but the usual suspects -- Sam Houston is especially popular -- are held up as inspirational examples of how even down-and-out alcoholics can overcome their addiction and live successful lives. According to the historical record, alcoholism never created a single tyrant. Based on my real-life experience, this seemed unlikely.

Exploratory visits to the biography sections of public libraries quickly convinced me that my hunch was correct. Concentrating, initially, on history's "bad boys," I soon assembled a number of famous evil-doers whose alcoholism had been missed by conventional historians. I uncovered others (Beethoven and Paine, for example) serendipitously, when I came across references to their heavy drinking while reading for my general amusement.

In gathering material on these famous over-looked alcoholics, I relied extensively on the research of others, especially biographers. This may present a minor problem for professional historians, who do not encourage reliance on secondary sources. But for this subject I think secondary sources are actually preferable. For one thing, because I cover so much territory I could not possibly have gathered the information from primary sources even if I had mastered the historians' techniques.

There is, however, a more important reason for my claim that secondary sources are superior. Alcoholism is probably the most under-studied of all complex subjects. No accurate information on it is provided in the academic programs available to undergraduate or graduate students of history -- it isn't "serious" enough. As a result, highly intelligent and well-educated individuals, who wouldn't think of writing a single paragraph about, for example, schizophrenia or cancer until they had consulted specialists in those complex diseases, will nonetheless toss off assertions about alcoholism without so much as cracking a book on it, or talking to a recovered alcoholic, or consulting a professional specialist.

So intense and pervasive is this cavalier attitude that of the scores of biographies of alcoholics I have read, I can recall only two or three in which the author seemed to possess some knowledge of the disease. All others make it implicitly clear in their texts, and in their bibliographies, that they considered it unnecessary to research alcoholism. I found myself musing that there might exist somewhere a Biographers' Academy, an institution that requires its graduates to take a Preservation of Alcoholism-Ignorance Oath -- a solemn promise that, whenever they encounter exceptional drinking or even rumors of drinking in a historical personage, they were to ignore the great body of alcoholism literature available (in public, if not academic, libraries) but were nonetheless to pontificate on the matter. Things are so bad that in more than one work, the biographer confidently assures his readers that a particular individual could not possibly be an alcoholic and then presents (in some cases on the very next page!) strong evidence to support exactly the opposite conclusion. (Waite's book on Hitler and Marek's on Beethoven contain especially good examples.)

This near-universal ignorance of alcoholism actually worked to my advantage. Unwittingly acting as my collaborators, many scholars gathered solid evidence of symptoms in their subjects. Because they displayed no awareness of the alcoholism-significance of particular facts -- Beethoven's bizarre changes of residence is an example -- the information is particularly trustworthy. Unintending to support the conclusion I reached (and in the case of Waite and Marek, being explicitly hostile to it), they gathered information more creditable than any that could have been assembled by an advocate of the alcoholism hypothesis. These diligent researchers, in other words, unintentionally honed a sharp edge to the axe I wield in the following pages.

I seem to be the first to identify a number of individuals of historical importance as alcoholics. More important, because I believe alcoholism is a powerful determinant of destructive behavior, I may be the first to assert that it is responsible for much wrongdoing of historical significance.

I have not systematically searched the literature for this purpose, so I will not list all my potential claims of priority. I may be the first to suggest that the question of why so many famous writers were alcoholics is answered by radically reformulating the question. I think it even likelier that no one else has said, as I do in Chapter Seven, that their addiction greatly influenced what these alcoholics wrote. Also, I may be the first to identify false accusation as a form of abuse favored by alcoholics, and to argue that this symptomatic behavior is what motivated some of history's more notorious false accusers. I might also be the first to notice that so many traitors were alcoholics and to suggest an explanation. And, for all I know, I might even be the first to offer a reasoned explanation for the rarity of baldness among alcoholics. But if others have reached these or other insights included in the book before me, I will cheerfully acknowledge their priority.

In fact, some ideas are deliberate extensions of those originated by others. The concept that alcoholism causes egomania is, at the very least, implicit in the work and writings of Bill Wilson, the founding genius of Alcoholics Anonymous. Although I don't recall reading the works of the psychiatrist Alfred Adler, his concept of ego compensation probably influenced my conclusion that the psychological effects of alcohol addiction drives many victims to extraordinary achicvement. Elias Canneti was another important indirect influence. I read his astonishing book *Crowds and Power* (Continuum, 1960) twice during the 1960s; his ideas were part of my mental inventory when I began to think deeply about alcoholism. Others, whose names I don't even know, undoubtedly influenced my thinking about this complex and fascinating (but ugly) subject.

The book may strike some as grossly unbalanced. I say next to nothing about some of the more flamboyant symptoms that can afflict alcoholics (delirium tremens, for example). When I write about well-known alcoholics, I write exclusively about their negative behavior -- saying little about their putatively attractive traits (with the exception of "alcoholic charm"), and even less about the accomplishments that made them famous. This is intentional. It is the nasty behavior that makes alcoholism such a terrible disease, not the drinking *per se*, or the serious physical damage it causes. Other diseases, after all, wreck bodies, but no other disorder does as much harm to those who come in contact with the victim. I am convinced, in other words, that my approach is correct; if the general reader wants to learn useful and basic information about this strange disease, this "unbalanced" book is the one to read.

My central assertion that alcoholism causes abusive behavior may cause some readers to may make one of two similar, and equally invalid, objections.

One objection may go something like this: "Okay, so most alcoholics are abusive, some extremely so, but many ugly characters have not been alcoholics. I've never heard of an alcoholic Mafioso. Saddam Hussein and Qadhafi aren't boozers, and there's no evidence that Son of Sam or that awful serial killer in the Ukraine were drinkers." My response to such anticipated criticism? "Correct, but so what?" The validity of my assertion that alcoholism causes violent behavior, for example, is not in anyway negated by violence committed by moderate drinkers, or by teetotalers. To quote my high school geometry teacher, Mr. Shields, "When I say that all horses are four-legged animals, I am not saying that all four-legged animals are horses."

Another objector might say, "My Uncle Fred is an alcoholic, and he wouldn't hurt a fly." Well, if you've already noticed that your uncle is an alcoholic he probably has reached the late stage of the disease (often called chronic alcoholism), is getting drunk every day, and has given up trying to "pass" as a normal nonalcoholic. As I explain in the main text, constantly-drunk alcoholics (not all of whom live on street corners) do indeed tend to hurt themselves rather than others. But if there are any not-yet-chronic active alcoholics functioning as well-behaved members of society -- holding down jobs, interacting well with nonalcoholics, treating their families and others decently -- they are the (extremely rare) exceptions that prove the general rule.

To avoid this sort of invalid thinking, I encourage readers to keep in mind, as they work their way through the book, what is both a caution and a claim to accuracy: Alcoholism explains *this* behavior of *these* people.

A few points about style. In most cases, I give the source of my information in the text rather than in a footnote or a backnote. I do this because of the generally negative nature of my assertions about people, many of whom are well known and some of whom (despite the fact that most of them are dead) have their admirers. When I claim, for example, that a well-known 1960s radical was a-bottle-of-brandy-a-day drinker and that he once brutally raped another well-known male radical, I think it best that I cite my source right there in the text.

Throughout the book I refer to alcoholism as just that, "alcoholism," or, occasionally, "alcohol addiction." I eschew the currently voguish term "alcohol abuse" because I consider it both too broad and too narrow. It is too broad because anyone can "abuse" alcohol, and it's too narrow because alcoholics do things that are far worse than their consumption, or abuse, of alcohol.

More often than not, I stick with tradition and use male pronouns when writing generically of alcoholics. I know this slights female alcoholics but I assure any of them who read the book that no insult is intended. I am fully aware of their representation in the ranks of boozers (to use a term, popular with AAs, that appears once or twice in the text.)

Now for the organization of the book. Most chapters are heavily anecdotal (alcoholism *is* anecdotal), with the bits of history and biographies organized to make particular points. In Chapter One, I set forth my premise that alcoholism causes egomaniacal behavior -- much of it destructive. I assemble in Chapter Two a small number of "Abusers and Accusers" (some well known, some not) to establish the disease's great power to cause heavily-patterned, harmful behavior. In Chapter Three, the reasons why most alcoholics are not recognized is discussed. In Chapter Four, I point out and explain the extraordinary occurrence of alcoholism in modern traitors. In Chapters Five and Six, I set down key symptoms of the disease. (Persons already familiar with alcoholism should at least take a cursory look at these chapters; certain behavior I identify as symptomatic has been generally ignored.) The strange matter of alcoholism's high incidence among writers (and its influence on their work) is covered in Chapter Seven and its role in homicides, especially serial murders, in Chapter Eight. In Chapter Nine, I cite a number of authorities on the disease's potential for harming children and then identify a small number of murderous sons of alcoholics. In Chapter Ten, I gather a collection of well-known contemporary and historical power-holders who were alcoholics and explain why their terrible behavior was caused by the disease. Chapter Eleven is devoted to establishing Joseph Stalin's alcoholism and to claim it as the fundamental reason for his murderous reign.

After giving it a great deal of thought, I decided not to add a concluding "What Is To Be Done?" chapter. Society is so lacking in awareness of the horror caused by this great disease that suggesting ways out of the monumental mess would be premature. My objective is to open the reader's eyes, not to offer facile solutions. There is no point in offering propositions unless and until a fundamental shift in perception takes place throughout society. This book is intended to encourage that profound change, to lay the groundwork for intelligent action.

I will, however, point out two reactions to alcoholism that ought to be avoided.

Alcohol is no more the cause of alcoholism than carbohydrates are the cause of diabetes; restricting the general availability of alcohol is not the answer. Besides being grossly unfair to those who drink moderately, experience in a number of societies, including, most recently, the former Soviet Union, has demonstrated the futility of trying to keep these addicts away from the substance they crave. The Gorbachev government's curtailment of vodka production led alcoholics not only to drink cologne and after-shave lotion, but to buy up great quantities of toothpaste and shoe polish. I don't know how they did it, but Soviet alcoholics managed to concoct home-made alcohol from those two products.

The other error to be avoided is to absolve alcoholics of responsibility for their behavior. Although it is nearly impossible to influence the *drinking* of alcoholics, society can limit, to some extent, their destructiveness. It is true, as I argue in the following pages, that if they weren't alcoholics they wouldn't commit evil acts, but alcoholics are influenced by society's reactions to their behavior. They should be swiftly punished for the wrongs they commit. It is unfortunate that many alcoholics are behind bars for behavior motivated by this disease (and sadder still that some have been executed), but it is even more tragic when alcoholics elude responsibility for the harm they cause. As is the case with many whose acts are described in the main text, most alcoholics incur no penalties for the great wrongs they commit.

This book has a very long prepublication history. I started to research and to write it in the late 1960s. By 1973, I had a manuscript that the late John Shaffner, a New York literary agent, thought he could sell to a publisher. But despite his rigorous efforts, no house agreed to take it. Although his efforts came to nought, John Shaffner did enlist in the project two people whose encouragement had a lot to do with my decision, many years later, to revise the manuscript and to see it through to publication. The late Dr. Frank A. Seixas, who was then Medical Director of the National Council on Alcoholism, read the manuscript and accepted John Shaffner's invitation to write the introduction to my book, if it was published. Illness prevented Dr. Seixas from any possible participation in the present publication, but his long-ago enthusiasm for the work of an unknown amateur added greatly to my conviction that I had something worthwhile to say.

Manon Tingue bravely took on the job of editing the earlier, messier manuscript. As she will notice, many of her wise suggestions have survived. I am deeply indebted to her not only for her skillful advice and guidance, which has made me a better writer, but for her personal generosity, hospitality, kindness and encouragement. I hope she will not be displeased with this version.

Another person who played an important role (although he doesn't even know I was writing a book) is my "cousin" and lifelong friend, Jim A. He was the first to explain, among other things, that alcoholism doesn't disappear when the blood alcohol level goes to zero and that ugly behavior is symptomatic. With his generous help and wise advice, I began the long journey toward an understanding of what the phrase "Alcoholism is a disease" really means.

As for the present volume, Robin Quinn skillfully corrected errors in grammar and spelling. John Allison, Aculeus Press's title meister, typesetter, indexer, part-time editor, and marketing genius contributed enormously. Truly, he is a man for whom the word "incredible!" says it all.

None of these persons are responsible for any factual errors, or for my opinions or conclusions. As for living individuals named in the text, in those cases where I express an opinion about the presence of alcoholism my reason for doing so is clearly stated. In other cases I neither express nor imply a conclusion of alcoholism for the simple reason that the information cited is insufficient.

JAMES GRAHAM

CONTENTS

VESSELS OF RAGE, ENGINES OF POWER

The Secret History of Alcoholism

1: VICTIMS WHO VICTIMIZE

There is only one good, knowledge, and one evil, ignorance.

Socrates

All great truths begin as blasphemies.

George Bernard Shaw

Many authors of books on alcoholism begin by defining the term "alcoholism," but I will not offer any brief definition. All short descriptions inevitably overemphasize the actual consumption of alcohol and ignore other behavior, things that alcoholics do which are far more grave than abnormal consumption of intoxicating beverages. Instead, the entire book will serve as a "definition" of this extraordinarily complex and baffling phenomenon.

What *is* useful at the start, however, is to understand what alcoholism specialists mean when they say "alcoholism is a disease"; knowing what they mean by "disease" is essential to the comprehension of the ideas in this book.

The National Council on Alcoholism has suggested the following definition of "disease," from *Dorland's Illustrated Medical Dictionary*, 24th Edition, (W.B. Saunders Company, 1973), as a basis for understanding alcoholism:

> A definite morbid *process* having a characteristic train of symptoms, it may affect the whole body or any of its parts, and its etiology, pathology, and prognosis may be known or unknown. [Emphasis added.]

Two important points must be made at the outset. The "characteristic train of symptoms" of any disease is what permits identification -- diagnosis -- of the disorder. Ordinarily, and properly, physicians can best observe symptoms and diagnose diseases; in some cases, only specialists armed with sophisticated diagnostic tools can make a sound medical judgment. But alcoholism is different; doctors have no special tools to help them identify this illness. Medical researchers may someday develop a fool-proof blood test or identify a physiological marker for alcoholism, but no such techniques now exist. Besides, most symptoms of this particular "morbid process" are *behavioral*, and physicians seldom observe the day-to-day activities of their patients. But people in close contact with alcoholics see and hear much of what they do and say. Anyone can learn to identify the behavioral symptoms of this disease and to match the observed behavior with the symptoms. Without a great deal of effort, many persons outside the medical profession can learn to diagnose alcoholism.

The second point is that because alcoholism is a *process*, it must, like any other process, have a beginning. Alcoholism starts sometime, and it seems to begin very early. Although there are exceptions, most recovered alcoholics -- the best primary source for learning what happens during alcoholism -- are convinced that their addiction began with their first drink. One important reason for believing this is the little-known fact that most alcoholics remember, for the rest of their lives, their initial encounter with alcohol. Not the first time they got drunk, which is something even nonalcoholics might remember, but their very first *drink*.

One famous alcoholic, Lillian Roth, described her first experience with alcohol (a glass of fermented prune juice) in her autobiography, *I'll Cry Tomorrow* (Frederick Fell, Inc., 1954):

I have a vivid memory of my first drink. *I had just turned seventeen...* It burned my throat, and I felt the blood rush to my face... "Gee... that's great. What is it?" [Emphasis added.]

Twenty-six years later, Lillian Roth had lived the equivalent of several lifetimes. She had conquered show business; she was an acclaimed night club singer while still in her early twenties. Then the disease destroyed her life. It transformed her into a destitute, hallucinating, late-stage alcoholic. Ultimately, she pulled herself out of the gutter and found sobriety through Alcoholics Anonymous (AA). But after her long years of harrowing alcoholism, and her dramatic recovery, the middle-aged Lillian Roth still remembered how she felt, as a teenager, when she drank that glass of fermented prune juice!

Nonalcoholics will find this incomprehensible. For them, the first consumption of alcohol is an inconsequential experience, a "So what?" event. Most can't remember it six months later, let alone when they are middle-aged. But alcoholics are *different* from nonalcoholics. They are *not* ordinary people who happen to drink more than the rest of us. *Most alcoholics never know what it is like to have a normal relationship with alcohol.*

If most alcoholics remember their first drink and most nonalcoholics do not, then we can conclude that *alcoholics were different from nonalcoholics before they had that first drink.* This is an important first step in understanding the modern concept of the disease which says that the ability to "get" alcoholism, to become addicted, is physical, and that this vulnerability is inherited. As Kathleen Whalen FitzGerald, Ph.D., put it in *Alcoholism: The Genetic Inheritance* (Doubleday, 1988):

> We know that it is transmitted *genetically*; not through the mind or the environment but through the body chemistry... One becomes an alcoholic because one is biologically vulnerable, and [then] tests this vulnerability by drinking.*

---

*Some alcoholics don't touch alcohol until a relatively advanced age, and in these cases, the devastating results strongly confirm the idea of inherited vulnerability. Marty Mann tells of the teetotalist 79-year-old matriarch of a prominent New England family who, when ordered by her physician to drink a glass of port once a day, became a street drunkard in a matter of weeks. Louise Bryant, wife of

The conflicting idea -- that alcoholics drink to relieve some *other* problem (psychological, economic, social, etcetera) -- is out of date. It is simply and totally incompatible with the modern disease concept of alcoholism. People who have had experience with alcoholism have rejected it for many years. (Members of Alcoholics Anonymous, which was founded more than fifty years ago, have always ridiculed the notion that childhood events caused them to drink.) Although the idea that "something else" must be behind the alcoholism was always seriously flawed and crumbles quickly under rigorous analysis, it did not die easily among alcoholism professionals. An important factor in its demise was the publication in 1983, by psychiatrist George E. Vaillant of Harvard Medical School, of his monumental work, *The Natural History of Alcoholism* (Harvard University Press, 1983.)

Vaillant reported on a comprehensive forty-year study of two groups of American males who had been closely monitored by scientific investigators from adolescence into late middle age. Many in this large, balanced sample (at the start, 204 were Harvard undergraduates and 456 were inner city youths) became alcoholics during the long investigative period. This gave the researchers a unique opportunity to observe the unfolding of the process from its earliest stages. At the end of the forty years, some of the alcoholics were still drinking and some had recovered; several were in Alcoholics Anonymous.

As Vaillant makes clear in the following excerpt, he began his research with a bias in favor of the "underlying cause" notion. But as he accumulated data about these intensely studied alcoholics, he changed his mind:

Far more surprisingly, *most future alcoholics do not appear different from [nonalcoholic] drinkers in terms of premorbid psychological stability.* However, not until several prospective studies

---

John Reed, the American journalist who reported on the Bolshevik Revolution, completely avoided alcohol as a young woman. Her father had been an alcoholic. She started to drink in her thirties, however, and died, destitute and alone, in a Paris hotel room of alcoholism at age fifty. These and other similar cases found in the literature are, like that remembered first drink, incompatible with any notion that addiction is caused by environmental factors.

were available... could such a hypothesis be seriously entertained. It was difficult to perceive that [personality disorders that supposedly lead to heavy drinking] might be secondary to the disorder, alcoholism. It was difficult to dismiss the *illusion* that alcohol serves as a successful self-medication for unhappy, diffident people... [But we had to conclude that] *premorbid family and personality instability no longer made a statistical contribution to the risk of alcoholism.* [Emphasis added.]

Although many people, including psychiatrists with little experience in the successful treatment of alcoholism, still hold to the "illusion" that hidden emotional problems cause alcoholism, despite its emphatic refutation by Vaillant and others, I accept completely the "genetic vulnerability" concept. Readers adhering to other notions (i.e., underlying causes) are forewarned: the evidence I have assembled in this book will give them no comfort.

To move to the next important step in understanding alcoholism:

Alcoholism itself causes severe psychiatric disturbances.

Addictive drinking usually begins when the alcoholic is a teenager -- when he or she takes that (unforgettable) first drink. After that, most *never* achieve sobriety.* They will probably abstain from booze from time to time. Going on the wagon is symptomatic, but sobriety is different from abstinence. Recovered alcoholics report that during these dry periods their minds were seldom free of the urge to drink. In AA terms, they were merely "dry drunks," not recovered, or sober, alcoholics.

Most cases of alcoholism endure for many years. Many alcoholics live to be more than 60 years old. Some even make it -- as active alcoholics -- into their eighties or nineties. This means the morbid process, the disease of alcoholism, often endures for forty years or longer. From the very beginning of that long process, the disease takes charge of the personality of the victim and influences it far more than any other factor -- *including childhood experiences.*

---

*One alcoholism specialist, Dr. LeClair Bissell, estimates that only ten percent of alcoholics eventually enter Alcoholics Anonymous or other effective treatment programs.

Although many will find that assertion startling, it isn't even new. The late Ruth Fox, M.D., a psychiatrist, the original Medical Director of the National Council on Alcoholism, and one of the pioneers in the successful treatment of alcoholics, made the point, forcefully, more than twenty years ago:

As the addictive process grows *all alcoholics, no matter what their background, tend to become very much alike in their behavior.* [Emphasis added.]

To those who resist this Copernican-like conception of alcoholism -- that adult addiction is a more powerful determinative of personality than early childhood experiences -- I suggest (1) that they open their minds to the possibility that it is correct, and (2) that they finish reading this book.

In the following chapters, I will compare the actual behavior of real alcoholics -- many of them well-known persons who are not usually identified as alcoholics -- to accepted symptoms of the disease. I will explicitly compare some of these people with each other, and I encourage the reader to make similar comparisons.

Some readers may resist the idea that it might be useful to compare, for example, the behavior of an American corporate executive (Henry Ford II) who has never been accused of a crime to that of a murderous sixteenth century English king (Henry VIII) or to a Nobel Prize-winning author (Eugene O'Neill), but comparisons across time and between cultures will make it clear that this entity, the morbid process called alcoholism, is a force of awesome power. It takes individuals of either sex, from entirely different backgrounds and cultures, and forges them into strikingly similar, pathologically-determined destructive personalities.

I am confident that by the end of the book, the reader will agree that the modern concept is correct; the disease determines personality. The nature and extent of the changes it wroughts will become clear as I consider specific cases, but at this point I will state the basic personality change:

Alcoholism causes egomania.

Alcoholics do not deliberately acquire bloated egos; egomania develops from profound psychological processes beyond their control. It is rooted in the insecurity and tension caused by addiction. From the beginning of the addictive process, the alcoholic's self-image is battered and assaulted -- daily! -- by his failure to do something that most other people do with ease: deal with alcohol on a "take it or leave it" basis. In response to this profound humiliation, the alcoholic, to quote FitzGerald, "assumes the omnipotence of an infant, the ego expanding and filling the psychic horizon." The alcoholic, in other words, adopts behavior patterns to *compensate* for the profound humiliation of addiction.

Some ego-enhancing activities of these sick people are socially acceptable; some even benefit society. But their fundamental purpose is selfish: to make the alcoholic feel better about himself. John Wallace, Ph.D., former Director of Treatment at Edgehill Newport, an alcoholism facility in Rhode Island, commented on alcoholics' strange obsession with success:

> many pursue obsessions in addition to alcohol... such things as compulsive sexuality, material goods, money, fame, *power,* and fortune... [Emphasis added.]

If alcoholics aspired only to the trappings of success, it would not be cause for concern. But sick egos seek *power,* and that means they want control over others, over *us.* The egomania, as I will explain, also causes them to behave destructively. Compulsive power-seekers with an urge to destroy are -- it is virtually a definition of the word -- a menace. Most alcoholics are transformed into evil-doers by this "disease of the total personality"; most commit heinous acts during their drinking years and the evil behavior of some has earned them a place in the history books.

Some of the destructive alcoholic behavior occurs when the alcoholic is actually drinking and the blood alcohol level is elevated, but many behavioral symptoms, particularly those relating to the alcoholic's need for power, *do not disappear when the alcoholic stops drinking and his blood alcohol level drops to zero.* Contrary to what we might expect, going on the wagon does *not* cause all symptoms to disappear. The egomaniacal -- or *power* -- symptoms go away *only* if the drinking stops *and* the bloated ego is deflated.

All modern alcoholism treatment programs are in accord on that point; *deflation* of the ego is imperative to recovery.

The well-known success of treatment programs (especially Alcoholics Anonymous) that emphasize ego *deflation* strongly supports the idea that alcoholism causes ego *inflation*. If removal of a component from a preexisting condition sharply alters that condition, we can conclude that the object of our action was essential to the continuation of the prior condition. If we cut off the supply of oxygen to a fire, the fire goes out. This informs us that oxygen is *essential* to fire. Similarly, if programs based on ego *deflation* have led to recovery in hundreds of thousands of alcoholics, we can conclude that ego *inflation* is essential to the condition of active alcoholism.

It usually takes years of alcoholic drinking for the ego-inflating effect of the addiction to reach its peak power, but significant, life-altering, ego inflation begins when the alcoholic starts to drink addictively. The power of this early inflation is so profound that it influences many of the life decisions made by young alcoholics.

Although I do not disagree with the assertion (oft-repeated in alcoholism literature) that alcoholics can be found in any occupation, I am convinced that egomania drives many young alcoholics into occupations that offer the possibility of quick ego gratification. Available statistics support my idea.

Writing -- creative writing -- is an egocentric occupation. If the idea that alcoholism-created egomania compels young alcoholics to seek short-term ego gratification is valid, then we ought to find a higher percentage of alcoholics among writers than among persons who pursue less egocentric activities. This seems to be the case. Donald W. Goodwin, M.D., in *Alcohol and the Writer* (Andrews and McMeel, 1988), cites one estimate of alcoholism incidence among American writers at one-third and another at 30 percent. Of the seven Americans who won the Nobel Prize for Literature, five (Sinclair Lewis, Faulkner, Hemingway, Steinbeck and O'Neill) were alcoholics. Five out of seven is 71 percent. Goodwin reports that statistics for fatal cirrhosis of the liver, which is usually caused by heavy drinking, show that writers rank second among all occupations.* (Bartenders rank first and letter carriers, last. Tending bar offers obvious advantages to an alcoholic; delivering mail does nothing for the demanding ego.)

Another profession that holds out the promise of ego gratification to young alcoholics is acting. The adolescent fantasy of becoming a famous Hollywood star is just that for most young people -- a fantasy. Few seriously pursue the dream by investing the time and effort required to succeed in what is, after all, a chancy, highly-competitive and demanding profession. But young people with an exaggerated, disease-created need for ego satisfaction are going to try harder than those who are less ego-driven. If this idea is correct, then we ought to find a lot of alcoholism among persons who have actually made it to the top of the industry; there ought to be a lot of alcoholism among real movie stars. Someone has already looked, and found alcoholism in abundance.

Lucy Barry Robe is an alcoholism researcher, writer, and a self-identified recovered alcoholic who worked for many years in the entertainment industry. She has intensively studied the phenomenon of alcoholism in movie stars and published her findings in *Co-starring Famous Women and Alcohol* (CompCare Publications, 1986). Robe used published reports of the stars' behavior and the Michigan Alcoholism Screening Test (MAST) to evaluate the possibility of alcoholism in now-deceased movie actresses and certain other well-known women. She identifies nearly 200 famous women as alcoholics.

Robe estimated the total number of winners of Oscars during the years 1928 to 1977 who might be alcoholics or heavy drinkers and came up with an incidence of 22 percent among female movie stars. She also looked at males nominated for the Best Actor award and estimated the alcoholism or heavy drinking incidence at 38 percent of the male nominees and 33 percent of the winners. These numbers, like those for writers, are exceptionally high. No one knows the incidence of alcoholism in the general population, but the consensus (among alcoholism specialists) is that it's about five percent.

If we assume that those whom Robe identifies as "heavy drinkers"

---

*Also of interest is the influence the disease has had on the content of their work. I explore this intriguing question in Chapter Seven.

were really alcoholics, this is how the incidence of alcoholism in two egocentric occupations compares with the general population:

Alcoholism in general population:	5 percent.
In writers [Goodwin]:	30 percent.
In female movie stars [Robe]:	22 percent.
In male movie stars [Robe]:	38 percent.

(A more recent study suggests that these statistics may be understatements. *The New York Times* of October 12, 1993 reports that a forthcoming book will place the alcoholism incidence at 60 percent for actors and 41 percent among novelists.)

In addition to these telling statistics, there are the valuable impressions of observant individuals. Goodwin quotes novelist (and physician) Michael Crichton:

> I know... many painters, famous and obscure, who drink to spectacular excess, and... alcoholic actors and directors... I have been surprised to see how many people in "the arts"... are heavy drinkers... [Or who do not] drink at all, in that careful, somewhat embarrassed manner which indicates a drinking problem somewhere in the past.

Sinclair Lewis, who was to die of the disease, once asked "Can you name five American writers since Poe who did not die of alcoholism?" Rising to Lewis's challenge, Goodwin does manage to prepare a rather short list of famous American writers who were not alcoholics. But then he dashes off another list, this one of alcoholic writers, and ends up agreeing with Lewis: "What is hard is to think of nonalcoholics among American writers of the twentieth century." (Dr. Goodwin's long list is quoted in full in Chapter Seven.)

When the estimated incidence of alcoholism in two groups of people who elected at an early age to enter occupations demanding exceptionally high levels of motivation (famous writers and movie stars) ranges from four to more than twelve *times* what we would expect among all occupations as a whole, then something is terribly wrong with our basic assumptions. What is wrong is the assumption that alcoholism has no influence on career selection.

There is only one explanation that reconciles (1) the statistics for alcoholism-incidence among writers and movie stars, (2) the inheritance of the vulnerability to alcoholism, (3) the absence of pre-alcoholism neuroses mentioned by Vaillant, and (4) the relationship of alcoholism and egotism. That explanation: the disease inflates the ego at an early age and the inflated ego influences the selection of a career.*

Well, so what? Who cares? If alcoholics gravitate to occupations that offer them high levels of ego gratification why not just relax and enjoy the books they write and the movies they act in? What harm is done if lots of actors and writers are alcoholics?

The answer is that the young alcoholic's thirst for power is never quenched by mere success. The sick need for ego satisfaction that puts them on a life-long power-trip also causes them to abuse power. This disease propels many victims into successful careers, but it also compels its victims to victimize.

I have focused on movie stars and writers in this chapter for the simple reason that the data for those professions are available. Other alcoholic power-trippers engage in activities that enable them to do more harm to more people. No one knows how many alcoholics are serving as prosecutors, but, as I show in the next chapter, public prosecution is an occupation that offers great opportunities for the perversion of power; innocents can be punished for crimes they did not commit. Other alcoholics are even more dangerous. Although we may not think of treason and serial murder as occupations, as I will make clear in future chapters, many well-known traitors and serial killers were alcoholics -- or, to put it more correctly, some alcoholics have chosen to satisfy their demands for ego satisfaction not by writing and acting, but by betraying and killing. My research has convinced me that the incidence of alcoholism in those two groups of evil-doers is actually

---

*Some alcoholics have engaged in both occupations. The late Tom Tryon, a self-identified recovering alcoholic, had been both a movie actor and a successful novelist. George C. Scott, who has identified himself as a "functioning alcoholic," turned to acting only after he tried, and failed, as a writer. Sterling Hayden was both a movie star and a novelist; he was identified as an alcoholic in his obituary.

higher than it is among actors and writers.

To begin our examination of alcoholics' dangerous impulse to abusive, egocentric behavior, I have gathered in the next chapter several examples of atrocious acts committed by now-deceased alcoholics, some of whom were rather well-known.

2: ABUSERS AND ACCUSERS

Power is nothing if it be consciously applied. The man who...
punishes only the guilty, who absolves only the innocent, whose
testimony is inexorably true, has really no power at all.

W. M. Ireland

When he punished for a reason, the Czar was conforming to the
will of God; when he punished for no reason, he became the equal
of God.

Henri Troyat

Power abuse begins in the family. The basic nuclear unit of
society is fraught with potential for damage by anyone afflicted
with an illness that compels destructive behavior. Families bear the
brunt of alcoholic nastiness and bullying, and if alcoholics never
attacked anyone other than close relatives, the disease would still
warrant society's intense concern. We can get some sense of just
how monstrously -- *and how much like one another* -- alcoholics
behave while hidden from public view from the published memoirs
of children who grew up in homes dominated by an alcoholic
parent.

Christina Crawford, daughter of Joan Crawford, the alcoholic
movie star, graphically described in *Mommie Dearest* (William
Morrow and Company, Inc., 1978), the rage that seizes many alco-

holics when they drink. One night, drinking, the movie star...

> erupted with a violence, a hatred and a suddenness that plunged
> both of us into an instantaneous struggle for survival. She leaped
> off the counter and grabbed for my throat like a mad dog... The
> choking pain of her fingers around my throat met the thudding
> ache of the blow to the back of my head... Her mouth was
> twisted with rage and her eyes -- her eyes were the eyes of a
> killer animal, glistening with excitement.

While drinking, alone and at night, Crawford would storm
through her Beverly Hills home, shouting and screaming at her
terrified children in fits of alcoholic madness.

Crawford's alcoholic need for power drove her to force her young
son to sleep -- every night! -- in a canvas harness that prevented
him from going to the bathroom. This was a cruel act committed
by the inflated ego, not by her booze-soaked brain. Crawford
didn't drink every night, but, drunk or sober, she forced the little
boy to sleep in the contraption.

At the time Christina Crawford's book was published, many
reviewers resorted to complex psychiatric explanations for the star's
abuse of her children. But only one explanation is needed: Joan
Crawford was an alcoholic, and alcoholism causes cruel, abusive
behavior.

Rage occurs when alcoholics drink because rage while drinking
is symptomatic of the disease. Research suggests that the alcoholic's brain reacts morbidly to the substance, unlike that of
nonalcoholics. Once ingested, ethyl alcohol apparently sets off reactions in the alcoholic's limbic system -- the portion of the brain that
controls rage. (According to biologists, we inherited our limbic
brains from reptiles.) Limbic rage would explain Crawford's
drunken fury, but she was nasty to her two children throughout her
life, even between drinking bouts. Sustained hostile behavior is
typical of alcoholics. Their capacity for viciousness, even while on
the wagon, is not rooted in the neurological reaction of the limbic
brain to ethyl alcohol, but in alcoholism-caused egomania.

Marguerite Courtney, the daughter of another alcoholic actress,
Laurette Taylor, wrote in her biography of her mother, *Laurette*

(Atheneum House, 1968), of the fear and bafflement she felt as a young adult because of her mother's deranged behavior:

> The wildest of fears began to obsess [me]. The unreasonable demands and accusations, the sudden savage scenes of jealousy and rage, the eyes black with hate, could mean only one thing; under some psychic compulsion that was almost madness Laurette had come to loathe and despise her daughter. So strong did the conviction become that on hearing the strange nocturnal movements, the ominous mutterings, [I was] filled with a nameless terror, and would rise and barricade [my bedroom] door.

Taylor's maniacal nighttime behavior while drinking is typical of alcoholics. So is their peculiar tendency to accuse other people of vileness. Beverley Nichols, the late British playwright and son of alcoholic John Nichols, describes in *Father Figure* (Simon and Schuster, 1972) his father's bizarre insistence that everyone else was afflicted with syphilis:

> Naturally all the members of his own family were accused, at one time or another, of having the disease; the circle broadened, my aunt had syphilis; it was written all over the letters of my remotest cousins; it was stamped on the handiwork of the gardener. Even a new housemaid would come under the ban.

John Nichols would get on his "everyone has syphilis" hobby-horse even when not drinking. He made other, even more obscene, accusations about his long-suffering wife, things so filthy that his son could not repeat them, even to close friends, forty years after his parents' deaths.

The son, as often happens, grew to hate his father. In fact, John Nichols's atrocious behavior led Beverley to try to kill him -- on three separate occasions. These attempts at parricide were not successful; the alcoholic survived. But Beverley Nichols made it clear in his autobiography -- he wrote it when he was an old man -- that he didn't regret trying to kill his father. He only regretted that he had failed. He was convinced that if he had killed him, the family's suffering would have ended. Instead, it continued for decades.

Although close relatives are the most frequent targets of their hostility, any alcoholic who has servants will abuse *them*.* Ludwig von Beethoven, the famous composer who was, in my opinion, an alcoholic, lived as a bachelor throughout his life and depended on servants for his daily needs. He devoted much energy to abusing them. Here's a quotation from George R. Marek's *Beethoven* (Funk & Wagnalls, 1969):

The couple he employs in 1809, the Herzogs are "wicked people." Out they go. The servant in 1811 is "a vagabond." He finds another couple in 1813... who stays with him almost three years. In 1816 he has other servants. He dislikes them. The following year he takes a housekeeper... and a kitchen maid. They are "stupid." A new cook appears... She cooks well. But she is "treacherous" and conspires against him. Out she goes with a new housekeeper... They are all "in league against him." His servant makes his way "into other people's rooms with counterfeit keys." He wants one without "murderous tendencies." He has reason to suspect another couple of committing a theft.

Vulnerability to alcoholism ran in Beethoven's family. His father, Johann, was arrested several times for being drunk and disorderly. Contemporaries described the father as a dissolute drunkard of whom "the tasting of wine was one of his early accomplishments." Johann probably inherited his alcoholic vulnerability from his mother, Ludwig's grandmother, who was "addicted to drink."

Although his biographers say little about Ludwig's own drinking, John N. Burk wrote in *The Life and Works of Beethoven* (Random House, 1943) that the composer could be found at his favorite tavern over a bottle of wine almost any day. Another biographer, Marek, inadvertently provides evidence that Beethoven had the reputation of a heavy drinker when he asserts that the composer was *not* an alcoholic. (If he didn't drink heavily, why deny the alcoholism?)** Fortunately, his biographies provide enough specif-

---

*As did Joan Crawford.

**Marek, like most biographers cited in this book, demonstrates no familiarity with the symptoms of alcoholism.

ic information about Beethoven to enable anyone with modern knowledge of the disease to conclude, even from this distance, that, contrary to Marek and other biographers, Beethoven most certainly was an alcoholic.

He had chronic liver problems which were diagnosed as cirrhosis in a post mortem examination. This is a strong sign of alcoholism in and of itself, and in view of the family history, it is compelling. Not everyone who is the son and grandson of alcoholics and who develops cirrhosis is an alcoholic. But the chances that Beethoven was not appear rather slim.

Beethoven's extraordinarily bad behavior toward others confirms the alcoholism. This is what his niece said about his nastiness: "He was very irritable, very jumpy, very sensitive, and therefore often unjust to and suspicious of his best friends." Marek, commenting on Beethoven's severance of a business relationship, writes that it was a matter of habitual false accusation -- "one more example of Beethoven's habit of suspecting people without cause." Beethoven's "trusts and mistrusts had a way of changing suddenly. [He has] raging swings [in his moods] and tempests of suspicion."

Beethoven's strange behavior both puzzled and fascinated Marek. "What is important -- and what repeats itself all through Beethoven's life -- is his protestations that his actions are 'upright and honorable' while he thoughtlessly wounds a friend."

Marek considers Beethoven's deafness as a possible cause for the bad behavior and then, correctly, dismisses it.

What is more natural that we should ascribe Beethoven's negative characteristics -- his suspiciousness, his quarrelsomeness, his sickly sensitivity... his arrogance... [to his deafness]?

[But] the more one studies this genius... the more one comes to sense that deafness cannot be the whole explanation. The [negative traits] were there before the ears gave out.

Beethoven had a strange compulsion to change his residence frequently. From 1792 to 1827, he occupied seventy-one different dwellings! We now know that alcoholics are often compulsive movers. AA members frequently tell of their experiences with the "geographic cure," frantic attempts, never successful, to escape from the addiction by changing their domicile. Those extraordinary relocations by Beethoven were the desperate acts of an alcoholic's battered ego.

Beethoven, who never married, was a promiscuous womanizer. Don Juanism occurs frequently in male alcoholics. It, like all of Beethoven's negative behavior, can be attributed to his alcoholism.

Alcoholics are also capable of attacking people they don't even know. A strange, but not untypical, incident is described by Carlos Baker in his *Ernest Hemingway: A Life Story* (Charles Scribner's Sons, 1969). Hemingway, an alcoholic, went out on the town one night with his wife, two male friends, and their wives. After many hours of drinking, the party entered a night club where Hemingway noticed the actors Charles Boyer and Ingrid Bergman sitting at the next table. Straightaway, Hemingway started to insult Boyer, asking his companions in a loud voice whether he ought not give the "back of his hand" to the "green-faced" Frenchman. His friends were embarassed and puzzled by his unprovoked hostility. The two actors tried to ignore him. But Hemingway continued his boorish behavior until Boyer and Bergman left the premises.*

Family members, friends, a movie star at the next table, complete strangers -- anyone who comes in contact with an alcoholic can be attacked. The danger zone increases dramatically if the alcoholic acquires political power; empowered alcoholics can harm more people.

Huey P. Long, the Louisiana politician who wielded enormous political power in the 1920's and 1930's, was an alcoholic. According to T. Harry Williams's *Huey Long* (Alfred A. Knopf, 1969), by 1927 when Long was conducting his successful campaign for Governor of Louisiana:

[He] had been drinking for years, probably since his earliest traveling salesman days. The habit took increasing command over him and was most likely to grip him in times of excitement, like a campaign... He tried to brush off criticism with impudence,

---

*Bergman is herself identified as an alcoholic by Robe.

by bragging about his addiction.

After holding the power of governorship for three years, Huey Long told one friend, "I've been under the influence of liquor more nights of my adult life than I've been sober, and out of this have come some of the most brilliant ideas of my career." While drinking, Long was often "loud and arrogant." He generally recovered from these binges quickly.* Belligerent behavior while drinking and the absence of hangovers are characteristic of alcoholics; they are symptoms of the disease.

Long abused his family. He would storm at his children with "sudden frightening fury." When he moved into the governor's mansion, he simply left his wife and children behind; he stopped living with them.

He maligned his brother Earl. He once told a friend, "You have to watch Earl. If you live long enough, he'll double-cross you. He'd double-cross Jesus Christ -- if He were down here on earth."

But Huey Long was more than a husband, a father, and a brother. He was a Senator as well as a Governor of Louisiana, and in the latter office Long came as close to being a dictator as is possible in a nominally-democratic society. Contemporaries considered him a power-hungry egomaniac. They were right, of course. Alcoholism caused the egomania.

Long's behavior while in public office reeks of alcoholic power-tripping. His favorite political weapon was the personal attack. His attacks, in 1921, on Governor Parker of Louisiana were so intense that Parker successfully pressed charges of criminal libel. (Long was let off with a nominal one dollar fine.) In the 1928 gubernatorial primary, one of his opponents sued for libel; the case was dismissed on a technicality. Although personal attacks were not uncommon in Louisiana in the Twenties and Thirties, they were usually kept within bounds. Long, however, "ignored the rules. Where others stopped at a recognized limit, he would ruin a reputation."

---

*In this book, binges are drinking episodes that end the same day they start. The term "bender" is used for drinking episodes that run two or more days. In general, early and middle stage alcoholics drink in binges, while benders are a symptom of the later stages.

In response to another slanderous attack unleashed by Long during the 1928 campaign, his opponent, the incumbent Louisiana governor, confronted him in the lobby of a New Orleans hotel and called him a liar to his face. The beefy Long struck the other, elderly man.

In a Senate speech, Long attacked Samuel Ansell, a Louisiana attorney, as "a scoundrel and a thief and a rascal and a crook." He claimed that Ansell, while employed in the adjutant general's office, accepted a bribe from an imprisoned draft dodger and then released the man from jail. Ansell sued for slander, and Long settled out of court.

While a United States Senator, Long launched a weird attack against Postmaster General James Farley who had been Franklin Roosevelt's campaign manager in 1932 and 1936. On the floor of the Senate (where he was immune from litigation), Long accused Farley of participating in an illegal racing wire service, of having a financial interest in companies constructing post offices, and of giving valuable stamps to his friends. He claimed to have an affidavit in a safe deposit box to support his claims, but refused to give it to a congressional committee because, he said, the committee was made up of Farley supporters. "Judas Iscariot would have had defenders just as Farley has them now," proclaimed Long before he dropped his campaign against the member of Roosevelt's cabinet. Not surprisingly, he produced no evidence to support his charges.

Nonalcoholic politicians do not often display *irrational* egotism. But all alcoholics are extremely egocentric, and sometimes their sick egos drive them to irrationality. Once, when he was meeting a delegation of citizens from Caddo Parish in Louisiana, Long snarled at the group of dumbfounded voters: "I will teach you to get off the sidewalk, take off your hat, and bow down damn low when Governor Long comes to town!"

Long boasted that he could "frighten or buy ninety-nine out of every hundred men." He kept dossiers on real or potential adversaries, and he insisted that his associates completely subordinate themselves to his own ego. One assistant said of Long, "He liked to break people, especially the strong... "

A journalist described the sense of threat that Long created, saying there was a "charged atmosphere which envelops him, the sense of danger that pervades the air about him."

Harley B. Bozeman, a former bodyguard, once revealed just how dangerous Long could be. Bozeman signed an affidavit stating that Long had told him to murder J.Y. Sanders, a political opponent. Bozeman swore that Long, *who had been drinking at the time*, said to him, "I mean for you to kill the son-of-a-bitch, leave him in a ditch where nobody will know how or when he got there. I'm Governor of this state, and if you were to be found out, I would give you a full pardon and many gold dollars."

Huey Long's life-long drive for power -- many were convinced he wanted to be President -- was stopped by an assassin's bullet.

One of the favorite attack techniques used by Long and other alcoholics is the false accusation. There's a simple reason for this. If a disease drives a person to shore up his sense of self-esteem (which is undermined by addictive drinking) by attacking others, the repertoire of available attack devices is determined by the social environment in which he functions. Some alcoholics will physically attack others, but violence involves obvious risks -- especially for a politician. False accusations not only involve minimal political risk, but also give the alcoholic the satisfaction of demeaning the target of his attacks. There is also a bonus; he can feel superior to everyone who believes the lies.

One extremely negative political figure in American history, a man whose name is synonymous with false accusations, was Senator Joseph McCarthy. McCarthy was an alcoholic, and his alcoholism explains his infamous behavior.

McCarthy died in Bethesda Naval Hospital in April 1957 of causes that were never made public. According to his assistant, Roy Cohn, he had been consistently disregarding physicians' warnings to abstain completely from alcohol. He had a hepatitis-impaired liver. *Time* said cirrhosis was the cause of death.

Fred Cook's account of McCarthy's end, from *The Nightmare Decade: The Life and Times of Senator Joe McCarthy* (Random House, 1971), has the ring of truth:

On the sixteenth floor of the Bethesda Naval Hospital was a series of private rooms... conveniently isolated. The area is... Tower 16, and it is reserved for the exclusive use of eminent leaders of our government establishment when they have become overloaded with more booze than their systems can tolerate. They are taken to Tower 16 to dry out...

McCarthy had been a frequent visitor to Tower 16. Toward the end, when he really went on a bender, he had a tendency to become a "mean drunk." The attendants at Tower 16 had had considerable trouble with him on previous occasions, but when he came in this last time he was literally uncontrollable. He grabbed a chair and broke it over the head of one of the enlisted personnel who were trying to take care of him, and the force on the floor, unable to control him, shoved him into... a padded cell where he could do no harm to himself or anyone else. There he passed out.

Poisons built up in his system, and by the time he was taken to his bed in his private room in Tower 16, the damage was irreversible.

"Bethesda was embarrassed by it," says one Washington insider. "There was some feeling that if they had put him in a straitjacket and gotten him to bed and treated him earlier, he might have lived. But there was no reason why anyone should have felt guilty, really. If it hadn't been this time, it would have been the next because he couldn't give up the liquor; he couldn't stop."

McCarthy was an alcoholic long before this last, fatal bender. It takes many years for a functioning middle class alcoholic, a former judge as well as a Senator, to progress to the stage where he is smashing chairs on the skulls of drunk-tank attendants. Roy Cohn claimed the Senator started drinking heavily only after he was humiliated by the Senate's censure in December 1955. This is impossible. McCarthy could not have been transformed from a normal drinker to the crazed Tower 16 drunkard in less than two and a half years.

Richard Rovere provides more evidence of alcoholic drinking in *Senator Joe McCarthy* (Methuen & Co., Ltd., 1960), when he manages to cram four alcoholism symptoms (high level of consumption, high tolerance and the absence of hangovers in the early years, and a sudden decrease in tolerance in the late stage) into one sentence:

His drinking prowess, until the last year of his life, was in fact notable. He could "belt a fifth,"... between midnight and five A.M., catch a couple of hours of sleep, and be at his office at eight or nine, ready for a hard day's work...

Rovere also says that the Senator "often went on the wagon (for him, this meant beer in place of whiskey) for days and weeks at a time." Heavy drinkers who go on the wagon (or who change their drinking patterns) are trying to control out-of-control drinking. People whose drinking is out of control are alcoholics. There is, in fact, no reason to think that Senator Joseph McCarthy was not an alcoholic for his entire adult life.

Certainly, the signs of a lifelong power trip were evident early on. One researcher, Mark Landis notes McCarthy's extraordinary completion of four years of high school in one year (a dropout, McCarthy had returned to school at the age of 21). Then Landis adds, "It is clear... that a sudden and dramatic change occurred in McCarthy's life just about the time he was achieving his majority... " Suddenly, McCarthy was fiercely ambitious, strongly suggesting that the alcoholic ego had come to life.

McCarthy went on to college, attended law school, and entered Wisconsin politics. By the time he was 31, he had been elected judge. While serving on the bench, he began to display the typical alcoholic disregard of conventions. He was soon well-known locally as the judge who specialized in quickie divorces, despite the fact that he was a Catholic at a time when divorce was strongly condemned by the Church. He even whipped through the formalities in one case as he and the two lawyers trotted up the courthouse steps. Egomaniacs do not like rules.

McCarthy's cavalier behavior blossomed when he entered the Senate as a freshman, years before he mounted the anti-Communism hobbyhorse. Robert Griffith makes the arrogance plain in *The Politics of Fear, Second Edition* (The University of Massachusetts Press, 1987):

What was remarkable about McCarthy's Senate apprenticeship was not policy positions... but rather his continued violation of the rules, customs, and procedures under which the Senate operates.

Alcoholism experts often speak of "alcoholic charm." John Hoving, one of McCarthy's political opponents, observed this phenomenon in the Senator:

Without doubt Senator McCarthy is one of the most cynical men I have ever known... [yet] I like him quite a lot and enjoy being with him.

McCarthy had a Jekyll and Hyde personality and superficial emotions, both signs of alcoholism.

"He can be the most affable man in the world," recalled one fellow senator, "and suddenly he will run the knife into you -- particularly if the public is going to see it -- and he will do it for no particular reason."

Another sign of an alcoholic ego at work is lying. Richard Rovere, after dutifully noting that a lot of American politicians tend to bend the truth, says this about the Wisconsin Senator:

But McCarthy was surely the champion liar. He lied with wild abandon; he lied without evident fear; he lied in his teeth and in the teeth of the truth; he lied vividly and with bold imagination; he lied, often, with very little pretence to be telling the truth.

Accusatory attacks are *the* favorite weapon of nonviolent alcoholics, and McCarthy's have guaranteed him a unique place in American history. The following are just two examples of blatantly false accusations, one involving a low ranking government official and the other one of the most respected statesmen of the time.

McCarthy once announced that a witness, a low-ranking Signal Corps employee, had cracked during a closed door investigation into espionage at Fort Monmouth. His pronouncement earned a page one headline in *The New York Times*: "Radar Witness Breaks Down: Will Tell All About Spy Rings." McCarthy said his witness, who had originally denied there was a spy ring, collapsed under vigorous cross-examination by Roy Cohn. But McCarthy asked reporters not to reveal the name of the witness who "has indicated a great fear of the spy ring which is operating within Government agencies, including the Signal Corps." Usually McCarthy favored innuendo, but in this instance (and in a few others) he simply lied. That he lied is a matter of record. A month later, the witness revealed that he had broken down because his mother had died two days earlier. He emphatically denied confessing to being a member of a spy ring. The United States Army believed him. They did not charge him with any offense, and he kept his sensitive job.

McCarthy made other assertions about espionage at Fort Monmouth, but he didn't find any spies. The United States Army subsequently exonerated all seven of the employees who had been suspended as security risks when McCarthy made his wild accusations.

McCarthy's slander of George C. Marshall, five star General, Secretary of State, and, as originator of the Marshall Plan, the savior of Europe, was perhaps his most egregious act. This is part of what he said from the floor of the Senate, where he was immune from libel suits:

> [Marshall is a] man steeped in falsehood... who has recourse to a lie whenever it suits his convenience... [part of] a conspiracy so immense and an infamy so black as to dwarf any previous venture in the history of man... [one in whose activities can be seen] a pattern which finds his decision maintained with great stubbornness and skill, always and invariably serving the world policy of the Kremlin.

Wild and unbelievable as his accusations were, many of his followers believed McCarthy's attempt to besmirch this impeccably loyal American -- a man who had served his country with honor and distinction.

Starting with his phony 1952 claim to have a list of 205 Communist policy makers in the State Department, this single alcoholic managed, in a few brief years, to do great harm to the United States and to many innocent citizens.

In a way, McCarthy couldn't help himself. The alcoholic is incapable of consistently exercising any authority he may hold without abusing it. If the alcoholic is a District Attorney, he may use his power to prosecute persons he *knows* are innocent. And if he does, his victims might suffer even more than those attacked by

McCarthy. An alcoholic District Attorney has at his command something McCarthy never acquired: the prosecutorial power of a state. Many alcoholics have held that awesome power, and I have uncovered two cases of rank injustice committed by two of them.

In 1916, Charles M. Fickert, the alcoholic District Attorney of San Francisco, framed two labor leaders, Thomas Mooney and Warren Billings. A bomb had been exploded during a Preparedness Day parade, killing ten spectators. Just two hours after the explosion, before he initiated any investigation, Fickert blithely told a group of reporters, "You know, men, I already think I know who did this."

Fickert used every means -- including steps that were blatantly illegal -- to frame Mooney and Billings. He suppressed evidence, used false witnesses, and suborned perjury. And he was certainly an alcoholic. Years after the frame-up, Fickert was a derelict: out of work, divorced (rare in those years) on a charge of intemperance, a poorly-dressed, public drunkard.

Mooney's death sentence was later commuted, but both he and Billings spent *twenty-three years* in prison. They were both pardoned only after their alcoholic-engineered frame-up had become "America's Dreyfus case," an international embarrassment.

Charles Becker, another victim of another alcoholic district attorney, was even less fortunate than the two labor leaders. He was executed for a murder he did not commit.

In 1912, four hired gunmen shot and killed Henry Rosenthal, the well-known owner of a New York gambling house. Becker, a police lieutenant, was charged with persuading a group of Rosenthal's competitors -- owners of other gambling houses -- to hire the killers. District Attorney Charles Whitman, an alcoholic, was determined to destroy the innocent Becker. He granted immunity to the four gamblers, all notorious, in return for their testimony. The four criminals swore that Becker had induced them to hire the four gunmen. If true, this charge meant Becker was guilty of first degree murder. The District Attorney arranged for the gamblers to remain in custody in accommodations so luxurious that reporters called them "Whitman's Ritz." He saw that they had ample time, and lots of rehearsals, to get their testimony down pat.

The Court of Appeals overturned Becker's conviction, saying that Whitman's case rested on testimony of six witnesses -- two of whose stories were "inherently improbable and subject to suspicion." The court found three of the four gambler-witnesses to be "indisputably... guilty of the murder and subject to the punishment of death." Instead of charging the men actually responsible for the murder with a capital crime, the alcoholic Whitman had offered them immunity if they would "furnish evidence to convict Becker." Whitman had claimed in court that the fourth gambler was a corroborating non-accomplice, but some of the Appeal Judges wrote in their opinion that the weight of evidence did not agree with that conclusion. In other words, they suspected that this fourth witness was also one of the murderers.

Despite the ruling of the Court of Appeals, Whitman had the same witnesses testify at Becker's second trial. They repeated their story. He also called three new witnesses. One of them had a criminal charge dropped by Whitman in exchange for his testimony against Becker. The second new witness later signed a complete retraction of his testimony. It was a brief-lived retraction, however; the witness issued a retraction of the retraction after Whitman's investigators got their hands on him. Becker was found guilty and sentenced to death.

In spite of his conviction, Becker would not have been executed if it were not for an almost incredible development. Billy Sulzer, Governor of New York at the time of the murder, wrote to an acquaintance that he was convinced Becker was innocent and that he intended to commute the death sentence. But by the time Becker arrived on Death Row, Sulzer was out of office. The newly-elected Governor -- the only person capable of preventing the execution of this innocent man -- was none other than Charles Whitman. The alcoholic prosecutor who framed Becker was now the alcoholic Governor with the power to grant, or to deny, clemency!

Several lawyers urged Whitman, because he had been the prosecutor, to recuse himself from the last judgment of Becker. Showing typical alcoholic contempt for the niceties, Whitman airily dismissed that advice, saying, "There never was a case... more perfectly proved in the history of jurisprudence."

Whitman's alcoholic compulsion to malign Becker remained at full strength. On the day before the execution, Governor Whitman announced to the press that Becker, who was locked in a cell on Death Row and unable to defend himself, had earlier committed another murder -- that of his first wife. The accusation was false.

Becker's second wife met with Governor Charles Whitman on the eve of the execution and begged him to spare her husband. While she made her desperate plea, the Governor was so inebriated that he had to be physically supported by two assistants. The intoxicated Governor rejected Mrs. Becker's plea, and Charles Becker was electrocuted the next day.

Whitman's alcoholism caught up with him in the end. He failed in his re-election effort after "more and more citizens became aware of the governor's problems with alcohol." It was too late, of course, to help Becker or any other unknown victims of his prosecutorial abuse.

Andy Logan, in her book *Against the Evidence: The Becker-Rosenthal Affair* (The McCall Publishing Company, 1970), presents a detailed account of the crime, the two trials, and the grisly execution.* She convinced me that Whitman knew from the outset that Becker was innocent. Anyone who reads her book knowing that alcoholism *causes* destructive behavior will conclude, as I did, that Becker would not have died if an alcoholic had not been the District Attorney and, later, the Governor.

We may like to think that our society does not routinely give power to people afflicted with an illness that compels them to abuse it, but anyone who does has an unrealistic view of the state of alcoholism in America today. Thousands of government officials, including prosecutors and other law enforcement officials, have the power to harm innocents. Because the disease is seldom diagnosed while the in its highly dangerous early and middle stages, it is certain that large numbers of them are alcoholics.

---

*The largest man electrocuted at the time, Becker suffered horribly. His three-jolt execution is still considered the most bungled in the history of Sing Sing.

3: THE INVISIBLE DISEASE

Hereafter, perhaps, some intellect may be found which will reduce
my phantasm to the commonplace -- some intellect more calm,
more logical, and far less excitable than my own, which will
perceive... nothing more than an ordinary succession of very natural
causes and effects.

Edgar Allan Poe

We are blind to alcoholism. We give these dangerous, sick people
great power. We elect them to high office, ignore their presence
in the cabinet, and watch blindly as they run, and sometimes ruin,
large business enterprises. We give them the power to investigate,
arrest, and prosecute, and when they abuse that power we never
connect the alcoholism to the abuse.

We trust them with more than power; we give them responsiblity.
Despite well-intended but ineffective procedures, active alcoholics
routinely pilot airliners filled with hundreds of passengers, and
others direct, as air traffic controllers, the landings and takeoffs of
hundreds of planes every day. We've even put one on the moon.

Edwin E. ("Buzz") Aldrin, Jr., who, in 1969, became the second
person to walk on the moon, has revealed that he was an active
alcoholic while an astronaut. While in training -- and under intense
medical and psychological scrutiny -- he would go on two-week-
long benders. He stopped drinking only two days before lift-off.

Some alcoholics have even made it to the highest levels of our
churches.

James Pike, the late Bishop of the Episcopalian Church, stopped
drinking in 1964. He had been named Bishop of California six

years earlier, and while in that exalted office was stopped (more than once) by San Francisco police as he wandered the streets late at night, drunk. According to one biography, *The Death and Life of Bishop Pike* by William Stringfellow and Anthony Towne (Doubleday & Company, Inc., 1976), he wasn't the only alcoholic Episcopal prelate at the time; Henry I. Louttit, Bishop of South Florida, "shared, with Bishop Pike, the condition of alcoholism."

We've had *many* active alcoholics in high government positions. The late Robert B. Anderson was a highly respected public servant whose long career in government included postings as Navy Secretary, Deputy Secretary of Defense, and Secretary of the Treasury under Eisenhower. President Eisenhower thought so well of him that he wanted him to run as his Vice President in 1956. (Anderson turned him down.)

Anderson's life ended on a decidedly down note. He pleaded guilty in the late 1980's to tax evasion and to operating an illegal offshore bank. He spent a year in prison. The sentencing judge had noted that Anderson "had been hospitalized for alcoholism ten times since 1981." Based on our current knowledge of the natural history of the disease, he was surely an active alcoholic when he served in the Cabinet and when Ike asked him to be Vice President. Just as certainly, Eisenhower didn't suspect that he was offering the job to a profoundly ill man.

I have concluded, based on direct personal observation, that another individual who has served for years in high government positions is an active alcoholic. To my knowledge, no hint of a drinking problem in this well-known person has ever appeared in the press.

Based on solid historical records, the United States has had three alcoholic Presidents. I name them in Chapter Ten.

Even in private life, persons close to the alcoholic fail to make the connection. Joseph Kellerman, a counselor with the National Council on Alcoholism, and author of several works on the disease, estimates that it takes an average of *nine years* for the spouse to *tentatively* diagnose alcoholism. Another expert has concluded that alcoholism is not noticed outside the home until the alcoholic reaches the advanced stage of the disease and starts to display the bizarre behavior associated with that condition -- such as showing up drunk on the job.

During its decades long time span, detection by others is, at best, spotty and sporadic. Although close observers may be reluctant to reach a conclusion, or can be blind to its symptoms, alcoholism is actually an either-or condition. A knowledgeable physician once told me that alcoholism is like pregnancy: either you have it or you don't. And like early pregnancy, alcoholism is not obvious to most observers in its earliest stages. Unlike pregnancy, however, the early stages of alcoholism may last, not for weeks, but for years.

The reason alcoholics among us go unperceived is not because they do not display blatant symptoms of the disease. They all do. Many are highly destructive and inflict great harm on the people they live with and, in many cases, the people they work with. But few of these victims of victims realize that alcoholism causes the bad behavior. Making the connection might not make life with an alcoholic any easier, but it would eliminate one factor contributing to the pain of the victim-observers -- the bafflement and mystification caused by the bad behavior.

Given the low level of alcoholism awareness, we should not be surprised when the alcoholism of public figures is missed by everyone. Joe McCarthy was not seen as an alcoholic by the public that watched his antics on television or read millions of words about him in newspapers. The media didn't report his fondness for alcohol. Until the end, some of his colleagues, too, were blind to it. So were his opponents, some even after he died.

Richard Rovere, in his decidedly unfriendly biography, denies that McCarthy was an alcoholic prior to his final collapse. As a journalist covering the Senate at the time, Rovere had lots of direct contact with McCarthy. Based on these observations, Rovere assures us that before his ignominious end, McCarthy "was not always drunk," frequently "went on the wagon," sometimes switched from whiskey to beer, spent time with friends, and "went deer hunting in the Wisconsin woods." But, Rovere confidently tells us, "he did not devote his life to drinking." The senator, says Rovere, "... was never a sot." Rovere manages in these passages to demonstrate that he knows nothing about alcoholism. None of the behavior he describes is inconsistent with the disease, and some of it -- going on the wagon, switching to beer -- is downright symptomatic.

There is nothing unusual about non-recognition. It is the norm.

Unless a conscious effort is made to acquire knowledge about alcoholism and then to apply that knowledge rigorously -- to actually appraise persons we encounter -- alcoholics, both those in our private lives and those in public view, will remain unrecognized.

Unlike most people, I have gone out of my way to spot alcoholics in my daily life. Working in large organizations, I tried to recognize as many alcoholics as possible among my colleagues in order to protect myself from their egocentric, destructive behavior. Like all large organizations, those I worked for all hired alcoholics and promoted them to important positions.

My "diagnostic skill" is such that I recognized many individuals as alcoholics upon meeting them for the first time. I've done this often and have seen my "instant diagnoses" confirmed by subsequent behavior. But I'm not the only one able to identify them on sight. As Richard C. Bates, M.D. wrote in *Applied Therapeutics*:

There is a certain *look* about alcoholics. I haven't been able to capture this look in words, but people who deal with alcoholics tell you that they can spot, many times, somebody who *just looks* like an alcoholic. [Emphasis added.]

But before I acquired my current level of knowledge -- and getting it was a very slow process -- I was as blind to the problem as anyone.

While serving as an Army lieutenant during the Korean War, I was outraged to overhear another officer refer to my company commander as a "boozer." I had never seen my friend Captain Smith drunk, or, for that matter, drinking anything but Coca-Cola. But six months after hearing that "outrageous slander" of my friend and immediate superior, I was to see Captain Smith stupefyingly drunk, remorsefully hungover, absent without leave, and -- mercifully -- hospitalized for alcoholism.

I grew up in a large extended family and had many aunts and uncles. Of that crowd of people, all of them now dead, there were two who were exceptionally and openly fond of drink. This aunt and uncle could always be counted upon to get "high" and "silly" at family parties to the delight of all. But I am as certain now as I am of anything that neither was an alcoholic. Why? Because neither ever displayed a single *symptom* of the disease -- never an ugly word while drinking, no blackouts, no high tolerance while drinking, no facial deterioration, and no family difficulties due to the drinking. This was true in spite of their well-above-average consumption of alcohol over many years.

Although those two most conspicuous consumers of alcohol were not alcoholics, three others among that large group (more than a dozen) of my parents' generation were, I am now convinced, alcoholics. I reached that conclusion about two of these relatives based on my present knowledge of alcoholism and my recollection of their behavior. The third person's son is currently a member of Alcoholics Anonymous, and he revealed to me that his father, my uncle, had been an alcoholic.

The existence of alcoholism in those three relatives was unknown -- was invisible -- to their nonalcoholic peers for as long as forty years. In each case, I came to the conclusion only after they were dead that each was an alcoholic -- and I thought I knew them very well.

I have asked children of alcoholics (members of Al-Ateen, a self-help organization formed on the Alcoholics Anonymous model) how old they were when they realized what was wrong with their parent. One girl was 14, and she didn't "get it," didn't understand that her father was an alcoholic, until her mother had taken her to several Al-Ateen meetings. She thought he picked a fight with her mother every Friday night because he was tired. All the children in this (most informal) survey said they were teenagers before they understood what the problem was.

Marguerite Courtney was 23 before she realized that her mother's terrifying nocturnal behavior was due to alcoholic drinking. And her mother was dead for many years before Ms. Courtney convinced Alfred Lunt and Lynn Fountaine, the famous husband-and-wife Broadway actors, that alcoholism was the reason why Laurette Taylor had insulted the two of them. Fed up with Taylor's gratuitous abuse, the Lunts had severed the decades-long friendship years earlier. They did not understand, until her daughter told them, that the friendship had been destroyed by alcoholism.

Although alcoholics are usually the last ones to know they have the disease, sometimes they figure it out before their families. I once met, at a meeting of Al-Anon (an organization primarily for spouses of alcoholics) two women who didn't know their husbands were alcoholics until the husbands joined Alcoholics Anonymous. When Billy Carter, the late brother of the former President, first entered AA, his wife Sybil reacted with disbelief. Dennis Wholey quotes her reaction. "... I was astounded... not aware that Billy was drinking as much as he was... "

Some families have buried alcoholic spouses, parents, brothers, and sisters without knowing they were alcoholics.

Most of these recognition failures occur when the alcoholic is still in the early or middle stages of the disease. Late-stage alcoholics, on the other hand, are often garishly identifiable on sight -- even by the alcoholism-ignorant. An unwashed, poorly dressed man staggering on a street corner while clutching a bottle of muscatel would be identified as an alcoholic by all. But even late-stage alcoholics go unrecognized if they don't fit this Skid Row stereotype, as was proven to me by the following experience.

I once hired a middle-aged woman, "Patricia Byrnes," to work under my direct supervision as Chief File Clerk at the headquarters of a large corporation. After being on the job for nearly a year, I began to suspect a problem. She was reasonably efficient, but absent about one day out of ten. After listening to her generally unconvincing excuses, I decided to talk to her former boss at another company. He not only confirmed that he had encountered the same problem of absenteeism, but told me she had worked for more companies than she had shown on our employment application. He also agreed with me when I told him I suspected that she was a drinker.

Armed with her poor attendance record, and the knowledge that she had signed a falsified employment application, I confronted Patricia Byrnes with my suspicion that she had a drinking problem. I gave her a choice: either go into AA or some other treatment program, or be dismissed. I agreed to give her a month to make her decision. She met with an AA friend of mine (who agreed with my diagnosis), but she came up with an excuse for not entering the program: "My doctor said there are too many rough people in AA."

To my consternation, in spite of her refusal to enter a treatment program, she proceeded to establish what was, for her, an astounding record of four straight weeks of daily attendance. She even looked better, and I concluded that she had gone on the wagon. That left me with the choice of extending her one month's "or else" trial period, or of firing someone who seemed to have made a dramatic change for the better. Her "doomsday" arrived, and I let it pass.

On the Monday of the fifth week, Patricia Byrnes telephoned, at about ten in the morning, and told me, in an ominously slurred voice, that she had been delayed but would be at work soon. Shortly before noon, Patricia Byrnes arrived at the office -- thoroughly intoxicated. She tried to sit at her desk and landed on the floor. In the ensuing uproar -- she worked in an open office and soon had several dozen open-mouthed witnesses -- I managed to get her out of the office, with the help of a nurse, and into a taxi. I thrust some money on the driver, gave him her home address, and never saw Patricia Byrnes again.

Now anyone who is heavily intoxicated at ten o'clock on a Monday morning and who lacks the sense not to go to work is on a bender -- a "lost weekend." Only late-stage alcoholics go on benders. In spite of her generally unhealthy appearance, her frequent absences, and her habit of being quietly "sodden" with alcohol during the workday, other than myself only one other person who worked in close contact with her (a woman married to an alcoholic) had suspected that Patricia Byrnes had "the problem." More than twenty persons had worked in the same room with her. Even her young assistant, who had worked alongside Patricial Byrnes for many months, told me she was astonished to see her boss drunk.

Patricia Byrnes did little harm in her job. Yes, she was frequently absent, and I suppose she misfiled documents occasionally because of her tippling. But, by-and-large, she didn't hurt anyone. Earlier-stage alcoholics in higher level jobs, on the other hand, can be dangerous.

Failure to recognize alcoholics and to deal warily with them can be tragic. When Joseph McCarthy was not perceived as an alcoholic and when the public failed to realize that the maligning of innocents is a favorite alcoholic pastime, many suffered unnecessarily.

Why do we fail? If the consequences of perceptual blindness are so severe, if most alcoholics behave so badly, why don't we "see" alcoholism? What are the reasons for this near universal and widespread inability to perceive a condition which is both dangerous and prevalent?

The reasons are many. Although together they add up to a complexity, most are simple and basic. Some result from our long, culturally-sensitive relationship with alcohol, others from characteristics of the disease, and still others from shortcomings of the observers -- those who ought to make the diagnosis but who do not.

An important factor in the near universal non-recognition is that for the great majority of its users, alcohol is non-addictive. Most nonalcoholics, the people who ought to perceive alcoholism as it develops in those close to them, use this drug themselves. These simple, self-evident truths -- that most users are not addicted, that most non-addicts are users -- lead nonalcoholics to assume that everyone else is also not addicted. Consider how different this is from the situation with heroin. There are very few non-addicted users. Most Americans have never even seen it, let alone tried it. Non-users assume (correctly) that most heroin users are addicts.

Even in the case of tobacco we don't have the problem, which we have with alcohol, of massive, non-addictive use. I've met a few non-addicted tobacco users, people who say they smoke only at parties, but such non-addicted smokers are rare. With tobacco, as with heroin, use and addiction go hand-in-hand.

But with alcohol, drinking nonalcoholics -- and in the United States, this means most adults -- develop their own set of attitudes toward the drug based on their own experience with it. This mindset contributes greatly to the inability to see alcoholism. Most nonalcoholics, for example, experience, sometime in their lives, various states of intoxication, and those experiences lead them to tolerate certain behavior in others. When an alcoholic behaves belligerently while drunk, many excuse the ugly behavior and blame it on overindulgence. They may say (if only to themselves), "Don't take him seriously. He's been drinking." Erroneously, they relate characteristic *alcoholic* behavior (belligerence while drinking) to their own, very different reactions to excessive consumption.

Many aspects of the reality of alcoholism interact with the attitudes of nonalcoholic drinkers. One factor which, paradoxically, contributes to the invisibility of alcoholics is the large number of them in our midst. Nearly all of us have encountered noisy, argumentative, heavy drinkers. Many of us have been exposed to crying jags, or even to violent drunks. There are an estimated ten million alcoholics in the United States, and they "teach" the rest of us that pathological behavior is not unusual. Because belligerent drunkenness is not rare, many find it difficult to grasp that it is symptomatic of a powerful disease.

Alcoholics themselves are leading participants in the game of pretending that alcoholism doesn't exist. Denial is a confirming symptom, and a major factor in non-recognition. If the person who is ill does not himself perceive that he is ill, the first step toward treatment found in virtually all other diseases -- self-realization that something is wrong -- is absent.

To appreciate the intensity and the tenacity of the alcoholic's denial, consider this true story: Two members of AA are summoned by the desperate wife of a man who, when they arrive at his house, is not only drunk, but is leaking so much blood from various orifices that the couch he is sitting on is one huge red stain. The reaction of this man when the two visitors identify themselves as members of AA? "Get outta here! My wife is nuts. I'm no alcoholic!" The men from AA, ignoring his protestations, call an ambulance. Thoroughly intoxicated, loudly and violently resisting, and still leaking blood, the man is driven off to a hospital where, a few days later, he dies. The AA members were not surprised. They knew that his hemorrhaging was caused by terminal cirrhosis.

If an alcoholic will deny that he is an alcoholic while on the threshold of death caused by *decades* of alcoholic drinking, it should not surprise us that the typical early or middle phase alcoholic is utterly *convinced* that he is not an alcoholic.

The attitudes of nonalcoholics support denial in many ways, the most harmful being the reluctance to diagnose. The idea that people we respect, people who function as rational, intelligent and even charming members of society might be secret alcoholics and totally incapable of accepting that fact is difficult to accept. We are reluctant to believe that our friends are doubly "bad," that they're both drunkards and liars, alcoholics and deniers.

But we would do ourselves a big favor if we were to react to the drinking and the lying coolly and objectively. They are as symptomatic of alcoholism as sneezes and coughs are to colds. Alcoholism demands both objectivity and, because the victims are master-deceivers, suspiciousness.

Decency and fairness are admirable traits. But if misguided loyalty and lack of knowledge cause us to fail to recognize alcoholism, no one benefits, and the risk of grave harm is enhanced.

Many widely-held attitudes toward alcoholism stem from the repulsiveness of late-stage alcoholics. In fact, the nature of late-stage alcoholism helps obscure the existence of alcoholics in the earlier phases. Late-stage alcoholics train us to pay attention to the wrong symptoms.

Late-stage alcoholics drink every chance they can. Early and middle phase alcoholics do not; they hold jobs and usually limit their drinking to one-night binges, getting drunk perhaps "only" four or five times a week. Many go on the wagon, sometimes for months. They can concentrate on other matters for long periods, seemingly unbothered by the hound of addiction.

Late-stage alcoholics are frequently noticeably drunk. In the earlier stages, the alcoholic shows few signs of drunkenness even when he has consumed large quantities. They can even carry out demanding tasks while their blood alcohol levels are significantly elevated. Some run meetings faultlessly; others perform surgical procedures.

Late-stage alcoholics are contemptible or piteous. Early or middle-stage alcoholics, on the other hand, are often skillful manipulators who are often superficially (but convincingly) contemptuous of the sober people close to them.

Late-stage alcoholics are usually shabbily dressed. Early or middle-stage alcoholics tend to dress *better* than nonalcoholics.

Late-stage alcoholics may look poorly and suffer from serious physical disorders caused by drinking. Younger alcoholics can be superb specimens; some excel at sports. Ty Cobb, perhaps the greatest baseball player who ever lived, was an alcoholic while playing. In recent years, several professional athletes in our most physically demanding sports -- football, basketball, and hockey -- have publicly identified themselves as alcoholics after entering treatment programs.

Late-stage alcoholics often have severe problems holding down a job. Early or middle-stage alcoholics are often perfectionistic overachievers. Some end up running large corporations, countries, or even empires.

Late-stage alcoholics are ego-deficient, sometimes obviously demented. Their lives are clearly controlled by booze. Early-stage alcoholics are ambitious, egocentric, and seemingly in control of their destinies. To unknowledgable outsiders (Rovere, *vis a vis* McCarthy, for example), they may even seem to control their drinking.

Most late-stage alcoholics are self-destructive, passive people who are seldom hostile. Early or middle-stage alcoholics tend to be domineering; they are destructive of others, not themselves.

Late-stage alcoholics are recognized by all as alcoholics, and early and middle-stage alcoholics, by few. Suggestions that they are alcoholics are met with outraged denials, by the alcoholic, by his friends, and even by his enemies. Unless and until they reach the final, self-destructive stages, alcoholics will be seen as a hero, villain, superstar -- anything but an alcoholic. Their alcoholism remains a secret, a phantom whose existence is denied by all, even when vivid signs are apparent to the knowledgeable, wisely *suspicious* observer.

4: THE TRAITORS' DISEASE

All spirits are enslaved which serve evil things.

Shelley

Nothing could be less appealing to an egomaniac than blind, unquestioning loyalty.

Common everyday loyalty presents no problem to the nonalcoholic who does not have an ego problem. As long as no ethical dilemmas or conflicts of interest intrude, most people can grant, effortlessly, a reasonable degree of fidelity to their relatives, to friends, to the organizations that employ them -- and to their country. But alcoholics have sick egos. Enslaved by addiction, they resist the demands of ordinary fidelity. Disloyalty attracts.

Alcoholic betrayal is an everyday occurrence. They routinely bad mouth others. Many cheat on their spouses. If they obtain organizational power -- to hire and fire, for example -- they abuse it, favoring inefficient lackeys over the truly competent.

Because everyday treachery is common, it should come as no

surprise that an extraordinary number of real traitors, people who have actually betrayed their country to its enemies, have been alcoholics.

For starters, consider what is the most infamous spy ring in history, that group of upper class Britons who successfully penetrated the highest levels of British intelligence services during World War II and in the early years of the Cold War. Four Soviet spies -- traitorous Britons -- were uncovered. I am convinced that each of them -- Burgess, Maclean, Philby, and Blunt -- was an alcoholic.

Many who have investigated these complex, interconnected cases suspect that yet another British spy, the so-called Fifth Man, was in place at a high level in counter-intelligence. Both leading suspects for the Fifth Man role also showed signs of alcoholism.

All who have written about them agree that Guy Burgess and Donald Maclean, the Foreign Office officials who fled Britain for the Soviet Union in 1951, were alcoholics. Drinking nearly ruined their careers.

Maclean once went on a two-day bender while on a diplomatic post in Cairo. He broke into the apartment of an American woman diplomat and, in a drunken rampage, demolished her furniture and bathroom fixtures. After this clear sign of alcoholism, Maclean was called back to London for "psychiatric treatment."

As for Burgess, his prodigious drinking bouts, drunk driving arrests, and brawling (not to mention his flamboyant homosexual escapades) eventually ruined his foreign service career.

Unfortunately, their heavy drinking didn't prevent these two from committing ruthless, highly successful treachery. They were both valuable spies for the KGB.

Maclean gave the Soviets, among other secrets, classified information about the United States atomic weapons program while he was posted in the British Embassy in Washington. As for Burgess, he furnished his Soviet controllers with a heavy flow of high-level information on matters of grave national importance. He also rescued Maclean from certain arrest, accompanying him on a spectacular escape to Moscow.

The Third Man, Kim Philby, has been called the most successful spy in history. Going to work for the Soviet apparatus as a young man, he was ordered to infiltrate British secret services. He not only succeeded in penetrating the intelligence corps, he nearly climbed to the pinnacle of power. Many are convinced he would have been put in charge of all British intelligence if he hadn't been thrown on the defensive by Burgess and Maclean's flight to Moscow. Although under a cloud of suspicion, Philby's skillful lying enabled him to avoid being charged with treachery for several years afterwards. Eventually, he too escaped to Moscow -- from Bierut, where he was working as a journalist.

In building the case that Philby (who was frequently described as a heavy drinker, but not an alcoholic, in contemporary reports) was, like Burgess and Maclean, indeed an alcoholic from an early age, we can begin with his mother. Philby himself told Phillip Knightley, the British author who interviewed him in Moscow near the end of his life, "My mother literally drank herself to death. Towards the end, she was drinking a bottle of gin a day." Clearly, she was an alcoholic. Not all children of alcoholics end up as alcoholics themselves, but we now know that the potential to become an alcoholic is inherited. If the son himself exhibited symptoms, then the mother's alcoholism should be viewed as supporting evidence for his own alcoholism.

There are many descriptions of Philby's heavy drinking over the years, including this one from *The Philby Conspiracy* by Page, Leitch, and Knightley (Doubleday & Company, Inc., 1968):

he was [in the 1940's,] a voracious and rather indiscriminate drinker. [known... for throwing down the most appalling mixtures of alcohol.] Not infrequently, he drank with the plain intention of getting speechless drunk... Most... who knew him knew he was an habitually heavy drinker... "

It's my impression and that of others familiar with them, that many *non*alcoholic contemporary educated British drink more alcohol than Americans of the same class. For this reason, it is especially significant that Philby's consumption was so excessive as to be remembered many years later.

The same authors describe Philby, when he lived in Beirut, routinely having his first drink *in the morning*. Morning drinking is a tell-tale sign of alcoholism.

While in Beirut, Philby seemed close to losing control. The periods of drunkenness became more frequent. He ended up literally "in the gutter" on more than one occasion. According to Phillip Knightley in *The Master Spy: The Story of Kim Philby* (Alfred

A. Knopf, 1989):

His family life broke down, and friends ceased to call as often, complaining they could not stand Philby's incoherence...

The drinking grew worse... His friends began to get used to him and often a party would continue over Philby's prostrate figure on the floor, staring glassy-eyed at the ceiling. When it was time to go, the men would carry him out.

After he defected and moved to Moscow, Philby went on "lost weekends" -- a sure sign of alcoholism. Knightley writes:

I know from other sources that he went on three and four-day [benders] in his Moscow flat; that he did not know night from day; that he would sometimes wake up and complain that the maid had not come to clean the flat and do the shopping, only to discover that it was 2 A.M.; and that during his travels he *would think he was in Moscow only to discover he was in Leningrad.* [Emphasis added.]

Members of Alcoholics Anonymous tell of similar bizarre experiences. Episodes of amnesia while drinking are called blackouts. People who have blackouts and go on benders are alcoholics.

Philby was clearly an egomaniac. Murray Sayle, a British journalist who interviewed him in Moscow, correctly rejected ideology as motivation for his treachery:

I doubt that Kim is a committed Marxist. He doesn't use Marxist language, doesn't think like a Marxist. In fact, whenever I talked to him he sounded for all the world like a transplanted British civil servant.

Brushing aside his phony claim of ideological motivation, Sayle correctly fingers Philby's egomania:

There is something about his psychology that gives him great satisfaction to have a secret that the people he's with every day don't know about.

The alcoholism-created personality is shallow. Alcoholics simply don't care about other people. What could be more egocentric and shallow -- and more alcoholic -- than Philby's incredible remark to friends at a cocktail party when he got the news, via telephone, that his ailing wife had just died? He cradled the receiver and said in a loud voice, "You must all drink to my great news. Aileen's dead!"

Alcoholics are as incapable of deep conviction to an ideology as they are of caring for others. Philby's motivation for his duplicitous life was not Marxism. It was his alcoholic ego.

The Fourth Man -- Anthony Blunt -- left the Secret Service after World War II and was not publicly exposed as a traitor until 1979. By that time he had been knighted for serving for many years as Surveyor of the Queen's Pictures.

According to Penrose and Freeman in *Conspiracy of Silence: The Secret Life of Anthony Blunt* (Farrar, Strauss Giroux, 1987), Blunt would start his daily drinking at 11 A.M. One of his MI5 interrogators told them that while being interrogated Blunt "had obviously been drinking a good deal." According to Stephen Koch, "He drank like a fish." Chapman Pincher in *Traitors* (Viking Penguin Inc., 1987) describes him as "a heavy gin drinker." Most revealingly, Pincher -- who was not making the case for alcoholism, thus enhancing the credibility of his information -- discloses that this genteel, upper class art historian, this vain and prissy homosexual who spent much of his time at Buckingham Palace and who relished his close contacts with the royal family, was "prone to violence when drunk." Marty Mann commented on this sort of behavior in her classic *New Primer on Alcoholism* (Holt, Rinehart and Winston, 1958):

[Alcoholism] is noticeable if a drinker displays marked "Jekyll and Hyde" characteristics when drinking, such as normally quiet and reserved person who becomes loud, argumentative, *belligerent or violent*, only when drinking... [Such] drinking behavior provides the most obvious signs [of alcoholism] to an informed onlooker... [Emphasis added.]

Blunt was power hungry. This was evident even after he ceased betraying his country. According to one of his art students, Patrick Mathieson, "No one dared criticize him... *he was on a shocking ego trip*. He had to keep proving his own *power*." [Emphasis added.]

The concurrence of treachery, egomania, heavy drinking, and violence when drinking convince me: Anthony Blunt was the Fourth Alcoholic in this notorious group.

Some students of this complex espionage operation are convinced that there was a Fifth Man, yet another high level Soviet mole, in British intelligence. Nigel West examines this possibility in *Molehunt: The Full Story of the Soviet Spy Inside MI5* (Coronet Books, 1987), and reports that internal investigators determined that either Roger Hollis, the Director of MI5 (the British equivalent of the FBI), or Graham Mitchell, the Deputy Director, had been a Soviet spy. There is no doubt that *someone* had tipped off Philby, warning him that he was about to be confronted with compelling evidence of betrayal, and enabling him to flee Beirut to Moscow. Both Hollis and Mitchell were among the few who knew that the authorities were about to pounce. There had been other serious counter-intelligence failures over the years, and West (among others) makes a convincing case for the Fifth Man hypothesis. West, who had the cooperation of at least one retired counter-espionage officer, concluded that Hollis was innocent and that Graham Mitchell must have been the betrayer.

Mitchell retired early, perhaps to avoid interrogation as a suspected spy. In his book, West casually mentions, "In later life [Mitchell] developed a drinking problem... " This sort of comment by an alcoholism-naive writer usually means that the person who was a functioning alcoholic for decades has begun to exhibit late-stage symptoms. As already explained, in most cases no one outside the immediate family knows of the alcoholism until the alcoholic is getting drunk at inappropriate times. Some take decades to reach that stage. The alternative explanation, that a moderate-drinking nonalcoholic suddenly becomes an alcoholic when past the age of 60, is so unlikely as to be impossible.

Another writer on the infamous British traitors, Chapman Pincher, who was apparently guided by another retired MI5 officer, thinks that Hollis, not Mitchell, was the Fifth Man. He makes a single off-hand reference to possible alcoholism in Hollis in *Traitors*. "A *history of drunkenness* has been no bar to entry... as evidenced by Maclean and Burgess in the Foreign Office, Philby in MI6, *Hollis*... in MI5." [Emphasis added.]

All six of these men -- Burgess, Maclean, Philby, Blunt, Mitchell, and Hollis -- are now dead. Of the six, there is sufficient evidence to conclude that four, Burgess, Maclean, Philby, and Blunt -- each an arch-traitor -- were alcoholics. As for Hollis and Mitchell, the comments by West and Pincher suggest that they too had the disease.

Because of the boozy lives the four spies led, some writers on this famous case have imagined that the pressures of leading a double life caused the heavy drinking. This is a romantic variation of the "underlying cause" notion -- that alcoholics medicate themselves with liquor because of life's pressures. Like the other versions, it is wrong. Based on current knowledge of the disease, we can say with confidence that the alcoholism came first. We can assume that each was an alcoholic before he betrayed his country. Since it is my contention that alcoholism creates an unquenchable thirst for power in its victims, I conclude that alcohol addiction caused the disloyalty, not the other way around.

Successful deception is mother's milk to the alcoholic's ego. It makes him feel superior to those he has deceived, and it is this need to feel superior that explains his treachery. It explains the extraordinary incidence -- one hundred percent -- of alcoholism in the four British spies, and its presence in an remarkable number of other modern traitors.

Richard Sorge was an alcoholic and a traitor. After fighting bravely for Germany in World War I (he was wounded three times), he not only became a communist in the 1920s but he actually switched his nationality. He secretly became a Soviet citizen and a spy for the GRU, Soviet military intelligence.

Sorge set up and ran a highly successful spy ring in Japan in the 1930's and in the early years of World War II. Discovered in 1941, Sorge was hanged by the Japanese. Because of his services to their cause, the Soviet Union put his image on postage stamps and practically deified him.

In *Target Tokyo: The Story of the Sorge Spy Ring* (McGraw-Hill Book Company, 1984) authors Prange, Goldstein, and Dillon describe Sorge's spectacular drinking. (Their index lists twenty-three entries under the sub-heading "Sorge, Richard, drinking.") As early as 1926, when he was 31, his first wife left him because of drinking and infidelity. While in Tokyo, witnesses report him showing the alcoholic's typical high tolerance; he polished off entire bottles of whiskey in single drinking sessions.

Sorge had the typical alcoholic ego: "he possessed a monumental ego... was a hard drinker, a womanizer, a man who loved to hold the conversational spotlight."

At one point he told his Japanese mistress that "Sorge is a god." Although his ego crumbled temporarily immediately after his capture -- the authors of *Target Tokyo* point out that he had to stop drinking "cold turkey" while in prison -- it soon reasserted itself. (Enforced abstinence will not, by itself, deflate the alcoholic ego.) Sorge volunteered to write a complete confession of his espionage activities, and the resulting narrative is described as "above all the work of an egotist... "

His alcoholism-induced bravado, as it does for all drinker-spies, helped Sorge in his espionage. He bluffed his way into the confidence of the German Ambassador, whom he then doubly betrayed by sleeping with his wife. His accurate warning to Moscow that Hitler was about to attack the Soviet Union could have saved hundreds of thousands of Soviet lives. Joseph Stalin ignored the warning, however, for reasons having to do with his own alcoholism, as I explain in Chapter Eleven.

Other probable alcoholic spies: Horst Eitner, a West German who was a partner of British double agent George Blake and who "loved his drink," according to his wife; Harry Houghton, the English civil servant who sold Naval secrets to Gordon Lonsdale and who had been kept in a sensitive job even though he was "inclined to insobriety"; Frank Gifford Bossard, who sold British secrets to the Russians and who was described as "a heavy drinker," and Otto John, the German triple defector (he defected to Britain during World War II, and, in the 1950's, to East Germany, and, finally, back again to West Germany) who was labeled an alcoholic by General Reinhard Gehlen, former head of West German intelligence.

Reino Hayhanen, a Soviet spy who was an illegal immigrant living in the United States, called attention to himself by having noisy drunken fights with his wife and drunk driving. Hayhanen switched sides and betrayed Rudolf Abel, an important Soviet professional spy.

Michael Bettaney, a 33-year-old senior counterespionage officer in Britain's MI5, attempted to betray his country in 1983 by approaching the KGB resident in London. His clumsy attempt was rejected by the Soviets, who simply didn't believe he was genuine. But MI5 found out about it and arrested Bettaney. He was sentenced to twenty-three years in prison for espionage. At the time, he had a record of arrest for public drunkenness and, according to Nigel West, was "under treatment by MI5's office doctor for an alcohol dependency requiring a bottle of whiskey a day... "

Pincher, in *Traitors*, identifies several other alcoholic traitors. He says Hans Joachim Tiedge of West German counter-intelligence was "a habitual drunkard." Tiedge defected to East Germany. Another West German, Jurgen Westphal, who had "a serious drink problem," was arrested after approaching the East Germans. Ruby Louise Schuler, a "serious alcoholic" who later died from its complications, was a secretary at a California technology company engaged in defense work. She enabled a friend to enter her employer's plant where he photographed secret plans for sale to the Eastern Bloc. Colonel Pyotr Popov, a GRU officer who was executed for spying for the CIA, "drank addictively."

In 1976, a 66-year-old Swiss general was accused of being a Soviet spy for fourteen years. He was a "hard drinking... loud-mouth," according to a contemporary press account.

In 1983, the United States Justice Department accused James Durward Harper, Jr. of delivering technical data concerning the Minuteman missile system to Polish agents. Harper was described as a "hard-drinking womanizer" in *The New York Times*.

Christopher Boyce is currently serving a long prison term for having sold the Soviets top secret details of an American spy satellite. Boyce, a former altar boy and son of a retired FBI agent, began his treachery while only 22 years old. His partner in espionage, who delivered the documents Boyce had stolen to the Soviet Embassy in Mexico, was Andrew Daulton Lee, a boyhood chum. In his book about the pair, *The Falcon and The Snowman* (Pocket Books, 1979), Robert Lindsey relates that at one point Lee told Boyce that if he wasn't careful he would become an alcoholic. Later, in a conversation with Lindsey, Lee actually refers to Boyce as an alcoholic. Boyce, who worked at a highly secret facility of TRW, a large California defense contractor, was known to drink heavily while on the job.

Young Christopher Boyce carried out one of most damaging espionage conspiracies ever uncovered. He betrayed the secrets of a $5 billion satellite system. If his partner is correct and Boyce is an alcoholic, then it was his alcoholism-dominated ego that caused this son of conservative, patriotic parents to betray his country.

Edwin P. Wilson is a former CIA agent now serving a fifty-two year prison term for various offenses, including selling twenty tons of C4, the plastic explosive frequently used by terrorists, to Qadhafi's regime in Libya. After being sentenced on those charges, Wilson tried to arrange -- from prison -- the murder of the prosecutor and eight others he blamed for putting him behind bars. Peter Maas, in *Manhunt: The Incredible Story of the C.I.A. Agent Turned Terrorist* (Random House, 1987), lists several entries in his index under "Wilson, Edwin P.: drinking problem." In addition to the heavy drinking, Wilson made clear by his extravagant duplicity and his history of trying to arrange murders that he has an extraordinary ego.

Clayton Longtree, the Marine Guard convicted of espionage while assigned to the United States Embassy in Moscow, is identified as an alcoholic by Ronald Kessler in *Moscow Station: How the KGB Penetrated the American Embassy* (Charles Scribner's Sons, 1989). (In contrast to most of the others mentioned in this chapter, Longtree seems to have been an underachiever; he grossly underperformed as a Marine. The fact that he voluntarily surrendered is also unusual.)

Philip R. Agee, a former CIA officer, earned the enmity of his ex-colleagues by disclosing the identity of many CIA agents and employees in his 1974 book, *Inside the Company: CIA Diary* (Stonehill, 1975). Although he denies it, some blame this renegade for the assassination of Richard Welch, the CIA Athens station chief who was shot dead outside his home. After he left the CIA, Agee travelled to Havana where he is believed to have volunteered information to Castro's intelligence service. Although I do not have sufficient information to determine if Agee is an alcoholic, British author Brian Freemantle noted in *CIA: The 'Honourable' Company* (Michael Joseph/Rainbird, 1983) that "Agee is now domiciled in Hamburg and there are reports of his drinking heavily... "

According to Ronald Kessler's *The Spy in the Russian Club*

(Charles Scribner's Sons, 1990), Glenn Souther, who committed suicide in Moscow in 1989, showed many signs of alcoholism before his defection. He drank in binges and during one drinking bout gave his young wife bruises and a split lip. He was a womanizer, an overachiever, a practical joker (it's good ego-inflating behavior), manipulative, and a traitor. Although he escaped to Moscow before the FBI could get any solid information about his treachery, Kessler makes a convincing case for assuming that this Indiana-born young man -- who asked, in his suicide note, to be buried in his KGB officer's uniform -- gave the Soviets everything he had access to as a US Navy photographer. Assigned to a top-secret intelligence unit, Souther probably gave the Soviet's details of our nuclear retaliatory strike plans, including escape routes to be used by American pilots who might be shot down.

Robert Lee Johnson, a U.S. Army Sergeant, stationed at the Armed Forces Courier Station in Europe, was arrested in 1965 and charged with spying for the Soviets. The information he gave the Soviets about NATO war plans was so highly valued by the Soviets that it was brought directly to Premier Khrushchev soon after receipt. According to Tom Mangold, U.S. intelligence considered Johnson the most damaging military spy in our history. According to Mangold, Johnson was an alcoholic.

Then there is the case of Edward Lee Howard, described in chilling detail by David Wise in *The Spy Who Got Away: The Inside Story of Edward Lee Harvey, the CIA Agent Who Betrayed His Country's Secrets and Escaped to Moscow* (Random House, 1988). Howard, who joined the CIA as a 28-year-old, was trained for a field assignment in Moscow. He was to run spies in the Soviet capital, under the watchful eye of the KGB.

Just before he was to leave for Moscow, his superiors got wind of Howard's heavy drinking. Ordered to take a polygraph, he failed four separate examinations. According to Wise's sources inside the CIA, he failed because he answered questions about his drinking deceptively. Howard (who met with Wise in Budapest after his escape to the Soviet Union) denied this. He claimed the CIA had been concerned about some petty theft that he had admitted to -- or that the polygraph machine gave false readings. Alcoholics lie about their drinking. There is no reason to think that this alcoholic -- Wise (correctly, in my opinion) identifies him as such -- was telling the truth when he was "fluttered" by the CIA, and there's no reason to believe him when he denies that his drinking caused him to be fired.

After the CIA dismissed Howard, he moved to New Mexico where he continued to drink heavily. He made drunken telephone calls directly to the U.S. Embassy in Moscow on the CIA's direct line. While in Washington on a business trip, he showed up one weekend -- unannounced and drunk -- in his ex-boss's driveway, complaining about the way he had been treated.

While still employed at the CIA, Howard had consulted with its in-house alcoholism counselor. David Wise quotes what the counselor told the young alcoholic:

> I've got people who sit in the parking lot at headquarters, drinking. I've got one lady who filled her windshield wiper dispenser with vodka and rigged the line so the hose comes inside the car. When she's caught in traffic, she can turn on the wipers and squirt herself.

This alcoholism specialist decided, apparently, that Howard's own drinking was not a problem:

> The counselor shook his head and fixed Howard with a kindly gaze. "You'll settle down," he said, "If it gets worse, come and see me.'"

Perhaps the CIA's "expert" didn't understand that alcoholism is an "either or" condition. Telling an alcoholic to "settle down" makes about as much sense as telling a diabetic that if he will just "take it easy" his body will soon react normally to carbohydrates. He also seems not to understand that it's the alcoholic's inflated ego -- not his consumption of booze -- that's the real threat to security. He may not have heard that the ego causes alcoholics' to resent perceived mistreatment more intensely than nonalcoholics. Or that Jekyll and Hyde behavior is symptomatic.

One night, while drinking, Howard fired a gun in a confrontation with three unarmed Santa Fe teenagers:

> It was almost as though there were two halves to his personality. The world knew Howard as a highly intelligent, successful young economist and former Foreign Service officer. [While in

the CIA he had used the State Department as his cover.] The other half was an angry alcoholic who packed a gun and acted irrationally. The two pieces did not fit, and now both were visible for the first time.

David Wise is wrong. The two pieces fit. The same entity that drove Howard to his early success also caused him to carry a gun and to use it. (Although he came from a modest background, Howard had successful careers in the Peace Corps, A.I.D., and a private company before joining the CIA, where he was selected for the prestigious Moscow assignment.) That entity -- alcoholism-induced egomania -- also causes "unreasonable resentments." After he was fired, this resentful, self-centered alcoholic contacted the KGB and told them everything he knew about the CIA's Moscow operation.

Armed with the traitor's information, the KGB seized Adolf G. Tolkachev, a Soviet citizen who had been furnishing the CIA with information about Soviet stealth technology. He was executed. The KGB swept up all the CIA's technical assets in Moscow, including multi-million dollar hidden listening devices. In the words of one CIA official, "The damage was tremendous."

After the CIA learned of Howard's treachery, he was placed under FBI surveillance. Unfortunately, he escaped and now lives in Moscow.

Of course, not all traitors are alcoholics*, and not all alcoholics employed in sensitive jobs turn out to be security risks. On the contrary, some may have worked rigorously *against* some well-known alcoholic traitors. William Harvey, a senior CIA official for many years and one of the major figures in the effort to nail Kim Philby, has been described (by Freemantle) as "a drinker" who once fired his pistol into his office ceiling to make a point. Barbara Walker, the ex-wife of convicted Navy spy John Walker (an apparent nonalcoholic), has been identified as an alcoholic in

---

*I could discover nothing in his biographies to suggest that Benedict Arnold was an alcoholic. His father, however, was a classic case. A much-respected merchant in his younger years, he ended up as the town drunk.

several sources. She reported her ex-husband's treachery to the FBI. (She waited seventeen years before making the call, however.)

One of the most damaging CIA alcoholics was apparently not, in the ordinary sense, a traitor.

James Jesus Angleton, longtime director of the CIA's counter intelligence unit, was supposed to catch Soviet spies. In his book, *Cold Warrior: James Jesus Angleton: The CIA's Master Spy Hunter* (Simon & Schuster, 1991), Tom Mangold has a (refreshingly blunt!) entry in the index:

    Angleton, James Jesus
      alcoholism of, ...

No less than eight pages are referenced under this heading.

Guests at Angleton's regular lunch table at a Washington restaurant came away astounded "by his capacity for alcohol." Archie Roosevelt, a senior CIA executive, simply couldn't understand how Angleton stayed on his feet after observing his normal midday consumption.

But if he didn't sell secrets to the Soviets, what did this powerful alcoholic do? Like McCarthy and the alcoholic prosecutors Whitman and Fickert, Angleton seems to have been a compulsive false accuser. Many loyal CIA employees' careers were cut short when Angleton accused them of being secret Soviet agents -- behind their backs, so they had no chance to defend themselves. His charges were so wildly wrong that the CIA agreed, years later, to award pensions to his innocent victims.

This alcoholic treated real spies far more kindly. After Angleton was fired for gross disregard of rules (he conducted illegal mail intercepts against American citizens), investigators discovered documents that had lain in his private safe for years. Placed finally in proper hands, these long-ignored papers led to an accomplishment that seemed beyond the capability of the alcoholic Angleton: the unmasking and the breakup in France of a *real* Soviet spy ring.

In view of their astonishing record, the CIA, the British Secret Service, and other intelligence services take horrendous risks whenever they hire an alcoholic for a sensitive position.

According to Brian Freemantle, of all the intelligence agencies, the CIA may be especially blind to these risks. He reports that although the Agency has a "rigid attitude" against homosexuality (he claims that whenever homosexuality is uncovered in a polygraph examination, the subject is eased out), "heavy drinking -- even alcoholism -- is tolerated."* They seem convinced that alcoholics in sensitive positions present no increased security risk.

Those who have written on the major spy cases report that the betrayers claimed other reasons to explain their treachery. Both the callow Boyce and the elderly Philby claimed to be motivated by ideology. Howard grandiosely announced to Wise that he is now "at war" with the CIA. But these alcoholic claims of ideological motivation for their treachery are as phony as alcoholic denials of addictive drinking. Some alcoholics became traitors for the same reason their brother-alcoholics and sister-alcoholics became actors, writers, and career criminals: betrayal offers an exceptionally big payoff to the alcoholism-battered ego.

---

*According to more recent information, the CIA no longer bans homosexuals.

5: POWER SYMPTOMS

The thing is that some people are just psychologically less ready
for failure than others.

Ted Bundy

The alcoholic's drive for power is his principal means of compen-
sating for the domination of self by a demanding and unforgiving
master -- alcohol addiction. *Nearly all the behavioral symptoms not
actually involving drinking are facets of the alcoholic's overriding need
to acquire and abuse power.*

Because alcoholics adopt deceptive drinking practices early in the
game, many people in daily contact with them will not notice the
heavy drinking. This makes the power symptoms most important,
for they, by their very nature, cannot be hidden. There are no
closet megalomaniacs.

This fact helped me enormously in researching this book. In
gathering my "collection" of historical alcoholics, I looked for
alcoholism in persons whose monumental egocentricity had demanded history's notice. I discovered, for example, alcoholism in
the biographies of Alexander the Great, Ivan the Terrible, and

Huey Long not because I had any prior knowledge of their drinking habits (I had none), but because their well-known egocentricity made me suspicious. I describe and explain in this chapter the most common of the power symptoms. Although I believe my collective designation of these behavior patterns as *"power* symptoms" is original, alcoholism specialists have long recognized many of these patterns, individually, as indicators of the disease.

As is the case with any list of symptoms for this complex disease, not all alcoholics will exhibit all the signs. Some -- those who succumb quickly and become derelicts at an early age -- will exhibit few of the power symptoms. But most alcoholics will display a *constellation* of symptoms from among those I describe.

It bears repeating that alcoholic egos are not equipped with a toggle switch; they do not acquire normal-sized egos just because their blood alcohol level has temporarily dropped to zero. Power symptoms survive during "dry" periods.

These then are the all-important power symptoms.

Denial. No matter how well educated, no matter how high the IQ, no matter what he has accomplished in his chosen occupation, the alcoholic will deny his alcoholism *to the point of absurdity.*

Although the late Congressman Wilbur Mills will be forever remembered by the public for his drunken romp in a Washington fountain with Fanne Fox, the "exotic dancer," as Chairman of the House Ways and Means Committee he was, in fact, greatly respected by tax professionals for his mastery of the complexities of the Internal Revenue Code. The man's competence was awesome and, after his downfall, he was sorely missed by the CPA's, tax lawyers and others who had to cope with the complexities of the nation's tax laws. "We never would have had this mess if Wilbur was still in charge," is what one tax partner in a major accounting firm told me not long after an overhaul of tax regulations created massive confusion.

So how did this highly intelligent and pragmatic man, who by his own admission was drinking two quarts of 100-proof vodka a day at the peak of his drinking career, react when an alcoholism specialist, a physician, first told him he was an alcoholic? (After leaving politics Mills spent many sober years practicing tax law and counseling alcoholics.) Dennis Wholey quotes him in *The Courage to Change* (Houghton Mifflin Company, 1984):

Lieutenant Commander Michael Bohan at the Bethesda Naval Hospital was the one who had the unmitigated gall to tell me I was an alcoholic. The first thing that flashed in my mind was, how the hell [was] a man like that... ever... admitted to medical school? How could he ever have graduated? Why would the navy ever commission him as a doctor? One thing [was] certain, he would never get to be a captain in the navy. I would see to that myself. I knew he was no good...

Although recovered alcoholics can, like Mills, laugh good-naturedly at their denial as they look back from the sanctuary (and the sanity) of sobriety, while they are active alcoholics the denial is as deep, profound, and as utterly irrational as Mills's reminiscence suggests. This bizarre behavior by people who display good judgment and high intelligence in other areas of their lives gives some hint of the potency of the disease's insidious control over the alcoholic's psyche.

But why do I call denial a power symptom, and why do I list it first in this chapter? Because denial is the foundation for all the other power symptoms. The alcoholic's ego would be severely deflated by an admission that it has no control over a substance that most people can handle on a "take it or leave it" basis. The "power" message that thunders upward from the ego is this:

I am in complete control! Alcoholics are not in control. Therefore, I am not an alcoholic!

I am convinced that without this deep-rooted assertion of power, which we perceive as denial, the alcoholic would either collapse into the abyss of terminal alcoholism and become a non-functioning daily inebriant, or he would enter a recovery program and begin the transformation of personality that is essential to permanent sobriety. Either course -- embracing daily inebriation or seeking sobriety -- is a form of *ego surrender.*

Recognition of the tenacity and depth of denial is essential to understanding the profound effect the disease has on alcoholic behavior and personality.

Lying. Psychologically healthy persons might lie to defend themselves in certain situations (to a highway patrolman, when caught speeding, for example), or for reasons of self-aggrandizement (exaggerating their accomplishments in a job interview), but most people are honest most of the time. There's a sound and simple reason for this: normal people have no reason to lie gratuitously. But alcoholics are different. For them, life is one long lie. Honest self-appraisal would lead them to accept the fact of their addiction. But honesty would force them to stop drinking or to turn to daily inebriation. Neither course is attractive, so they adopt a pattern of glibly lying about their drinking. If all they lied about was their drinking, it would be bad enough. But they become as addicted to telling falsehoods as they are to ingesting alcohol.

The alcoholic soon learns that lies empower. Telling a falsehood places the liar in a position of superiority over others: he knows he's lying and they do not. Turning others into fools (for believing the lie) is raw meat to the alcoholic ego.

Practice does make perfect, and most alcoholics become slick fabricators. But they cannot fool all of the people all of the time. Sometimes they're caught in monumental whoppers. Whenever a major falsification is uncovered, red flags ought to go up; the alcoholism-wise should look for other symptoms of the disease.

One very deceptive gentleman who warrants a close retrospective look is Admiral Richard E. Byrd, a man once revered by millions for his exploits as an aviator-explorer of arctic regions.

One of Byrd's most famous feats was accomplished in 1926 when he, and his co-pilot, Floyd Bennett, were the first to fly over the North Pole. The truth is, this great achievement never happened. He and Bennett didn't reach the Pole. As Richard Montague made clear in *Oceans, Poles and Airmen* (Random House, 1971), Byrd's claim is "a fraud that has persisted for nearly half a century... [a] monumental deception."

Based on the performance capability of Byrd's airplane, Montague convincingly demonstrates that it was simply impossible for him to have flown to the Pole and back to his base at Spitzbergen, Norway, during the fifteen and one-half hours he was aloft. It would have taken twenty-two to twenty-four hours to make the round trip. According to Montague, after Byrd returned from his flight, he asked Bernt Balchen, himself a pioneer airman, to make some computations. These same figures appeared on Byrd's flight chart -- the one he himself supposedly had kept during his flight "to the Pole." Byrd used Balchen's calculations to falsify his chart.

To further support his assertion of Byrd's mendacity, Montague quotes a 1960 study by G.H. Liljequist, a Norwegian meteorologist, showing that Byrd would have required a northerly gale of forty-five to fifty knots on his return flight in order to have made the flight in the elapsed time. After examining meteorological charts for the day of the flight, Liljequist concluded that there had been virtually no wind.

To this compelling circumstantial evidence, Montague adds that Floyd Bennett once confessed to Balchen that the plane had developed an oil leak, shortly after taking off from Spitzbergen. Byrd ordered Bennett not to continue towards the Pole, but to fly in circles. They did so for fourteen hours. During the entire flight, they were no more than fifteen miles from Spitzbergen. They never got close to the Pole!

Montague tells of another well-documented case of fraud by Byrd. While exploring Antarctica in 1929, three members of Byrd's expedition returned from a seven-hour flight and said they had discovered a large mountain peak. When they excitedly reported this news to Byrd, he asked them to show on a map just where the newly-discovered peak was located. They pointed to the location, and Byrd coolly congratulated them on having confirmed the discovery he had made -- but failed to mention to anyone -- that very morning. He went to his office and closed his door. In a few minutes he popped out, waving a map showing a large "X" at the same spot. It was obvious to those present -- all of them Naval personnel well below the Admiral's rank -- that the "X" had been written with a different pencil than the one Byrd had used to make other, authentic notations during his flight. Two other flyers had been with Byrd on the morning flight, and they told their infuriated colleagues that their plane had turned back about 100 miles short of the mountain peak.

So much for Byrd's fakery. Now for his drinking. According to Montague, he carried several pints of cognac in his flight bag during his flight to the *South* Pole. When the aircraft landed at a refueling stop on the way back, he was barely able to stand. He staggered around shouting, "We made it! We made it!" Four and a half hours later, he was back at the base camp in Little America and in full control of himself -- displaying the alcoholic's typical ability to recover quickly from a binge.

Montague writes of another incident. After returning from a flight that lasted seven hours, Byrd, thoroughly intoxicated, was "struggling and cursing loudly... raving mad" in front of the entire Little America population.

In a brief article about Montague's book, *The New York Times* referred to the author's references to Byrd's "personal frailties." *The Times* went on to say that "some of Byrd's associates who had known those frailties but were also indebted to Byrd for starting them on a variety of careers were dismayed by public airing of charges against him." The "newspaper of record," unlike Montague, did not mention his drinking.

There is no justification for hiding alcoholism in a public official or in a national hero like Admiral Byrd. In Byrd's case, knowing as we now do, of alcoholics' potential for lying, knowledge of the Admiral's drinking lends considerable weight to Montague's already convincing case that he falsified historically-important records. The alcoholism-induced need to lie explains the otherwise inexplicable behavior of a man who was admired by millions.*

Overachievement.   Their strong need to compensate for the destructive power of the addiction frequently causes alcoholics to rise quickly in their chosen profession. I am convinced that if the innate ability is there, *early* success is the norm for drinkers. Young alcoholics have exceptional needs for ego assurance, and, for most, the drinking does not impair that quest.

David J. Pittman made the point in his book, *Alcoholism: An Interdisciplinary Approach* (Harper and Row, 1959):

The alcoholic must prove he is better than his fellow man so that he will not have to feel so guilty... when he is sober. Therefore,

---

*Sadly, Admiral Byrd's son, Richard E. Byrd, Jr., died a few years ago, an alcoholic derelict. A former Naval officer and Harvard graduate, he disappeared while en route from his home in Massachusetts to Washington, D.C. He was to attend a ceremony honoring his father, but never arrived. His body was discovered in an abandoned Baltimore warehouse, dressed in dirty clothes and wearing one shoe. A watchman had been the last to see him alive, carrying a bottle in a brown paper bag.

*he must do things better than most people and consequently
becomes compulsive and perfectionistic.* [Emphasis added.]

Of course, if they move into the later stages of the disease and
get drunk virtually every day, alcoholics will be unable to function
in demanding occupations. Many young over-achievers become
middle-aged wrecks. This is what happened to several famous
American alcoholic writers. Fitzgerald, Hemingway, and Capote (to
mention only three) were already famous while in their early twenties but became nonproductive late-stage alcoholics in middle age.

Ethical Deterioration. In addition to lying, infidelity, and other
signs of unethical behavior, alcoholics frequently get involved in
more complex improprieties. Sometimes, the disease-caused
unethical deterioration brings down an alcoholic who had risen to
lofty heights while his alcoholism went undetected by the public.

I have already mentioned the case of Robert B. Anderson, the
former United States Secretary of the Treasury who went to jail for
bank fraud. After serving as Assistant to President Reagan,
Michael Deaver was found guilty of perjury. At his trial, Deaver
admitted to active alcoholism at the time the offense was committed.

The explanation for Anderson's and Deaver's behavior? The
alcoholic's battered ego cannot accept the normal boundaries
established by ethical norms. Playing by the rules is easy for most
nonalcoholics most of the time. But people with addiction-battered
egos find rules burdensome. Their egos already functioning on
overload, they ignore the rules.

Trouble. This is -- all too frequently -- an end result of the power
symptoms, and not a symptom in itself. But if we have a large
population of people with a condition that causes egomania and
that manifests itself in lying, craftiness, inability to follow rules, a
desire to debase others, serial destruction, ethical deterioration, and
addiction to an intoxicant, it should come as no surprise that they
are over-represented among those who have run-ins with the
authorities for various infractions. These will range from relatively
petty matters to the peccadillos of Anderson and Deaver to
homicide and treason. And to accidents.

The alcoholism of Joseph Hazelwood is well established. He was captain of the Exxon Valdez whose 1989 oil spill was the largest in North American history. Although there seems to have been no convincing evidence that Hazelwood was drunk at the time of the accident, he was absent from the bridge while his ship was sailing through dangerous waters. Disregard of other rules has been alleged in a suit filed before the accident. Bruce Amero, who had served with Hazelwood prior to the accident, claimed in his suit that the captain had ignored Exxon regulations regarding fire and boat drills, had once ordered his officers to shut down electronic navigation equipment and to rely on celestial observations although the stars were not visible, drank on board in violation of Exxon regulations, and failed to appear on the bridge during course changes as required by company rules.

At this writing, two well-known individuals are at the center of developing news stories; alcoholism may be involved in each case. Senator Robert Packwood has been accused of sexual harassment by several women. After the charges were publicly revealed, Packwood entered Hazelden, a Minnesota alcoholism treatment center. He checked out a few days later, far too soon to have completed the usual program. Marge Schott, owner of the Cincinnati Reds baseball team, has been suspended from baseball for repeated use of racial epithets. During an interview on national television, Schott denied that she had a drinking problem. Stay tuned.

Craftiness. The alcoholic develops a crafty, cunning nature.

As with lying, this symptom will be used initially to enable drinking. If, for example, a young male alcoholic is drinking at a bar with a friend and the friend suggests they either go bowling or to a movie, the choice is simple. He's going to choose bowling because bowling alleys have bars and movie houses do not. But the alcoholic cannot say that. Instead, he'll smoothly tell his friend that he heard the movie is a stinker and, besides, they are more likely to meet some girls at the bowling alley. The end result is that the alcoholic continues drinking, and his friend never knows why they didn't go to the movie.*

This craftiness carries over into matters not directly related to the drinking, and has obvious ego-enhancement potential. Manipulation makes the sick ego feel better. Their slyness greatly complicates the general difficulty of dealing with these often dangerous people.

False Accusations. Those with sick egos can enhance their own self image by tearing down others. This leads to false accusations.

The reasons they accuse the innocent are not that difficult to understand. A sick ego gains nothing by attacking someone whose behavior has already earned widespread disapproval; you cannot ruin the good name of someone who doesn't have one. Unable to attack those known to be guilty, the alcoholic can only destroy those who, if not universally admired, are at least respected. The alcoholic might, of course, destroy someone by uncovering and exposing something real, an actual dirty secret. But, unfortunately for the desperate-to-destroy, most people are not secretly guilty of serious wrongdoing. Only false accusations can destroy the innocent.

Most alcoholic maligning is private; neither the accuser or the victim is well-known. But some alcoholics have attacked public figures. McCarthy maligned not only low level government employees but George Marshall and Dean Acheson. In future chapters, I will show that many other well-known figures, including George Washington, Abraham Lincoln, and Henry Wadsworth Longfellow were maligned by alcoholics.

Perhaps the most common private false accusation is that of spousal infidelity, which can be carried to ridiculous extremes. The alcoholic wife of one man I know even accused her (completely innocent) husband of having affairs with her *entire* circle of girl friends. Other husbands are baselessly accused of homosexuality. Recently, a young married friend of mine had this experience: he retired to his bedroom to read and to avoid his alcoholic wife, who

---

*Members of Alcoholics Anonymous have told me that, unlike going on the wagon (which they found relatively easy), trying to stop drinking once a drinking session is underway is extremely difficult. The craving for alcohol is greatly amplified by the first few drinks, and any interruption (especially one long enough to watch a movie) will cause the alcoholic to experience intense physical discomfort.

was drinking heavily. One of his small children had climbed into bed with him and was sleeping alongside. Suddenly his booze-sodden wife barged in, called him a "perverted creep," and took the child away.

The nature of the alcoholic's accusation will be determined by the situation. Bosses will accuse their most efficient subordinates of incompetence and, as has been shown, alcoholics with prosecutorial or investigative authority will attack the innocent with all the power at their command.

Grandiose Behavior. Alcoholics frequently act like little gods, taking taxis when they're broke, compulsively spending on luxuries they can't afford, and excessively using credit. Grandiosity is rooted in egomania.

"Door-matting." Tallulah Bankhead, according to Lee Israel's generally sympathetic biography, *Miss Tallulah Bankhead* (G.P. Putnam's Sons, 1972), once blew a screen test because she drank a fifth of liquor for lunch. An alcoholic who led a promiscuous sex life, Bankhead loved to disparage her many partners:

> She has a romantic interlude, and, afterwards, discusses it with lurid details and complete unreserve... She is said to dilate upon his ways and wiles, his abilities and his disabilities, his prowess or lack of prowess, with such considerable abandon that the unfortunate male, if present, can think of no recourse except immediate suicide.

She would also describe her partners genitalia to "anyone within earshot the morning after... Tallulah's evaluation of [her husband's] masculine prowess was... opprobrious."

This sort of verbal debasement is typical of alcoholics; ridiculing others makes them feel better about themselves. Members of Al-Anon have an excellent term for the practice: "door-matting."

Serial Destruction. Alcoholics who hold power over others will use it continually to shore up their egos. As a result, they favor drawn out campaigns against a single individual or a series of attacks against a number of people. An alcoholic executive, for example, will fire a number of people, for no valid reasons, over a long period.

Alcoholics favor serial destruction because the addiction never lets up; the need for ego-aggrandizement doesn't go away.*

Multiple Marriages and Divorces. This power symptom will not be available to all since it requires financial resources, as well as a supply of willing partners. Some celebrities known for multiple marriages and divorces (Elizabeth Taylor and the late Richard Burton, for example) have identified themselves as alcoholics. Other much-married well-known persons have been tagged as alcoholics by people who knew them well; Tommy Manville, the millionaire playboy of the 1940's and 1950's who had eleven wives, was identified as an alcoholic (on a 1960's television talk show) by two of them. I identify, in this book, certain historical figures known for multiple divorces as alcoholics. Henry VIII (described in Chapter Ten) who got rid of several wives, one way or another, is perhaps the best-known example.

Divorce initiated by a belligerent alcoholic is an expression of egotism and satisfies the need for serial destruction.**

Rejection of Friends. Over the course of a lifetime, the typical alcoholic rejects scores of friends. Although some of these are preemptive strikes (if an alcoholic senses that he's going to be criticized or even rejected because of his drinking, he might make the first move), most are just one more ugly means for the alcoholic ego to build up its self-esteem.

Aggressive Sexual Behavior. Many male alcoholics are Don Juans; they use their pathologic charm to seduce. If sex were only sex, this would not be a problem. But sex and power are interrelated, and any sexual relationship involving an alcoholic will ultimately be a stormy one. A male alcoholic might continue womanizing after he marries, adding another victim to this power game -- his cuck-

---

*As I show in Chapter Eight, the inclination to destroy serially has lead some alcoholics to become serial killers.

**Of course, many alcoholics are divorced by their spouses. One authority, Richard C. Bates, M.D., estimated that between 50% and 70% of all divorces involve alcoholism.

old wife.

Many female alcoholics, like Tallulah Bankhead, also exhibit aggressive sexual behavior.

Unreasonable Resentments. Alcoholics tend to get angry over petty things and unreasonably resentful over matters that nonalcoholics shrug off. They will rant for days about some minor run-in with a sales clerk or a bus driver. Exaggerated fault-finding makes them feel better about themselves.

Superficial Emotions. The same people who get extremely upset over imagined slights and have crying jags when drinking are incapable of normal emotional responses to real events. Perhaps one of the most disturbing things about alcoholics is that they seem *incapable of grief.*

Kim Philby's nasty remark upon hearing that his wife had just died (which was quoted in the last chapter) was an especially ugly manifestation of typical alcoholic emotional shallowness. A few years ago, I witnessed an even more chilling reaction to death -- this time in a female alcoholic. A woman neighbor received news in the early afternoon that her only daughter, 20 years old, had been killed in an automobile accident. That evening, over the objections of her distraught teenage son, she calmly put on a festive outfit and went out to "dinner party," which was nothing more than a thinly-disguised drinking occasion with three alcoholic girl friends (her drinking partners). In the days and weeks that followed, she showed no signs of grief over a loss that would have devastated a normal, i.e., nonalcoholic, mother.

Having a normal human reaction to real events outside their own control is beyond alcoholics' capability. The disease-battered egos cannot handle the additional load of grief, or, for that matter, any decent human emotion. Alcoholics may say "I love you" to someone they want to control, but that phrase is just another lie served up by the ego.

This distressing lack of normal human emotion and sentiment, like all other power symptoms, disappears after *successful* treatment. Recovered alcoholics are as affected by the death of loved ones, and life's other emotion-laden events, as are the rest of us.

Charm (Jekyll and Hyde Behavior)   All alcoholics develop "Jekyll and Hyde" personalities. Although this book is about the evil, "Mr. Hyde" side of their behavior, the charm they can display should not be underestimated for it too is a power symptom.

Alcoholics use charm to assure themselves that they are in control; the person who elicits a warm response to a flattering comment or a smile to a little joke is exercising control over the target of his manipulation.

Although it may seem innocuous, this symptom actually compounds the destructiveness. It misleads those close to him. We are all susceptible to charm, and persons near the alcoholic have a difficult time accepting that someone who is often amiable and pleasant is capable of shocking nastiness. It is even more difficult to realize that the charm, like the blatantly bad behavior, is also caused by the disease.

"Telephonitis."   Alcoholics, particularly female alcoholics, love to telephone others at all hours of the day and, especially, at night. The telephone is an excellent means of extending power: the person telephoned is summoned by the egomaniac and is required to listen to whatever the alcoholic wants to talk about at that time.

Lucy Barry Robe identified the late Martha Mitchell (wife of John Mitchell, Nixon's Attorney General and convicted Watergate conspirator) as an alcoholic. According to Robe, she was hospitalized more than once for alcohol problems. Martha Mitchell was known for her habit of telephoning members of the press late at night -- barely coherent. Her convoluted "inside" stories of the unfolding Watergate scandal were published by a few journalists who either gullibly took her drunken ramblings seriously, or knowingly published the inane comments of a sick woman.*

Careful Grooming.   Most alcoholics take exceptional care of their appearance, which will surprise those who think of them as derelicts. Actually, specialists estimate that Skid Row alcoholics make up less than five percent of the total alcoholic population in the United States.

The misapprehension is widespread, however, as was made clear

---

*In my opinion, John Mitchell was also an alcoholic.

during the uproar surrounding the nomination of the late Senator John Tower to Secretary of Defense. Many journalists, in discussing the charge that Tower was an alcoholic, made a point of mentioning his neat appearance, including his fondness for custom-made London suits. Obviously, the reporters erroneously thought that Towers' habitually spiffy appearance countered the allegation that he had a drinking problem.

Female alcoholics typically keep neat homes, unless and until they slip into late-stage alcoholism with its constant, heavy inebriation. Again, as with the exceptional personal grooming, it is the inflated ego that compels them to maintain a front of respectability.

Association with Social Inferiors. Alcoholics will seek out their social inferiors as drinking companions. The graduate of an Ivy League university who frequents a bar favored by blue collar workers deliberately places himself in an environment that lets him feel superior to the people around him.

This symptom may not appear until late in the game. Many early stage alcoholics, on the other hand, are successful social climbers. It's a form of over-achievement.

The "Geographic Cure." Some alcoholics change their residence frequently. These moves are attempts, usually unsuccessful, to obtain control over their lives -- and their drinking.

Rejection of Religion. Alcoholics who are reared in a religious faith tend to reject that faith after the addiction takes hold. This is another expression of egotism.

As with all the power symptoms, there are exceptions. Most alcoholic clergy do not become atheists, or change their religion. Some of them do, however. James Pike, an alcoholic Catholic priest, switched to the Episcopal Church.

But even if the alcoholic maintains, on the surface, a pattern of religious observance, there will be no depth to their convictions. True adherence to a religious faith, like a steadfast personal relationship or loyalty to a nation, requires subordination of the ego. That is incompatible with active alcoholism.

Further evidence of the ego-inflating effects of alcoholism beyond its power symptoms, lies in the critically important role that ego *deflation* (often including a return to religion) plays in recovery. One of the first psychiatrists to become interested in the mechanics of Alcoholics Anonymous, Harry M. Tiebout, M.D., observed that there were two elements in the AA program which account for its success. It requires the alcoholic (1) to give up "without reservation his irrational desire to run things, to dominate events and people," and (2) to awaken spiritually.

Anyone approaching Alcoholics Anonymous and its relationship to religion, to "spiritual awakening," or to any concept of God, can do so on one of two levels. He can approach it as a believer and accept at face value AA's assertion that there is a spiritual basis for the recovery from alcoholism. Or he can accept the alternative psychological explanation (to which I subscribe) that the acceptance of religion helps the alcoholic to achieve ego deflation.

The over-inflated ego has to be beaten down if the alcoholic is to achieve true sobriety. Alcoholics Anonymous, the most successful approach to the problem of alcoholism yet devised, is soundly based on this need for deflation. A careful reading of the famous Twelve Steps clearly shows that each has been carefully crafted to help suppress the over-inflated ego:

1. We admitted we were powerless over alcohol -- that our lives had become unmanageable.

2. Came to believe that a Power greater than ourselves could restore us to sanity.

3. Made a decision to turn our will and our lives over to the care of God as we understood Him.

4. Made a searching and fearless moral inventory of ourselves.

5. Admitted to God, to ourselves, and to another human being the exact nature of our wrongs.

6. Were entirely ready to have God remove all these defects of character.

7. Humbly asked Him to remove our shortcomings, became willing to make amends for them all.

8. Made a list of all persons we had harmed, and became willing to make amends to them all.

9. Made direct amends to such people wherever possible, except when to do so would injure them or others.

10. Continued to take personal inventory and when we were wrong, promptly admitted it.

11. Sought through prayer and meditation to improve our conscious contact with God as we understood Him, praying only for knowledge of His will for us and the power to carry that out.

12. Having a spiritual awakening as the result of these steps, we tried to carry this message to alcoholics and to practice these principles in all our affairs.

Bill Wilson, the founder of Alcoholics Anonymous, said that deep deflation of the ego is a basic objective of the AA program. It is clear that he had deflation in mind in developing the Twelve Steps; no egomaniac can sincerely practice any one of the steps, let alone all twelve, and remain an egomaniac.

Other successful treatment programs pay great attention to the importance of ego deflation; no detail is overlooked. For example: although it may seem trivial to the unenlightened, in successful residential programs patients are required to maintain their own living quarters. The alcoholic may be a movie star, a billionaire, or a four-star general, but while in treatment he makes his bed and sweeps his room. The professionals who run those programs know that if employees cleaned up the patients' rooms, it would work against ego deflation.

Of course, not all destructive, egocentric people are alcoholics. In order to distinguish alcoholics from nonalcoholics who are flagrantly egocentric for reasons having nothing to do with alcoholism, we need to take a careful, intelligent look at the drinking.

6: OTHER SIGNS AND SYMPTOMS

An alcoholic is someone who can take it or leave it.
So he takes it.

Charles Jackson

In addition to the power symptoms described in the last chapter, alcoholics distinguish themselves from the general population in many other ways. They drink, of course, and because their drinking surpasses that of nonalcoholics they develop certain tell-tale physical signs. I describe both drinking symptoms and physical symptoms in this chapter.

As is the case with the power symptoms, not all of these symptoms will appear in all alcholics.

Drinking Symptoms

Some workers in alcoholism include in their lists of symptoms, drinking and drinking-related behavior that might also be found, under certain circumstances, in some heavy-drinking nonalcoholics. The widely used Michigan Alcoholism Screening Test (MAST), for example, asks the testee questions to determine if he is an alcoholic, including:

> Do you ever feel guilty about your drinking?
> Have you gotten into physical fights while drinking?
> Have you ever been arrested for drunk driving?
> Has your drinking ever created problems between you and [your family]?

In my opinion, some nonalcoholic "Saturday Night" heavy drinkers, particularly young American males, could answer "Yes" to some or even all of these particular questions. If there were no other positive answers, the drinker may not be an alcoholic. Heavy drinking young nonalcoholics (think of the stereotypical college fraternity member) sharply curtail their drinking as they mature, with no help from anyone. Some authorities claim that most nonalcoholic Americans seldom get drunk once they pass their mid-twenties.

I think it is not helpful to consider the ambiguous behavior addressed in these particular questions in trying to identify, with a high level of certainty, alcoholism. But there are enough other clues, peculiarly alcoholic behavior, that we can focus on. Alcoholics make it easy for us to identify them. They do things with booze that nonalcoholics simply cannot accomplish -- not even healthy, but foolish, young drinkers. It is this *distinguishing* behavior -- hard-core alcoholic drinking behavior -- that I concentrate on in this section.

Extraordinary Consumption. Here are some examples, all from published works, of actual alcohol quantities consumed by well-known alcoholics on specific occasions:

F. Scott Fitzgerald: Thirty-three cans of beer in one day.

Ernest Hemingway: Sixty ounces of eighty-proof rum in one night.

Billy Carter: Half a gallon of booze a day, plus beer.

Wilbur Mills: Two quarts of hundred-proof vodka in one night.

Graham Chapman: Sixty fluid ounces of gin per day.

John Steinbeck: Twenty-seven martinis in one night.

No *non*alcoholic drinker could consume these quantities. They could not physically manage to get that much booze into their systems. They would vomit, fall down drunk, pass out, or otherwise become incapacitated.*
But alcoholics are *different*.
Just how different is clear from this account by novelist Elmore Leonard in Dennis Wholey's *The Courage To Change* (Houghton Mifflin Company, 1984) of an encounter with a foolish nonalcoholic. While on a business trip in Colorado, Leonard was challenged to a drinking contest.

... I was out for the evening with a trucker. We were drinking whiskey and we had dinner. [Later] we were drinking brandy and he said, "I haven't met a low lander yet I didn't have to put to bed." I thought, "What is this? I know skinny guys back in Detroit who drink four to five martinis for lunch. They could kill this guy sitting at a table. He wouldn't last an hour with these guys in three-piece suits." Before that evening was over, he was chasing a waitress down an alley. The next morning, I went to see him at his office, after I had gotten a couple of beers in me for my equilibrium. He looked up, red-eyed, and said, "Oh, my God. I never want to see you again."

Morning drinking. As Elmore Leonard demonstrated by his beer drinking the next day, alcoholics drink in the morning -- especially after a night of heavy drinking. For nonalcoholics, the very thought of a serious morning drink while hungover is repugnant. Alcoholics, because they are physiologically different from the rest of us, feel better if they can ingest alcohol the next morning.

---

*Perhaps they could "succeed" if they guzzled the booze so quickly their system had no time to react. But quick consumption of large amounts of alcohol can be fatal. Every year, otherwise healthy American youngsters die of acute alcohol poisoning as part of fraternity hazings.

Cross Addiction. Some authorities have proposed that alcoholism ought to be called "sedativism." This is because, as most modern alcoholics discover, when booze is not conveniently available a sedative pill will usually give them the buzz their bodies crave.

To understand how peculiarly specific cross-addiction with pill-form sedatives is to alcoholics, imagine the host of a well-lubricated party suddenly announcing that he's run out of booze but -- not to worry, he suddenly tells his guests -- he is placing a big bowl of phenobarbital at the bar. The nonalcoholics in the crowd, even those who want to continue drinking, would think their host had lost his sanity. But an alcoholic would understand and might even gulp down a few pills.

With the introduction, in recent decades, of a variety of mood-altering prescription drugs in the market place, alcoholics now have many more alternative substances available. Valium and other tranquilizers are now popular alternatives to alcohol.

Cross Tolerance. Not only do many alcoholics turn to other seda-tives to satisfy their craving, they all develop amazing tolerance for all substances that are pharmacologically similar to alcohol. This can cause unexpected medical problems.

I once heard a corporate executive casually mention over lunch that he had awakened in the middle of his gallbladder surgery. Alerted by this bit of information, I kept my ears open for any reports of heavy drinking by this man whom I did not know very well. Within a few months, I had heard enough to conclude that he was an alcoholic.

Anesthetists are increasingly aware of the problem. Patients are now routinely asked about their alcohol intake in pre-surgical interviews.

Overwrought Behavior While Drinking. Ugly, highly-charged emo-tional behavior during drinking episodes is a sign of alcoholism.

Part of the "Jekyll and Hyde" syndrome, these transformations can result in loud, accusatory harangues, crying jags, the smashing of furniture, and violence. The extreme behavior is, almost always, unprovoked. It's triggered by the alcohol's effect on the alcoholic, not by the behavior of others who happen to be present.

Nonalcoholics rarely display *unprovoked* nasty behavior while inebriated.* They rarely become agitated to the point of rage. When drinking they are usually more cheerful, less inhibited than when sober; in the apt popular phrase, they're "happy." If they continue drinking they might fall asleep or get sick -- but they don't start breaking chairs.

Blackouts. These are episodes of amnesia while drinking. Blackouts do not necessarily occur during periods of heavy drinking. More than one recovered alcoholic has told me an episode can be triggered by a single drink. They can last for a few hours or for weeks. During a blackout, the alcoholic will not necessarily appear drunk and may be capable of functioning at a high level of competency.

One recovered alcoholic, an insurance salesman, told me he had no recollection of selling the largest policy he ever wrote. According to the late Frank A. Seixas, M.D., former Medical Director of the National Council on Alcoholism, an alcoholic surgeon once performed a successful tracheotomy during a blackout.

The scariest blackout story I've heard was of an airline pilot whose blackout ended while he was at the controls of an airliner. His most pressing problem? To find out, without alarming his companions in the cockpit, exactly where the plane was headed.

Again, normal drinkers do not have these bizarre experiences; for the blackout experience, "alcoholics only" need apply. The nonalcoholic who has a fuzzy memory the morning after an especially heavy drinking session isn't even coming close.

Benders. These are drinking episodes that last two days or longer, and they are strong alcoholism symptoms. Usually, benders do not appear until the late stages of the disease. Again, nonalcoholics simply cannot drink, heavily and continually, for two days or longer.

Going on the Wagon. Alcoholics sometimes try to "prove" to themselves (and to others) that they are not alcoholics by abstaining. They stay off booze for weeks, or even months, at a time.

---

*The drunken brawls that occur among young males are an exception. These probably have more to do with crowd psychology and testosterone levels than with alcohol, although the disinhibiting effect of booze undoubtedly contributes.

This behavior tags them as alcoholics. Nonalcoholic heavy drinkers may cut out alcohol to lose weight, or if they develop a medical problem. But the complete temporary cessation of alcohol consumption by a heavy drinker for reasons relating to the drinking is a strong indication of alcoholism.

"Switch" Drinking. Alcoholics may alter their drinking patterns in attempts to "solve" the problem. A favorite move is to substitute wine or beer for distilled drinks. The alcoholic is kidding himself, of course, since all he's doing is changing the package in which the addictive substance, ethanol, is delivered. (Some alcoholics drink beer exclusively; others, wine.)

Others use more imaginative stratagems. One female alcoholic, a suburban housewife, voluntarily promised her husband (who had expressed his concern about her heavy drinking) that she would henceforth drink only when they entertained. Within a matter of weeks, this normally reclusive woman became the most active hostess in the neighborhood. Dinner party invitations suddenly spewed out to people she barely knew and even to some she couldn't stand. After a few weeks of this frenzied hostessing, she gave up and returned to her normal pattern of solitary drinking.

Again, nonalcoholics -- people who have no continuing problem with alcohol -- seldom attempt radical revisions of their drinking routines.

Sneak Drinking. This is hard to spot, for obvious reasons. One recovered alcoholic, a salesman, described a technique he used whenever he had lunch with a group of slow-drinking nonalcoholics. After the first round of drinks was served, he'd gulp his down and then excuse himself to go to the men's room. On the way, he'd stop at the bar and have a quick double. After leaving the men's room, he'd belly-up to the bar again and have a second double. Rejoining his companions with those four extra drinks under his belt, he'd promptly order another round for everyone.

Closely related to sneak drinking is the secreting of booze. Alcoholics are fearful of running out of their addictive substance. This leads them to stash bottles away in drawers, on closet shelves, and, particularly if they are living with a concerned nonalcoholic, in odder places, such as inside toilet tanks.

Predrinking Drinking. When invited to a social event, alcoholics will gird themselves against an expected insufficient flow of booze by drinking *before* they party. The "alkie" always keeps a stiff drink on the dresser. As with other drinking symptoms, this is virtually exclusive to alcoholics; nonalcoholics have no desire, and no need, to predrink.

Physical Symptoms

Alcoholics, eventually, *look* like alcoholics. Most people have no problem identifying late-stage alcoholics. But during the earlier phases, most alcoholics are not recognized. Many physical signs show up early, however, and knowing them can help in identification.

Premature Aging. Alcoholics look older than their years. After Lillian Roth had sobered up, a friend told her of the first time they had met: "I remember asking you how old you were, and you said 34. I thought you were lying. 'She's closer to 54,' I said to myself."

When Charlie Parker (the legendary saxophone player, and an alcoholic) died, the attending physician had to guess his age for the death certificate. He wrote down 55. Parker was 35.

Puffy Eyes. Alcoholics tend to develop puffiness below the eyes. In photographs, their eyes may look smaller or "squintier" than most people. (More than all other physical signs, puffiness around the eyes is *not* exclusive to alcoholics.)

Glassy Eyes. Sometimes, when they are drinking, the only outward sign is a peculiar glassiness in the eyes.

I think this look may have been captured, inadvertently, on film. A few years ago I read a television critic's strong recommendation of the film *Freud*, starring Montgomery Clift as the famous psychiatrist. The reviewer gushed enthusiastically about a luminous look in Clift's eyes, suggesting some sort of acting triumph. Intrigued, I watched the movie and concluded that Clift -- an alcoholic who died of liver failure -- had been drinking on the set. The magical gleam in the eyes of the famous psychiatrist in certain scenes was just Monty's way of letting us (at least some of us) know that he'd had a few belts between takes.

The "Chipmunk" Look. Heavy drinking can cause enlargement of salivary glands, leading to swelling in the cheek area which gives the drinker a facial appearance suggestive of a chipmunk. The late Senator John Tower, whose reported heavy drinking was a major factor in the Senate's rejection of his appointment as Secretary of Defense, had this symptom, in my opinion. So did W.C. Fields.

Hair. Believe it or not, here's a physical *benefit* of heavy drinking!

George DeLeon, a psychologist, investigated the "old drinkers'" tale that "There are few bald alcoholics." With the help of a group of students, he compared the heads of Skid Row alcoholics to those in a control group. All the subjects were between the ages of 41 to 55. He reported in *Psychology Today* (October, 1977) that within the control group, 82% were bald, but that only 32% of the derelicts had lost their hair.

The explanation for this odd little fact lies, I think, in a pharmacological property of alcohol; it causes dilation of peripheral blood vessels, those, like capillaries in the scalp, most distant from the heart. The alcoholic's dilated vessels deliver more nourishment to hair follicles, keeping the hair healthy. The same effect is probably responsible for the lush, heavy eyelashes I've noticed in many younger alcoholics.

Needless to say, this is only a confirming symptom. Most people with healthy hair are not alcoholics, and some baldies are.

(The bad news about blood vessel changes is that alcohol constricts the ones nearest the heart. Coronary accidents, including fatal heart attacks, are an increased risk in heavy drinkers.)

Smoking. Many alcoholics are heavy cigarette smokers. According to one authority, "Nine out of ten male alcoholics smoke cigarettes. Sixty percent of them smoke more than a pack a day, and a whopping one-third smoke two or more packs a day."

Not all alcoholics smoke (Hemingway never did), and some (Tennessee Williams, for example) quit smoking but continue to drink. The nation-wide reduction in cigarette smoking in recent years has probaby diminished the value of this symptom. But since the incidence of cigarette smoking among alcoholics remains higher than among nonalcoholics, the incidence of alcoholism among smokers remains higher than among nonsmokers.

Hypochondria. Perhaps this belongs among the "Power Symptoms." Alcoholics might imagine nonexistent illnesses in order to call attention to themselves. Or it may be that all the booze they consume causes a variety of physical sensations that they misinterpret as signs of different illnesses. In any event, hypochondria is listed as a symptom in the AMA's *Manual on Alcoholism* and it turns up in some of the characters that appear in these pages.

Throughout this book I use published reports of these and a few other standard symptoms (which are mentioned in passing), as well as the power symptoms described in the last chapter, to conclude that a number of historical figures were alcoholics.

7: ALCOHOLISM WRITES

Print is the sharpest and strongest weapon...

Joseph Stalin

Odium had to be cast on their ideas, their personalities, even their very names.

George Katkov,
on Stalin

Many alcoholism investigators have puzzled over the extraordinarily high number of writers who are alcoholics. Most ask "Why do writers drink?" and come up with a number of explanations -- none of them very persuasive. I ask "Why do alcoholics write?" and the question answers itself. Alcoholism causes egomania. Some turn to writing because it is an occupation that holds out the possibility of ego-satisfying recognition at a very young age. As already noted, it is the prospect of youthful ego gratification that attracts other young alcoholics to careers in the theatre, movies, and other arts. This match-up, in early adult life, of the egomaniacal needs of budding alcoholics with ego-gratifying occupations explains the stream of middle-aged celebrities to alcoholism treatment centers that we have witnessed in recent years. According to out-of-date notions, "success" somehow or other compelled people to suddenly start ingesting alcohol in extraordinary quantities.

Writing for publication offers something else to the alcoholic ego: the chance to attack others. The enormous body of modern literature produced by alcoholic writers contains a lot of ill-concealed malicious attacks on persons known to the authors.

These alcoholics' pens were sharp and wounding, but they were two-edged weapons. By recording the sort of personal attacks that less talented alcoholics merely vocalize, they have left a testimonial to alcoholism's power to incite malice. The written attacks support both the diagnosis of alcoholism in the individual suspect, as well as my idea that the disease itself had a powerful influence on *what* the alcoholics wrote.

The literature produced by these alcoholism-controlled writers is substantial -- enormous, really -- for the simple reason that there have been an awful lot of them. Donald W. Goodwin, M.D., listed in *Alcohol and the Writer* (Andrews and McMeel, 1988) dead American writers who were "considered alcoholic by contemporaries or biographers, or who drank enough to get the reputation of being alcoholic... " Here's his list:

Edgar Allan Poe, Edwin Arlington Robinson, Ambrose Bierce, Theodore Dreiser, Hart Crane, Sinclair Lewis, Eugene O'Neill, Edna St. Vincent Millay, Dorothy Parker, F. Scott Fitzgerald, Ring Lardner, Ernest Hemingway, John O'Hara, William Faulkner, John Steinbeck, Dashiell Hammett, Thomas Wolfe, John Berryman, J.P. Marquand, Wallace Stevens, E.E. Cummings, Theodore Roethke, Edmund Wilson, James Thurber, Jack London, Tennessee Williams, Truman Capote, William Inge, Robert Benchley, Jack Kerouac, O. Henry (Willam Sydney Porter), Mr. Dooley (Finley Peter Dunne), John Cheever, Conrad Aiken, Woolcott Gibbs, Stephen Crane, Philip Barry, James Jones, Robert Ruark, William Saroyan, Irwin Shaw, Delmore Schwartz, Robert Lowell, Randall Jarrell, Jean Stafford, James Agee, Ralph Maloney, Raymond Chandler, and, according to its nonalcoholic drama critic Brendan Gill, almost every writer for *The New Yorker* during the thirties.

Goodwin also mentions two non-American writer-alcoholics in his book: Malcolm Lowry and George Simenon.

J. Anthony Lukas came up with his own list in *The New York Times Book Review* (December 1, 1985) of writers who were "excessive drinkers." Understandably, he repeats most of those on Goodwin's list, but he added others:

Carson McCullers, Lillian Hellman, Don Marquis, Ben Hecht, Charles MacArthur, Shirley Jackson, Harry Crosby, James M. Cain, Maxwell Bodenheim, Bernard De Voto, Jane Bowles, Thornton Wilder, Stanley Edgar Hyman, Katherine Anne Porter, Louise Bogan, James Whitcomb Riley, Gene Fowler, A.J. Liebling, and Charles Jackson.

Upton Sinclair* named in *The Cup of Fury* (Hawthorn Books, Inc., 1956) many authors who later appeared on both Goodwin's and Lukas's lists. Others he named: William Seabrook, George Sterling, and Dylan Thomas. Lucy Barry Robe adds women writers Margaret Mitchell, Marjorie Rawlings, and Jill Robinson (who has identified herself as an alcoholic.) Other deceased alcoholic writers (not all Americans) that I can add, based on my own research, are Thomas Paine, James Boswell, Brendan Behan, Frank O'Hara, Evelyn Waugh, and Raymond Carver. Carver had ten years of productive sobriety before his death in 1988. Among living writers, Elmore Leonard has revealed that he is a recovered alcoholic. There are others.

As for the malice in their works, perhaps an appropriate place to start is with Thomas Paine, the Revolutionary War pamphleteer. He was certainly an alcoholic. Late in life he developed a face like W.C. Fields** and was often collected from taverns with a "two week growth of beard and his body giving off a most disagreeable

---

*A lifetime teetotaler, Sinclair avoided drink because of a strong family history of alcoholism; his father died of alcoholism, and three uncles "had the problem."

**The "chipmunk look," mentioned in Chapter Six, was more significant than Field's famous red nose. The red nose was caused by rosacea, a bacterial infection that afflicts many nondrinkers.

odor."

During the Revolutionary War, Paine accused well-known patriots, including Gouverneur Morris, of profiteering from the war effort. One of Paine's biographers bluntly labeled a particular charge -- that Silas Deane tried to silence him with money -- a falsehood. When Deane demanded that Paine substantiate his allegation, Paine lamely explained that "he had given particulars... to Congress and would do so again if asked, but that he could not reveal them to the public."

Paine attacked Benjamin Franklin, who had been his mentor, in a series of published accusations. At the time, Franklin's daughter told her father, "the most rational thing [Paine] could have done was to have died the instant he finished *Common Sense.*"

After, in effect, dropping his American citizenship to serve in the French Assembly (as he had earlier discarded his British citizenship), Paine flew into a rage because he thought George Washington didn't do enough when he was briefly imprisoned by the French.

According to this alcoholic, the father of his adopted country was possessed of a "cold hermaphrodite faculty" and capable of "mean and servile submission to the insults of one nation." He meant that Washington, who would have been hanged if captured during the war, was serving the interests of those who would have executed him -- the British. Paine also accused Washington of personal treachery, "... I shall continue to think of you as treacherous until you give me cause to think otherwise... As to you, Sir, treacherous in private friendship (for you have so been to me, and that in the day of danger) and a hypocrite in public life, the world will be puzzled to decide whether you are an apostate or an imposter; whether you have abandoned good principles, or whether you ever had any." George Washington was also a lousy general and a rotten president, according to this boozer.

Paine eventually settled in New Rochelle, New York, where he was exceedingly unpopular. His attacks on Washington and his public benders had a lot to do with his neighbors' attitude toward the former hero.

Paine did not write fiction, and all his written attacks were direct and undisguised. Although Edgar Allan Poe, whom Goodwin good-naturedly calls the "Chairman of the Board" of American alcoholic writers, is remembered as a writer of fiction and poetry, he too resorted to direct written attacks on vulnerable targets.

Poe displayed a weird tendency to accuse everyone else of plagiarism. He had a special persistence to so accuse Longfellow, the most widely respected and popular American poet of the time, of stealing from the works of others. Although he was severely limited by nineteenth century literary mores -- Poe did not write realistic fiction -- he found an outlet for his alcoholism-induced compulsion to malign others by resorting to direct false accusations.

Modern alcoholic writers of fiction have greater opportunities for mischief; they can avoid the risk of libel inherent in direct journalistic assaults because, unlike Poe, they are expected to write realistic fiction. This gives them excellent "cover" for the malice. But the trend toward realism has affected biographers as well, and the more comprehensive biographers of alcoholic authors have rounded up the empties, so to speak, giving us portraits that reek of booze. Thorough biographers have also gathered an abundance of evidence of malicious behavior by these alcoholics who chose to write, including Thomas Wolfe.

Wolfe wrote lengthy and highly autobiographical novels that are full of attacks on people close to him.

There is no doubt he was an alcoholic. His biographer Andrew Turnbull doesn't call him one, but he gives many reasons for the knowledgeable reader of *Thomas Wolfe: A Biography* (Charles Scribner's Sons, 1947) to conclude that he was. Wolfe had a tolerance for alcohol which, despite his exceptionally large size, can only be explained by alcoholism. While visiting Germany, he consumed eight liters of beer in one session and spent the following six days in a hospital, recovering, not from the effects of all that beer, but from injuries received in a fight he had started.

A friend once saw him pour a pint of whiskey into a glass and "[drink] it down as if it were a mild red wine." He then stood up and walked six miles. Turnbull cites many other incidences of excessive drinking and high tolerance.

He had the typical alcoholic hostility toward his family. He said to his brother, Frank, whom he had portrayed as a lush in *Look Homeward, Angel*, and who was suffering from a constriction of the esophagus at the time, "Why don't you just kill yourself, Frank -- drink enough to kill yourself? You don't amount to anything. Why don't you die?"

While drinking, Wolfe would sometimes take a sudden dislike to a complete stranger -- to the point of violence. He once punched a man at a bar for having a "grey face."

Of course, friends were also at risk. He once threatened to knock down Maxwell Perkins, his editor, while in a "state of murderous intoxication." Fortunately, he was distracted by an admiring female and didn't attack the older, and much smaller, Perkins.

Alcoholics reject other people; their lives are littered with broken friendships. Wolfe was no exception. He dismissed Perkins, who had turned his chaotic manuscripts into publishable books, estranged himself from his mistress, Aline Bernstein, from friends, family (in an off-and-on pattern), and many others. In some cases, the estrangement resulted from Wolfe's ridicule of others in his fiction. "Sooner or later there always was [some flaw found] with everyone."

Wolfe displayed the false accusation symptom. He wrongly accused Bernstein of unfaithfulness, the charges preserved in his letters to her.

Anyone who read his earliest novels will remember that the mother of Eugene Gant (the thinly disguised author) was a miser. In real life, Wolfe complained to friends that he was forced to teach because his mother stopped sending him an allowance. Actually, as Turnbull points out, Wolfe's mother "had financed his graduate work without reimbursement to herself, had sent him money when he couldn't make ends meet on his N.Y.U. salary, and had paid for a large part of his year abroad. Why, in any case, should he have expected his family to go on helping him?" Why indeed? But more important, why did this man falsely accuse his generous mother of being stingy?

After their relationship ended, Wolfe accused Maxwell Perkins, who, by all other accounts, was a loyal and supportive editor, of plotting to destroy him. As quoted by Andrew Turnbull, he wrote to an agent who had recently seen Perkins:

Please... don't tell him..anything about me... For six years he was a friend -- I thought the best I ever had -- and then... he turned against me... it's as if he were praying for my failure...

A weird incident -- and alcoholism is a lifetime of weird incidents -- involved Wolfe and Sherwood Anderson:

Wolfe, Anderson, and his wife, Eleanor, had attended a dinner party where someone had spoken of the Southern propensity for smearing liberals on grounds other than their liberalism. In corroboration, Mrs. Anderson, who had recently been in North Carolina, said she had heard it rumored that Wolfe was Jewish. Jumping to his feet, he called the imputation outrageous, while Anderson and the others defended Mrs. Anderson and accused Wolfe of anti-Semitism for taking offense.

Wolfe's behavior on this occasion ended the long relationship between him and the Andersons.

Wolfe died of tuberculosis at age thirty-eight. His physician believed he had contracted the disease when he drank whiskey from the flask of a stranger.

In his biography of Dorothy Parker, *You Might As Well Live* (Simon and Schuster, 1970), John Keats recounts Parker's propensity for verbally attacking others.

She regularly blasted both her husbands. Edwin Parker, her first husband and a fellow alcoholic, was an inept fool who was unable to cope with the simplest challenges of everyday life -- or so his wife told her friends at the famed Algonquin Round Table. She later elevated her calumnies to include a false accusation of morphine addiction. Her second husband, Allan Campbell (another alcoholic), "couldn't act... couldn't write anything but Hollywood trash... never understood her... couldn't cook... was a political cretin... was weak... afraid... married her for her money... wasn't a man... was a pansy." Parker once told friends that Campbell had beaten her and was responsible for the bruises on her face. Unfortunately for her, these friends knew that her husband was thousands of miles away at the time. She got the bruises falling down drunk.

According to Keats, Dorothy was practically a non-drinker in 1917 when she married Edwin Parker. By the mid 1930's, her drinking was such that a friend recommended she join Alcoholics Anonymous. It is likely, then, that her alcoholism was in full flower during the 1920's, when she acquired her famous reputation for wittiness.

Friends feared her rapier wit, and with reason. When at the Round Table, her companions hated to use the bathroom; whoever left the table became the instant target of Parker's clever malice.

She'd flatter the person she was talking to, but drip malice about mutual acquaintances -- displaying a pattern that's as characteristic of alcoholism as is heavy drinking. Most alcoholics do not have the talent of a Dorothy Parker, however (or of an Oscar Levant, an alcohol and sedative addict "blessed" with similar wit). Parker's fame is based on her unusual talent in expressing a rather ordinary, and in less skilled hands, tiresome symptom of a common disease.

In the final years of late-stage alcoholism, her famed wit deteriorated to witlessness; she called one of her friends a "Jew-hating Fascist son of a bitch." Although her maiden name was Rothchild, and she had been an anti-Hitler activist in the months before Pearl Harbor, she called another acquaintance a "Jew-Fascist." She said this while sitting on the floor of her apartment, surrounded by empty whiskey bottles.

During her final years, Parker tried to dictate an autobiography. After listening to her tapes, her friend Wyatt Cooper decided they included so many "outrageous things about Jews and about her father" that he destroyed them.

Parker was not a particularly prolific writer and most of her malice was expressed vocally.

Eugene O'Neill, like Thomas Wolfe, drew upon his own family as the source for some of his major works, and, like Wolfe, he maligned his closest relatives. In *Long Day's Journey Into Night*, he portrays his father as a penny-pincher. In reality, James O'Neill was an exceptionally generous man -- especially to Eugene.

His father sent Eugene to two private prep schools, and to both Princeton and Yale. He arranged for him to get a job on a New Haven newspaper, going so far as to surreptitiously (to protect Eugene's pride) reimburse the paper for his salary. He gave Eugene and his other alcoholic son handouts when their drunkenness prevented the brothers from getting and holding jobs. And when Eugene married, his father gave him and his bride, as a wedding gift, *a house on Cape Cod!*

Both of O'Neill's major biographers emphatically reject as false the most abominable accusation leveled against his father in *Long Day's Journey*: that his stinginess was directly responsible for his wife's morphine addiction. (In the play, the father, to save a few dollars, hires a quack doctor to treat the mother, and this doctor prescribes the narcotic.)

The alcoholic O'Neill did not want this play published until 50 years after his death. Although he said he did this to "protect" others, it is now clear that he figured that half a century later anyone who knew the real O'Neill family, and who could have countered his evil lies, would have long since died. Fortunately for the truth, O'Neill's widow ignored his wishes; the play was published a few years after he died. This enabled two biographers, the Gelbs and Sheaffer, to look at the facts and clear the principal target of O'Neill's alcoholic malevolence. They concluded that James O'Neill was a generous husband and father. Another biographer, Doris Alexander (who published her work before the play was released), describes James O'Neill, who was a hugely popular actor, as a "soft touch" who freely gave handouts to his down-and-out theatre colleagues.

Regrettably, despite the correcting biographies, this alcoholic's lies seem to have succeeded. *Long Day's Journey* is considered a masterpiece by many, and is frequently described as "searingly honest." Actually, it has as much honesty in it as the transcript of one of Joseph Stalin's purge trials. *Long Day's Journey Into Night* is an evil and thoroughly dishonest play -- the sick work of a sick mind.

Tellingly, as both the Gelbs and Sheaffer make abundantly clear, the man who maligned his father behaved badly toward his own children. The playwright had separated from his first wife before she gave birth to Eugene O'Neill, Jr., and he didn't bother to even meet the boy until he was twelve. His other son, Shane, became a drifter who would occasionally ask his father for a loan. Unlike *his* father, O'Neill refused to help. He even refused to assist financially while Shane was in treatment for heroin addiction. He practically disowned his daughter, Oona, when a newspaper published a photograph of her in a nightclub. And when she married Charlie Chaplin, he *did* disown her. He forbade the mention of her name in his presence and never spoke to her again, rebuffing more than one attempt she made at reconciliation prior to his death.

Rejection of children is not uncommon among alcoholics; neither is the maligning of others, including parents. O'Neill's alcoholism was responsible both for his mistreatment of his offspring and the lies he wrote about his father.* I say this in spite of O'Neill's apparently sharp reduction in alcohol intake in his later years.

AA members and others have made it clear that abstinence and sobriety are not the same. An abstaining alcoholic who has not gone through the ego deflation that is central to any successful treatment program may be as miserable and as abusive as a drinking alcoholic. The misery can last through years of abstinence. Gary Crosby, the entertainer, didn't drink for *nineteen years* before he turned to Alcoholics Anonymous. As he told Dennis Wholey, the nineteen years were full of unhappiness and rage that destroyed his marriage. But within a week of joining Alcoholics Anonymous, Gary Crosby felt at peace.

Arnold M. Ludwig, M.D., wrote of the great difference between "dry" and "sober" alcoholics in his *Understanding the Alcoholic's Mind* (Oxford University Press, 1988):

As bad as many alcoholics can be when drunk, they can become even worse when dry, demonstrating the need for attitude changes as part of the recovery process.

Ludwig quotes John Berryman, the late alcoholic author, on this important difference:

The condition aimed at in treatment is "mental sobriety" or "comfortable sobriety." Just being dry was just being in hell.

I think O'Neill was "dry," but not "sober" during the long periods he stayed away from booze in middle age. His "dry" alcoholism

---

*Although no playwright is required to tell the whole truth about his family in an autobiographical work, O'Neill seems to have gone out of his way to make both his parents look bad. Most people who have seen his "masterpiece" would be surprised to learn that although O'Neill's mother was indeed addicted to morphine for many years, she eventually, and courageously, overcame the addiction.

would explain his awful treatment of his children, his stormy third marriage, and, finally, the malignant and deceitful play he wrote about his own family.

In *his* final days, F. Scott Fitzgerald may have been on the road to recovery. He not only stopped drinking, but seemed to have undergone the necessary ego deflation. Aaron Latham in *Crazy Sundays: F. Scott Fitzgerald in Hollywood* (The Viking Press, 1971) quotes Anita Loos, "Scott has that unhealthy humility of the reformed alcoholic."

In the years before his ego seems to have been deflated, at least temporarily -- a step toward recovery which, contrary to Anita Loos's snide and ignorant comment, is most healthy -- Fitzgerald lived through what is perhaps the world's most thoroughly recorded case of alcoholism. His biographies are full of detailed accounts of specific drinking feats such as a three-day bender while he was a 1920's Princeton student and the consumption of thirty-three cans of beer on a single day in 1935. During his many years of drinking, Fitzgerald, unsurprisingly, treated people badly. His biographies record a lot of nastiness.

The most damaging hostility was directed at his wife, Zelda, and may have contributed to her decline into insanity. She probably witnessed (and, at least in the early years, participated in) thousands of one-day binges during the ten years of their marriage prior to her first commitment. Many of those drinking episodes were marked by abusive attacks by Scott and, on some occasions, by violence.

His hostility toward Zelda showed in his writing. Nancy Milford, in *Zelda: A Biography* (Harper & Row, 1970), reported that Fitzgerald used his wife's letters and diaries in his works and always made the fictional characters he patterned on her appear less than wholesome. He continued to do this even after she was hospitalized with mental illness. His portrait of Zelda in *Tender is the Night* was particularly harsh and accusatory, and was probably responsible for her relapse.

Fitzgerald attacked others in his literature, including Gerald and Sara Murphy, a wealthy American couple who, despite Scott's ugly behavior, had befriended the Fitzgeralds.

He was virtually non-productive during his final drinking years and unquestionably had moved into the late stages of the disease, which is characterized by, among other symptoms, the inability to carry projects through to completion.

Fitzgerald had been working on *The Last Tycoon* during a seemingly sober period immediately preceding his death, in 1940, from a heart attack. It is perhaps significant that he suffered his final coronary while doing something AA's recommend to newcomers to counter the craving for alcohol: he was eating chocolate.

Ernest Hemingway's alcoholism was already underway in 1918. In that year, while hospitalized with war wounds, the 19 year-old Hemingway kept a bottle of cognac under his pillow; eventually, one of his nurses discovered a closet-full of empty bottles. Hemingway may have been drinking all that cognac to relieve the pain of his wounds. If he was, it's a strong sign of alcoholism. In 1976, a team of researchers lead by Henry S.G. Cutter, Ph.D., concluded that the anesthetic effects of booze are not the same for everyone. "[Ingesting alcohol] reduced the level of pain reported by alcoholics but had no effect on that reported by nonalcoholics." Because of that closet-full of empties, it looks as if Hemingway, typically, had begun his alcoholic career as a teenager.

Nothing in his biographies suggests that Hemingway underwent successful treatment for alcoholism prior to his death in 1960. His addiction, in other words, seems to have lasted more than forty years.

During his long alcoholic life, Hemingway frequently exhibited characteristic hostile behavior. He abused friends, relatives and complete strangers. His four wives* were all subjected to verbal abuse and to physical violence. Hemingway's biographer, Carlos Baker, writes that while the author was living in Paris in the 1920's, he "looked in vain for evidence of decency and intelligence among most of his fellow ex-patriates in Paris." He maligned T.S. Eliot, Ezra Pound (he claimed Pound once faked a nervous breakdown to avoid some household chores, a typically preprosperous and belittling alcoholic's slur), Ford Madox Ford ("a liar and a crook"), and Fitzgerald ("a rummy").

---

*According to Tom Dardis, Hemingway's fourth wife, Mary, was also an alcoholic.

A.E. Hotchner, in *Papa Hemingway* (Random House, 1966), listed some of his rejections: "Kenneth Tynan was brutally executed... Peter Buckley was run through... Slim Hayward was summarily guillotined... Peter Vietrel was shot down... Spencer Tracy and Leland Hayward were simultaneously executed."

Many other victims are identified by Carlos Baker in his *Ernest Hemingway: A Life Story* (Charles Scribner's Sons, 1969). Hemingway was contemptuous of other writers. James Jones was a "battle fatigue type." Thomas Wolfe was "a one-book glandular giant with the guts of three mice." Fitzgerald was not only "a rummy" but "a liar with the inbred talent of a dishonest and easily frightened angel." Norman Mailer's *The Naked and the Dead* was "poor cheese, pretentiously wrapped." He was glad he didn't write like Faulkner, the author of "Octanawhoopa" stories. John Dos Passos was "a one-eyed Portuguese bastard." He viciously parodied Sherwood Anderson in his second novel *The Torrents of Spring*.

He mounted an especially cruel attack on Sinclair Lewis in *Across the River and Into the Trees*. Although it was supposed to be fiction, Hemingway gave enough clues in the book to ensure that readers would know that he was writing about his fellow Nobel Laureate (and fellow alcoholic).

He ridiculed, at great length, Lewis's face. As Hemingway knew, Lewis suffered from a disfiguring skin disease. Among other cruelties, Hemingway said he looked as if he had been "run one half way through a meat chopper." He added some sneering comments about Lewis's companion, an elderly woman who looked like an "illustration in *The Ladies Home Journal*." (I say more about her later.)

Lewis was not the only writer Hemingway ridiculed in print. He accused F. Scott Fitzgerald, in *A Moveable Feast*, of behaving like an insecure sexual idiot. He claimed, years after Fitzgerald was dead and unable to rebut the tale, that Fitzgerald was so concerned about the size of his penis that he once asked Hemingway, in a men's room, to tell him if he had standard-sized equipment. In my opinion, this famous episode, involving two alcoholics, never happened because (a) alcoholics avoid, like the plague, playing the fool, (b) alcoholics like to make *others* appear foolish, and (c) alcoholics lie and falsely accuse. It would have been as out of character for one egotistical alcoholic (Fitzgerald) to ask such a ridiculous question as it was in character for another alcoholic

(Hemingway) to make up a malicious lie about the dead Fitzgerald. Alcoholics sometimes even manage to malign others who are themselves noted for *their* skill at malice; Hemingway once insinuated that Dorothy Parker had stolen his typewriter.

"Terrible and unjust" -- that's how Carlos Baker characterized Hemingway's attack (in a portion of *A Moveable Feast* deemed unsuitable for posthumous publication) on Gerald and Sara Murphy. This talented and rich couple had befriended Hemingway in the 1920's. After falsely blaming them for his own decision to leave his first wife, Hemingway accused the Murphys of bringing "bad luck" to many others, and to themselves: "They lived to have all their bad luck finally; to the very worst end that all bad luck could go."

What bad luck? What misfortune befell the Murphys? What happened to the Murphys that the alcoholic Hemingway thought they somehow deserved?

This is what happened. Their two beloved sons, one a teenager and the other only 10 years-old, had died within eighteen months. Not being alcoholics, the Murphys were devastated by their losses.

When he agreed to travel to Stockholm to collect his Nobel Prize, William Faulkner had a problem. He needed to stop drinking several days before he left. If he quit too late, he would be in withdrawal agony during the ceremony. Stopping too early, he might fall off the wagon in Sweden. Somehow, he managed it. He quit drinking two days before he left and avoided any embarrassment in Stockholm.

In Joseph Blotner's comprehensive two-volume work, *Faulkner: A Biography* (Random House, 1974), the author includes "drinking" as a subheading in his index. There are 134 separate references.

Although an alcoholic, Faulkner, at first glance, would seem to refute the idea that alcoholics malign others in their fiction. A white Southerner with aristocratic pretensions, Faulkner wrote with admiration and apparently sincere respect for both Negroes and poor whites. The only people he seemed to dislike were the Snopses, and anyone who has read Faulkner knows that to know a Snopse is to dislike a Snopse. Faulkner appears to be an exception: an honest alcoholic writer who didn't use his talent to abuse others in print.

But there *is* something wrong. Not all white Southerners in

Faulkner's day were poor or descendants of Confederate field commanders. Were the others all bad, had they no saving graces? His brother, John, in *My Brother Bill* (Trident Press, 1963) puts his finger on the problem when he writes that Faulkner's Snopses were nothing "but a massive put down of a whole class of white Southerners," who were seen by Faulkner as "termites who undermined a social order." This entire class of people, his brother points out, "were never presented... in any stage other than their most objectionable one."

I suspect that William Faulkner created the Snopses (brilliantly -- one easily joins the author in disliking them) not because he was honestly portraying a social phenomenon of some significance, but because his alcoholism-dominated ego needed objects of debasement and ridicule. Rather than ridiculing his family or friends, this alcoholic writer chose the entire Southern middle class.

Sinclair Lewis, one of America's five Nobel Prize-winning alcoholic writers, died in Rome at the age of 66 after a series of heart attacks. His life followed the classic alcoholic pattern: outrageous acts against others (including the women who loved him, his children, and his friends) and, then, in the end, his own intense suffering as the disease moved into its final stages. Although he spent his final years in a luxurious Italian villa, behind its walls he endured as much alcoholic agony as any Skid Row derelict.

Lewis had visited Italy two years before his final trip, accompanied by his housekeeper, Mrs. Powers, a simple woman whom Lewis insisted on taking along to all social gatherings. (This was the woman mentioned by Hemingway.) She was the mother of a young actress who had had an affair with Lewis. According to his biographer, Mark Schorer, Mrs. Powers would "sit silently or comment on the weather" while surrounded by the witty sophisticates who flocked around the famous novelist. Bernard Berenson, the art critic, was puzzled by "the enigma of Mrs. Powers." His puzzlement would have evaporated if Berenson had known that alcoholics seek the company of their social inferiors as the disease intensifies its grip.

In his last, terrible years, Lewis was continually drunk and, at the end, afflicted with delirium tremens. After his last heart attack, the Nobel laureate lingered for ten days, uttering not a rational word.

In 1925, twenty-five years before his death, Lewis was already so far gone in his alcoholism that he spent several days at Bill Brown's Training Camp -- a "well-known establishment located in a suburb north of New York for the... rehabilitation of drunkards who could no longer help themselves." Lewis was 41 at the time. Twenty years before *that*, in 1905, he wrote in his diary, "Had enough whiskey to go to sleep at seven thirty." His illness spanned forty-five years, and, during that time, Lewis committed many bizarre acts of hostility.

When Lewis and his second wife, Dorothy Thompson, the well-known journalist, were close to divorce, a friend wrote that "they came to blows that were actual and not rhetorical." Thompson implored Lewis to cut down on his drinking. She wrote him a letter (a typical, but futile, measure) begging him to stop, "because it was only when he was drinking that his rages came upon him." Shortly afterwards, Lewis went on a drunken rampage in a New York hotel room; he smashed the furniture to bits and was carried out in a straitjacket.

Schorer relates other incidences of hostile behavior. These range from a rude "go to hell" to the wife of the Secretary of State who complimented him on *Main Street*, to thanking a hostess for a very "dull evening" upon leaving a dinner party, to the acrimonious termination of his two marriages.

Lewis displayed "Jekyll and Hyde" behavior. Schorer in *Sinclair Lewis: An American Life* (McGraw Hill Book Company, Inc., 1961) quotes from a note to Thompsom from one of her servants:

He worshipped the ground you walked on. When he heard you were coming home from a trip, he would send for the barber to shave him, insist that all of his clothes were in apple-pie order, dress as though he were going to court. And then, after you'd hardly be in the house... he'd start a quarrel, and then, as likely as not, he'd call the car and leave... I never understood why he acted so.

Thompson perceived in Lewis a little known (by other than alcoholism experts) physiological symptom: "Sometimes when he came to his wife in the night, drunk and demanding, Lewis exuded an odor, she remembered, that was -- she paused in the recollection as she sought for the exact analogy -- that was like rotting weeds." Marty Mann, in *New Primer on Alcoholism*, describes a "sweet-sourish" odor that emanates from the entire body of alcoholics and which is due to the oxidation of alcohol through the pores of the skin.

Lewis drew malicious portraits of his wives in his fiction. Dorothy Thompson's stepson, Wells Lewis, wrote to his father about the cartoon portrayal of Dorothy in *Gideon Planish*: "the attack on Dorothy was unfair, one-sided, and pretty damned unkind, even worse than Fran Dodsworth." (Wells was referring to an earlier book in which Lewis included another unflattering portrait of Dorothy.) In an earlier novel, *Half a Loaf*, Lewis had done a similar hatchet job on his first wife, Grace Hegner.

Typically, Lewis rejected friends and broke relationships throughout his boozy life as a means of asserting false control over his destiny. Not surprisingly, lists of rejected friends appear in some alcoholics' biographies, including Schorer's, who includes an entry from Lewis's journal, recorded near the end of his life:

FRIENDS
How lose: Paul Hilsdale, Irving Fisher, Soule, Hal Smith, Updegraff, Noyes, Tinker, Billy Fay, Bill Collins, Bob Pfeiffer, Hal Smith [sic], Connie, DeKruif, Grace, Woodward, Dorothy, Harcourt, Brace, Benets, Gunther, Florey, Birkhead, Molly, Edith Summers, Upton Sinclair, Mary Vorse, Fay, Bevil Rudd, H.G. Wells, Banning, Mrs. Mallick, Mrs. Nolan, Ben Huebach, Geo. Macy, C.N. Thomas.

According to Schorer, the list could have included all of the following:

Leonard Bacon, Anna Louise Strong, Michael Williams, Grace MacGowan Cooke, George Sterling, Arthur S. Hoffman, Albert Payson Terhune, Charles Norris, Charles Hanson Towne, Phillip Goodman, Hugh Walpole, Frazier Hunt, Charles Breasted, Lloyd Lewis -- on and on, down to Dr. Benjamin Camp, James Roers, Sturges Riddle, down even to Hooper, Dick Marshall, Flowers, Cook, Mary Parrish, Chet Syms, Reynolds and Denton, Davy Deans, 2 Stans, Oley and we would still not have named half of the lost, not even a tenth.

The existence of these lists in Lewis's biography (and in Hemingway's) is more important than the actual names. Alcoholics become addicted to the *process* of rejection. They destroy friendships and marriages, and they estrange their children. If they become famous, the rejection process is facilitated for the simple reason that fame attracts more potential rejectees.

Lewis, as alcoholics frequently are, was scornful of entire groups of people. He ridiculed small-town businessman in *Babbitt*, maligned women in *Cass Timberlane*, and dozens of barely concealed public figures in *Gideon Planish*.

Lillian Hellman is listed by J. Anthony Lukas as a writer who drank a lot and is among the famous women whom Lucy Barry Robe classifies as an alcoholic. In *Lillian Hellman: The Image, The Woman* (Ballantine Books, 1986), the biographer William Wright cites many instances of Hellman's behavior (including heavy drinking) that are consistent with Robe's opinion (and mine) that she was an alcoholic.

Hellman showed classic alcoholic behavior in exhibiting unreasonable resentments. She would become infuriated by "a slight at a checkout counter, a child stepping on her foot, or an adult brushing against her in a crowd... [She] terrorized waitresses, secretaries, sales people." Hellman also had the usual collection of ruined friendships that result from the alcoholic's need for serial destruction: "She had terminal blowups with many who had been close to her."

A successful playwright while a young woman, Hellman created a storm in her later years by writing best-selling "memoirs." Although some criticized her for ridiculing others (Ernest Hemingway's ex-wife Martha Gellhorn nailed her for "relentlessly portraying Hemingway -- and everyone but Hellman -- as a posturing fool"), the memoirs became a bit of a problem for the elderly Hellman because she was caught indulging in that second-favorite pastime of alcoholics: lying.

The most flagrant of these frauds was the tale of "Julia," told by Hellman in *Pintimento* and later made into the popular film of the same name.

As a result of the film, the central event she described -- a bit of youthful heroics -- became the best known "episode" in Hellman's life. The problem is that it never happened. Hellman claimed to have undertaken the dangerous mission of delivering money to a young American woman (whom she called "Julia") active in the anti-Fascist underground in Austria just prior to the outbreak of World War II. Her veracity was seriously questioned by several critics, including Gellhorn, who pointed out several grave inconsistencies in her story. Then the lie exploded in Hellman's face. The real "Julia" -- alive and well and living (unbeknownst to Hellman) in New Jersey -- published *her* memoirs and destroyed whatever remained of Hellman's tattered reputation as a truth-teller. The memoirs of the elderly American woman (Muriel Gardiner Buttinger) left no doubt: she was "Julia." Unfortunately for Hellman, Doctor Buttinger (she had become a highly respected psychiatrist) had never even met Hellman!

But how did Hellman know *about* Julia? Wright uncovered a link. Buttinger and Hellman had a mutual friend, a socially active lawyer, known to tell dinner-table stories in New York during the war about "Julia's" exploits. Hellman had heard of "Julia" but she never met her, and she never acted as a courier. Her story was a fabrication.

Lillian Hellman lied for the same reason Joe McCarthy and Admiral Byrd lied: to empower her alcoholic ego. Alcoholics are usually very good liars, but sometimes their arrogance gets the best of them. Hellman's egomania prevented her from checking to see if "Julia" was still alive.

It might be enlightening, in the midst of this parade of "distinguished" literary alcoholics, to note briefly the career of Dorothy Kilgallen, the late Hearst gossip columnist. After all, she too was a writer of sorts. If the disease really does cause alcoholics to behave very much like one another, regardless of their backgrounds, we should expect to find patterns of abuse in Kilgallen's work that's similar to those in the products of her (presumptive) literary betters.

Kilgallen, who died of an overdose of alcohol and pills, is tagged an alcoholic in Lucy Barry Robe's book. Her gossip column, "Voice of Broadway" which appeared several times a week in the Hearst newspapers, was notorious for its "blind" references to unseemly behavior by celebrities and near-celebrities. In writing her column, Kilgallen, I'm now convinced, did what any alcoholic with the disease-created compulsion to malign would do: she simply fabricated sleazy accusations. She lied. She got away with this despicable practice because she veiled her slanderous comments with descriptions that might fit more than one person.

I recall that at one stage in her career, when Kilgallen seemed obsessed with accusing obviously heterosexual public men of homosexuality (a more serious charge in the 1950's than it is today), she insinuated that one of New York's most popular, and macho, major league baseball players was having an affair with his -- equally macho -- manager.

Although she got away with these outrages for many years, one of Kilgallen's targets did take her to court. As reported by Lee Israel in her biography *Kilgallen* (Delacorte Press, 1979), Elaine Shepard, who worked in the Eisenhower White House, regularly accompanied the White House press contingent whenever they traveled with the President. It happened that at that time all the reporters on the press plane were males. Kilgallen published an item suggesting that a female member of the White House staff (as usual, Kilgallen did not use a name) engaged in simultaneous sexual relations -- an orgy -- with a number of reporters while in flight. Elaine Shepard sued, claiming, as the only female on the aircraft, that there could be no doubt Kilgallen meant her. At the trial, Kilgallen took the stand and coolly denied that Shepard was the target. She was taken aback when Shepard's attorney stuck another slanderous item under her nose: an earlier column claiming that an unnamed female reporter had gone to bed with movie star Clark Gable in order to get an interview. The lawyer established that Shepard had been Kilgallen's target of this earlier, equally false, accusation. Unfortunately, the jury did not find for the victim of Kilgallen's false accusation; the columnist walked out of the court room with a favorable verdict. But Israel quotes one of the jurors who regretted they could not bring in a verdict against Kilgallen, since he knew she was a "character assassin."

Truman Capote, son of an alcoholic mother who committed suicide, was himself an alcoholic. He was treated for alcoholism at Chit Chat Farm in Pennsylvania and at Hazelden in Minnesota, but never achieved permanent sobriety. He died in 1984, at the age of

60, of cardiac arrhythmia, a disorder common to long-term alcoholics.

As shown in Gerald Clark's *Capote: A Biography* (Ballantine Books, 1989), alcoholism influenced both Capote's behavior and his writing -- particularly as the addiction tightened its grip.

Capote used his talent to ridicule others who were either present or past friends. He portrayed Tennessee Williams as a repugnant homosexual "queen" who lived in a Plaza Hotel suite littered with dog feces. The composer Ned Rorem was pilloried by name; he was "A Quaker queer... an intolerable combination of brimstone behavior and self-righteous piety." The writer Katherine Anne Porter, herself caricatured by Capote, said of him at the time, "Apparently [Capote's] life has turned into a kind of poison that he's spitting out over the world."

Capote, a personal friend of many social leaders of his time,* went too far in *"La Côte Basque, 1965,"* a story that appeared in the June 1975 issue of *Esquire*. He portrayed many friends and acquaintances -- including Babe and Bill Paley, his closest friends for many years -- viciously. (The Bill Paley character was a "rich and attractive Jew who yearned to be a WASP patrician.") One of those he skewered -- Anne Woodward, who had shot her husband ten years earlier under mysterious circumstances -- swallowed a fatal dose of Secanol shortly after this work of "fiction" was published.

In the event, Clark reports that Capote's powerful friends were outraged:

> Truman had been accepted, pampered, and allowed into the inner recesses of their private lives; in return, he had mocked them and broadcast their secrets. He was, in their opinion, a cad and a traitor.

Capote's social life was finished by the publication of this

---

*In his later years, Capote, a homosexual, combined his sexual needs with the typical late-stage alcoholic's habit of associating with social inferiors. He had affairs with stupefyingly dull and ordinary men. One fellow, an air-conditioning repair man from a small town in Illinois, had much the same puzzling effect on Capote's rich and sophisticated friends as had the frumpy Mrs. Powers on the (resolutely heterosexual) Sinclair Lewis's European acquaintances.

malicious work. Although much of the printed comment that the episode engendered focused on the question of whether or not "the artist" had a right to use gossip told to him in confidence, I think *"La Côte Basque, 1965"* was just another alcoholism-determined work of malice. Capote used his talent and his access to publication to do what all alcoholics *must* do: he debased others to compensate for the battering inflicted on his ego by the addiction.

These alcoholics who wrote were more destructive than the average alcoholic because they had the means, and the talent, to attack lots of people in an especially harmful way. But although the pen is said to be mightier than the sword, it isn't, really. Some alcoholics do greater harm. They kill. They kill *because* they are alcoholics, and we need now to take a look at the blood-drenched record of this most destructive of all human maladies.

8: ALCOHOLISM KILLS

I started to drink... I had this here -- I don't know what you call it --
maybe a blackout... I am just thanking God that I didn't kill my son.
Why I killed my wife I do not know because I loved her.

An Alcoholic

I killed [a fellow officer] in New Guinea, just at dusk... he was shaving
and the bullet went through his throat...

An Alcoholic

Violence is the expression of impotence.

Hannah Arendt

The United States Government determined, in a 1983 survey, that
forty percent of the inmates serving time in state prisons for rape,
burglary, or assault said they drank heavily the year before they
entered prison. The survey also found that forty percent of habitual offenders -- those with five or more convictions -- drank heavily
between prison terms. No attempt was made to distinguish be-

tween heavy drinking nonalcoholics and alcoholics, but there can be no doubt about it: alcoholics are responsible for a large percentage of violent crimes. In the decades of drinking experienced by most alcoholics, I am convinced that most commit *some* violent acts. This is certainly true of famous alcoholics who have been the subject of comprehensive biographies; their stories are replete with violent episodes.

One night's wildness by F. Scott Fitzgerald was recalled by Anita Loos. A guest at the Fitzgeralds' home, she and Zelda were trying to ignore Scott, who was drunk and angry. Aaron Latham described what happened next in *Crazy Sundays: F. Scott Fitzgerald in Hollywood* (The Viking Press, 1971):

> Finally he jumped up from the table and said, "I'm going to kill you two." And he tried. He jerked off the tablecloth with everything on it and then started throwing candelabra and other big, heavy things at us. Scott had locked all the doors, but the butler -- he will always be a hero to me -- broke through a glass pane in one of the doors and came in and held Scott. Then Zelda and I ran across the street to Ring Lardner's house."*

Arnold Gingrich, former editor of *Esquire,* told Latham that Fitzgerald was "a real Jekyll and Hyde character -- a vicious drunk, one of the worst I have ever known."

Malcolm Lowry, another alcoholic novelist, threatened murder while drinking. More than once he menaced his mentor, Conrad Aiken.**

Lowry's propensity for domestic violence may have led directly to his death. Drinking heavily one night, he attacked his wife with a broken bottle. She fled to a neighbor's house. When she returned the next day, she found Lowry dead. He had taken twenty capsules of sodium amatyl. Lowry had openly fought his addiction for many years; his wife believed he had been overcome with remorse for attacking her.

---

*Although himself an alcoholic, Lardner did no harm to the two women. He gave them shelter until Fitzgerald passed out.

**As already noted, Aiken was also an alcoholic.

Jackson Pollock, the artist, committed wild and senseless violence while drinking. B.H. Friedman in *Jackson Pollock: Energy Made Visible* (McGraw Hill Book Company, 1972) says that Pollock "tried to throw Gaston off the roof... tried to push Baziotes out a window... [and] tried to strangle Siqueiros." He once rammed his car repeatedly into a Larry Rivers' sculpture, trying to destroy the work of a fellow artist. While drinking in a cabaret with Friedman and other friends, he suddenly turned on a stranger, a college student who had done nothing to antagonize him:

Just as a number ended and everyone was beginning to applaud, Jackson grabbed the boy by the shoulder, turned him so he faced Jackson, then squared off and socked him in the jaw.

While serving in Cairo, Donald Maclean, the British traitor, wrestled a rifle away from an Egyptian guard and tried to smash his skull. He was on the bender that ended when he trashed the apartment of an American woman diplomat.

Eugene O'Neill once vented his drunken rage on a roomful of furniture. He destroyed it with a machete. He hit at least two of his three wives and on one wild night tried to drag one of them home by the hair.

James Thurber and Sinclair Lewis also broke furniture while drunk. George C. Scott (a self-identified alcoholic) once destroyed an entire hotel room.

It would be bad enough if they only wrecked furniture. But alcoholics frequently attack people, and sometimes they kill. The victim is most often the spouse, or someone else close to them. Because they all possess this potential for mayhem, and because they dissemble easily, one shudders to think of the number of alcoholics who murdered and got away with it.

One homicide that remains officially unsolved is the July 3, 1954 slaying of Marilyn Sheppard.

Her husband, Dr. Sam Sheppard, was accused of the crime, found guilty, and sentenced to life imprisonment. But he was freed in 1966 by the United States Supreme Court on grounds that his first trial had been unfair because of a prejudicial atmosphere marked by headlines like, "Sam Called a 'Jekyll-Hyde'." Sheppard's second trial ended with an acquittal.* No one else was ever charged with the crime.

Sam Sheppard went through two more marriages in the brief life (less than four years) left to him after his release from prison. He became a professional wrestler, a rather unusual occupation for a former surgeon. When he died, *The New York Times* quoted his mother-in-law who said he had been consuming a bottle of vodka a day. In his book on the affair, *Dr. Sam, An American Tragedy* (Henry Regnery Company, 1972), Jack Harrison Pollack wrote that Sheppard polished off whole bottles of vodka in single drinking sessions.

Sheppard's second wife divorced him in 1968 and requested the court to restrain him from seeing her lest he "perpetrate bodily harm." She said that Sheppard had thrown empty bottles at her and threatened her with a pistol.

At his death, Sam Sheppard was estranged from his brother Steve who had led the long fight to overturn the murder conviction. He had accused his brother of wanting to keep him "in jail because it gave him status." He also seems to have been estranged from his son, who did not attend his funeral.

During his second trial in 1966, his attorney, F. Lee Bailey, refused to let his client testify because, according to Pollack, Sheppard was "drinking heavily -- straight vodka... and was mixing alcohol with a variety of pills."

To his credit, Pollack uses a word that most biographers of heavy drinkers avoid; he refers to Sheppard's *alcoholism*. Indeed, heavy drinking probably killed him. The coroner attributed death to "a prelude to cirrhosis," and added "this was not something that happened all of a sudden."

If Sheppard was an alcoholic in 1970 (and by all appearances a late-stage alcoholic), and if, as was the case, his heavy drinking frightened his attorney in 1966, then he was most likely an alcoholic in 1954 -- the year his wife was slain.

---

*One key item of evidence used by his attorney (F. Lee Bailey) in his presentation to the Supreme Court was a deposition by Dorothy Kilgallen, whose alcoholism is described in the last chapter. Kilgallen accused the judge in Sheppard's first trial of having said, before the trial began, that Sheppard was guilty. At the time Kilgallen gave her deposition the judge was dead and unable to defend himself against her accusation.

Here's Sam Sheppard's account of the murder: That night, after a party, he had fallen asleep on the living room couch. He was awakened by his wife's screams sometime past 12:30 AM. He rushed upstairs to his wife's room and, seeing a "white form" standing next to his wife's bed, started to grapple with the intruder until he was knocked unconscious by a blow from behind. After an undetermined period, he awoke and found that his wife had been beaten to death while he was unconscious. He then heard a noise on the first floor and, after running down the stairs, encountered what appeared to be a male figure. He and this stranger fought, and Sheppard was knocked out for the second time. At 5:45 A.M., five and one quarter hours after he had last been seen by someone outside the family, Sam Sheppard reported the murder. He drank alcohol the previous night, but in quantities unknown.

The prosecution claimed that Sheppard had committed premeditated murder. The defense argued that if he had wanted to kill his wife, he would have drugged her or used some method other than beating her with a sharp, heavy instrument. The first trial's verdict of second degree murder shows that the jury didn't believe either the state's claim of premeditation or the defense's claim of innocence.

If I am right, and Sheppard was an alcoholic at the time, it is not difficult to imagine what may have happened. Perhaps Sheppard, well into a Saturday night binge, attempted to make love to his wife when, for some reason, he became enraged. (There was evidence of sexual assault.) Perhaps Marilyn, who was pregnant, objected to his drunken advances. Perhaps he was temporarily impotent as a result of too many drinks. Perhaps whatever happens inside an alcoholic's booze-soaked brain when he becomes enraged just happened. Then he struck his wife in a rage, repeatedly smashing her head and face with a hatchet. (His second wife later said that he habitually carried one around the house, after he was acquitted.)

The police counted thirty-five blows to Marilyn Sheppard's head. If he killed her he could have used the rest of the night to get rid of the weapon and his T-shirt -- neither of which was ever found. Because alcoholics can drink large amounts without becoming rubber-legged or slurred of speech, a state of non-sobriety would not interfere with attempts to hide evidence of a murder. And the police, who did not administer a sobriety test when they answered his call, probably saw none of the signs of heavy drinking that appear when nonalcoholics overindulge.

If an alcoholic commits a murder while drinking he does so *because* he is an alcoholic. Once the deed is done, if there is any chance of getting away with it, the alcoholic can call on his practiced ability to lie skillfully. Sheppard apparently kept his parents, his brothers and their wives, his second wife and even the biographer who labeled him an "alcoholic" convinced that he did not murder Marilyn Sheppard.

There were no witnesses to this killing. But the fact of Sam Sheppard's alcoholism and the probability that he was a non-sober alcoholic on the night of the murder is something that anyone interested in this famous case must consider in deciding whether to believe Sheppard's story that the "bushy-haired stranger" who beat Marilyn Sheppard to death only managed to knock him out. Twice.

Two famous female alcoholics who shared more than their addiction in common were Libby Holman and Anne Woodward. They both killed their husbands.

Holman, a popular singer who married an heir to the Reynolds tobacco fortune, claimed complete memory loss when her husband, Zachary Smith Reynolds, was found dead in their bedroom in 1932. According to Jon Bradshaw in *Dreams That Money Can Buy* (William Morrow & Company, 1985), Holman, who had been drinking heavily the night of the murder, years later confided to a friend, "I don't know whether I shot him or not." She was indicted, but, pregnant with his child, she was released at the request of her husband's family. The realization that she may have killed her husband during an alcoholic blackout was not enough to lead Holman to sobriety; she reportedly indulged in drugs as well as liquor in her later years. She committed suicide in 1971. Her husband's murder remains officially unsolved.

Unlike Holman, Anne Woodward never said she didn't remember blasting her rich socialite husband with a shotgun. She told the police she thought he was an intruder. In spite of the fact that her prowler story seemed most implausible (her husband was emerging, naked, from the shower when she shot him), it was nonetheless accepted by the authorities; she was not charged. Anne Woodward was known to drink heavily and to have "insane rages." She lived for many years after the shooting, but committed suicide a few days after the alcoholic Truman Capote published his thinly-veiled fictionalized account of the killing.

Another infamous murder attributable to alcoholism -- this one in the early nineteenth century -- was the execution of a 17 year-old male slave who committed the "crime" of breaking a pitcher. He was slaughtered with an axe by his owners, two nephews of Thomas Jefferson, who had summoned their other slaves to watch the killing. Boynton Merrill, Jr. writes about the case in *Jefferson's Nephews* (Princeton University Press, 1976). He ascribes the homicides, wrongfully, in my opinion, to a number of vague psychiatric reasons, but he does a more than adequate job of convincing me that both killers were alcoholics who killed in a drunken rage.

Getting *inappropriately* angry about perceived wrongs is typical alcoholic behavior, and to most people, the accidental breakage of crockery does not justify homicide.

Although relatives, servants, and others closely involved with alcoholics are usually at risk, sometimes alcoholics kill complete strangers.

On the night of July 14, 1966, Richard Speck knocked on the door of a nurses' residence in Chicago. Once inside, he tied up eight young female nurses and stabbed them to death -- one by one. All were strangers to him.

After his arrest, Speck was examined by a number of psychiatrists. None of them, to my knowledge, diagnosed him as an alcoholic or suggested that his alcoholism caused the massacre. They labeled him a "sociopath" which seems to be the psychiatrists' way of saying he was essentially sane, but not very nice.

Then someone discovered that he had an extra Y chromosome, and a new theory was proposed. According to this idea, double Y chromosome males had a high propensity for violent behavior. Although studies showed that the incidence of double Y chromosomes among the population of males convicted of violent crimes was four times higher than in the general population, other researchers found that most individuals with the abnormality were not violent. Then someone took a second look at Speck and discovered that he did not, after all, have the extra chromosome. That ended the double Y chromosome explanation for the rampage.

Marvin Ziporyn, a psychiatrist, describes various symptoms of alcoholism in Speck in the book he co-wrote with Jack Altman, *Born To Raise Hell: The Untold Story of Richard Speck* (Grove Press, Inc., 1967). Ziporyn does not, however, call him an alcoholic.

Speck drank and used barbiturates. He had been drinking heavily the day of the murders, and since he was physically capable of the individual knife-murders of eight young women (and the rape of one of them), he was clearly not incapacitated by his alcohol intake. Displaying high tolerance, he was drinking and acting like an alcoholic.

Ziporyn is convinced that Speck had no recollection of the murders. Although many murderers make that claim to avoid punishment, Speck comes across in Ziporyn's book as totally without guile. He accepted the fact that he murdered the nurses; he had been puzzled by the blood on his hands when he awoke on the morning after the massacre. Because of his failure to recollect the killings, I think Richard Speck murdered the nurses while in an alcoholic blackout.

While under observation by Ziporyn, Speck exhibited increased tension and agitation after receiving sedatives. The normal reaction -- normal to nonalcoholics, that is -- to sedatives is to become sedated. Speck's contrary reaction strongly suggests alcoholism.

Richard Speck told Ziporyn that he had many prior violent experiences while drinking or while on barbiturates:

Whiskey makes me wild. When I'm on that I can do some terrible things. Like once I was aboard ship on the Randall there was this sailor -- he was a good guy, but I just went after him and beat him up. I was drunk and threw some coffee in an officer's face, don't know why. I've attacked some of my best buddies and never knew anything about it. That's the funny thing. I don't know what happens to me till they tell me. Last year, I was in Dallas and I had a few drinks with some "drivers" you know -- pep pills. Them and Wyman's glue make my headaches go away -- wish I had some now. Anyway, I was talking to this guy, I think he was queer. Suddenly everything blacked out. Next thing I knew, the guy was on the ground covered with blood, and I was battering at him with a tire handle. My buddy, Al Butts, pulled me off. He said I was a crazy man.

Speck went on to tell the psychiatrist:

Don't you think my mother begged, pleaded, cried, trying to get me not to drink? I only drank a little till I was fifteen, and then a little more, but later -- man when those headaches started, I really poured it in me. My mother didn't like it, didn't like it at all.

Despite this expression of affection for his mother, Speck told Ziporyn that he had struck her while on sedatives.

In his conclusion, Ziporyn likens Richard Speck to Doctor Jekyll and Mister Hyde, but fails to note that this pattern is common in alcoholics. He attributes Speck's rampage to a mishmash of physiological and psychiatric reasons.

After having examined Speck regularly for more than a year, Ziporyn asked Speck's prison friend, Mark Clancy, for his opinion. Clancy said:

Well -- I'm no psychiatrist, of course, but just as a friend of his. I think if he did it, he must have been drunk or out of his mind. I can't see him doing it deliberately. He's just not made that way. The way I figure, he was drunk or on the pills and went in to rob the joint, and something happened to snap him. I don't think he remembers. I don't think he knows any more about it than we do.

Doctor Ziporyn goes on --

Clancy's views obviously did not add any professional weight... but this personal impression on the part of a sensitive individual was certainly not without value.

Speaking as someone who listens with a great deal of skepticism to what most psychiatrists say about alcoholics and alcoholism, it is my opinion that Clancy states, in fewer words, a more accurate appraisal of Speck's motivation than does Ziporyn.

In my opinion, Richard Speck was an alcoholic. His alcoholism caused him to kill those nurses in the same way *his* alcoholism caused F. Scott Fitzgerald to attack his wife and Anita Loos. But in Speck's case, there was no one there to restrain him.

Both Speck and his alcoholism adjusted to life behind bars. According to an 1981 article in *The Wall Street Journal*, he spent his time painting and making moonshine liquor. Said Joliet's warden, "He told me he doesn't want to spend these 1,200 years sober."

Speck didn't last that long. He died in 1992.

The United States Justice Department recently surveyed 12,000 prisoners and determined that about 60 percent had been "very drunk" just before committing their crimes. "Rapists and assaulters were most apt to be drinking immediately before their crime... " One researcher, R.T. Rada, has found alcohol use among rapists and other sexual offenders to exceed that of noncriminals. *He also found that in cases where the criminal was an alcoholic, the criminal sexual activity ceased if there was recovery.* This finding lends strong support to the idea that the alcoholism itself was the root cause of the criminal behavior.

Here, from John M. MacDonald, M.D.'s *The Murderer and His Victim* (Charles C. Thomas, 1986), are the percentages of murderers who drank alcohol prior to killing in various cities: Memphis, 86 percent; Columbus, 83 percent; Chicago, 55 percent; Helsinki, Finland, 66 percent; and Glasgow, Scotland, 55 percent. Although we have no way of knowing how many of these drinking killers were alcoholics, in view of their propensity for violence and the high incidence of alcoholism in the three countries where the data were gathered, the number must be high. MacDonald cites another study in which thirty murderers who were arrested immediately following their crime had their urine alcohol level tested. The testers found alcohol in 83 percent of the cases.

According to MacDonald, "the *only* psychological disorders found more frequently among criminal offenders then in the general population were sociopathic (antisocial) personality disorder,*

---

*Psychiatrists have a notoriously poor record of diagnosing alcoholism, especially in its early or middle stages. I suspect that many in the "sociopathic" category were undiagnosed alcoholics.

alcoholism, and drug dependency." [Emphasis added.]

The F.B.I.'s Behavioral Sciences Unit recently undertook an in-depth study of thirty-six convicted and incarcerated murderers who had 111 dead (and nine surviving) victims between them. Only seven of these killers had murdered only once; all the others were multiple murderers. All of them had committed sexually-related homicides. The results of the F.B.I.'s study were published in *Sexual Homicides: Patterns and Motives* (Lexington Books, 1988), by Robert K. Ressler, Ann W. Burgess, and John E. Douglas. Al-though the F.B.I. team shows no apparent appreciation of the ego-inflating power of alcoholism, they did gather a number of facts that make it clear that alcoholics constituted an important segment of their sample.

Nearly 70 percent of the murderers in the F.B.I.'s sample came from families in which one of the parents "had histories of alcohol abuse." Although it is impossible to tell from this single statistic how many of the murderers themselves inherited the vulnerability to alcoholism, the number who did is probably high.

Out of the 118 victim-cases, half of the murderers told the F.B.I. investigators that they had been drinking prior to committing the crime. These are the words of one rapist-killer:

> It was the same as with the other one. I had been drinking at the bar. I don't even remember leaving. I don't know what made me kill her. I don't even know why I raped her. I had a good-looking wife at home. I saw her get into her car and I walked up and got in the car with her, yelled at her, took her down there where I raped her. I kept telling her I didn't want to hurt her, but I just started choking her.

Another murderer went AWOL from the Army while --

> on a drinking [bender.] While out on the street, he beat a drunk to death after the man grabbed him... He then beat to death a second man. Finally, he abducted a female acquaintance. When he awoke the next morning, her dead body was beside him with a broomstick thrust into her vagina with such force that it had penetrated her lungs. Although he believes he killed her, he claims no recollection of the incident.

In my opinion, this man, like Speck, killed during an alcoholic blackout.

Yet another killer gave the F.B.I.'s interviewer his insight into the relationship of alcohol and career criminals. He sounds like an alcoholic:

If it hadn't been for beer and whiskey, I wouldn't be [in prison] today. I've seen a lot of men come in and out since I've been here. They go out and they come in. The only reason they do that is they get hold of a bottle. Ninety percent of the guys that are in here are pretty good people, but when they get hold of that bottle, it makes them feel like they are superman.

Joel Norris, a consulting psychologist who has interviewed many imprisoned multiple murderers, stated in *Serial Killers: The Growing Menace* (Doubleday, 1988): "Most multiple killers whom we have studied, *serial killers* as well as *mass murderers*, are *consistently addicted* or dependent upon drugs or *alcohol* or both." [Emphasis added.]

Serial killers, those who kill a lot of people, but in separate episodes, need certain "qualifications" to succeed, characteristics not required by mass murderers like Richard Speck who kill in a single outburst. The serial killer, by definition, isn't apprehended after his first murder. He goes on killing. But between murders he lives among us, pretending to be normal. He plans each murder. He coldly calculates how to locate the victim, how to do the actual killing, and how to dispose of the body. Unlike Speck-type spree murderers, *serial killers need more than rage.* If serial killing were looked upon as an occupation it would be seen to demand craftiness, manipulation, and the ability to deceive. Also helpful is a strong desire to control and to humiliate. In a word, serial killing demands egomania.

Based on my research, several of America's most notorious serial killers were victims of the disease that causes egomania; they were alcoholics.

Ask most Americans to name one serial killer and they will probably respond, "Ted Bundy." A handsome ex-law student, who was executed in 1988 by the State of Florida, Bundy killed at least twenty-one, and perhaps as many as forty young women. He was an alcoholic.

In *The Only Living Witness: A True Account of Homicidal Insanity* (Simon & Schuster, 1983), Stephen G. Michaud and Hugh Aynesworth provide more than enough information on which to diagnose alcoholism.* While on Death Row, Bundy granted them interviews in which he provided details about his behavior in the years when he was killing women in Washington, Utah, Colorado, and Florida. Bundy, who still hoped to escape execution, wanted to avoid inadvertently confessing to his crimes, but he couldn't resist the opportunity to impress the authors (and through them, the public) with his brilliance. The solution? He agreed to answer the journalists' questions "as if" he were talking about a third party. Michaud and Aynesworth went along with this fiction. Later, they played their tapes to psychiatrists who agreed that Bundy was actually talking about himself. The authors also interviewed third parties who knew Bundy.

One intended victim, a young Colorado woman who escaped from Bundy's car before he could club her to death, told the police that her abductor "smelled of liquor." An acquaintance said, "When Ted drank, he often got drunk." Bundy himself told the interviewers he would "down two or three quick beers before going on a shoplifting spree." (Alcoholics usually understate their alcohol intake. He probably had more than "two or three" beers.) He told of once leaving a bar "where he had been drinking a great deal," seeing a woman on the street and having the urge to assault her. He invited another girl to his room where they both "became intoxicated." On another occasion, he picked up a hitch hiker, and "they both got drunk." (These two very lucky women weren't harmed.)

Bundy told Michaud and Aynesworth that he drank before each murder.

Bundy was convicted of murder in Colorado, but escaped. Fleeing to Florida, he settled in a boarding house. "He started drinking heavily that first week in Tallahassee -- his neighbors at the Oaks remember seeing Ted repeatedly drunk... "

On his most murderous night, Bundy broke into a Florida sorority

---

*Michaud and Aynesworth seem not to consider that possibility themselves, or, if they do, do not treat alcoholism as a motivating factor.

house armed with a heavy club. He bludgeoned four sleeping coeds, killing two of them, and badly injuring the others. He had been in a bar drinking before he entered the sorority house. A witness who saw him fleeing the crime scene told the police that Bundy was drunk.

A few days later, Bundy checked into the Lake City Holiday Inn where two clerks noticed he was drunk and slurring his words. Shortly after that he was seen driving his van. He was noticed because the van was "weaving and lurching" on the highway. On the day before he was captured, "He drank heavily." When arrested he was "drunk and disoriented."

Bundy even had access to alcohol while on Florida's Death Row. His own investigator said he was drunk during a prison interview. On another occasion, he was seen ingesting eight-hundred milligrams of Valium.

While on Death Row, Bundy married Carole Boone. According to Michaud and Aynesworth, Boone was known to "[lead] a circle of her closest co-workers on a three-hour liquid [lunches]." Bundy and Boone had been friends before he was imprisoned, and although there is not enough evidence to conclude that his bride had a drinking problem, alcoholics tend to associate with other heavy drinkers. According to one specialist, Richard C. Bates, M.D., "alcoholic males tend to marry alcoholic females." Boone smuggled vodka and Valium to her new husband until caught by the authorities.

Bundy is described as "defeated" when first arrested, but his egomania soon reasserted itself. In fact, it probably cost him his life. Early in the proceedings his lawyer plea-bargained a life sentence in exchange for a guilty plea. But Bundy denounced the deal. He pleaded not guilty and announced that he would defend himself. An observing psychiatrist said Bundy wanted a trial and wanted to represent himself in order to "confront and confound various authority figures." He needed to be seen as the center of attention, a "handsome courtroom dazzler" who would beat the rap. It didn't work. Bundy failed to convince the jury and was sentenced to death.

Bundy displayed a full array of power symptoms. He was a crafty charmer. (Diabolically so -- he tricked his victims into going with him.) He was arrogant and felt superior to the police who were trying to put him away. He "took meticulous care of his appearance and dressed with casual, studied tweediness." And he displayed no remorse whatsoever for his crimes.

Because Bundy frequently raped and sexually mutilated his victims, the psychiatrists (and those who automatically turn to psychiatric explanations whenever they encounter abnormal behavior) had a field day developing psychosexual models to explain this serial killer. Being ignorant of alcoholism, they do not understand that if Bundy had been diagnosed and successfully treated for *that* disease at an early age, he probably would not have murdered anyone. Like all recovered alcoholics, his ego would have been deflated. *People with normal egos cannot commit egomaniacal crimes.* But what about those sexual urges? What would a recovered alcoholic have done about them? The answer is he would have done what other men do: fantasize and masturbate, or fantasize with a willing partner and act it out in a harmless way, or repress the urges. Bundy's sexual hunger did not kill those women. His sick ego did.

In his final television appearance, made a few hours before he was to be strapped in the electric chair, Bundy looked defeated. The cocky alcoholic ego had finally collapsed. But it was too late. Too late for Bundy, and too late for his victims.

John Wayne Gacy, who tortured and murdered thirty-three boys and young men over a six year period, is another widely-known serial killer. Like Bundy, he was drunk when arrested. Like Bundy, he is, in my opinion, an alcoholic.

Gacy probably inherited his vulnerability to alcoholism from his father, an abusive drinker who died of cirrhosis. According to Tim Cahill's book *Buried Dreams: Inside the Mind of a Serial Killer* (Bantam Books, 1986), Gacy drank Scotch and 190-proof pure grain alcohol. He devoured Valium "like popcorn."

In his "straight" life, Gacy was something of an overachiever. Before his arrest, he had been active in local politics, the church, and the Junior Chamber of Commerce. He performed as a volunteer clown at hospitals, and once had his picture taken with the First Lady, Rosalyn Carter. Cahill says Gacy was a "fussy" dresser who once ridiculed a detective investigating the killings for wearing a "shit brown" suit. He was "composed of lies, misrepresentations, and false ideals." He had a puffy face, and when arrested "his eyes were glassy, dull, and dead. He [looked] like a man insane. Or on drugs." That morning John Gacy drank Scotch before 9 AM. Like Bundy, he showed no remorse.

What kind of crimes did Gacy commit? A contractor in suburban Chicago, he would entice teenage boys to his house on the pretext of offering them employment. Once in his house, he would trick them into letting him handcuff them. Then Gacy would rape them -- orally and anally -- and torture them. After his arrest, neighbors said they had sometimes heard boys screaming for hours. The neighbors hadn't suspected torture. They thought it had something to do with drugs. He finished off his victims with slow strangulation, then buried the bodies under his house until that space was filled up. He dumped the last four victims in a nearby river.

John Gacy is now on Death Row.

Henry Lee Lucas has been convicted of eleven murders, but he probably killed many others. At one point following his arrest, he claimed to have killed hundreds -- but later recanted. The son of an alcoholic mother and an alcoholic father, Lucas began drinking when he was 10. He was only 15 when he committed his first murder. According to Norris, author of *Serial Killers: The Growing Menace*, Lucas was drunk every time he murdered. He killed for ten years, sometimes with another alcoholic named Toole, before he was arrested. Frequently they would torture their victims before killing them. They would press lighted cigarettes into their skin or burn them with red hot metal. Although most of his victims were strangers, Lucas killed both his mother and his common-law wife. He is currently imprisoned in Texas.

Norris includes in his book the case of Bobby Joe Long, a serial killer (nine victims) and rapist (more than fifty). Norris says Long "routinely consumed large amounts of alcohol in the strip bars where he was searching for new victims."

Gary Schaefer committed two murder-rapes and one rape. According to Norris, Schaefer "admitted to having a drinking problem."

Between the years 1971 and 1972, twenty-seven teenage boys disappeared in Houston. The disappearances ended when another teenager, Wayne Henley, shot and killed Dean Corll, a homosexual in his thirties. Henley and another boy, David Brooks, admitted to the police that they had procured victims for Corll and assisted him in burying the bodies. Henley also actually committed some of the murders.

Despite Henley's and Brooks' admissions of their own guilt and the dead Corll's inability to defend himself, the Houston authorities were convinced that Corll was indeed the mastermind and actual killer of most of the boys. (Like Gacy, he tortured and raped before killing.) One reason the police believed Henley and Brooks was their age. They were in their early teens when the first murders occurred, and it was thought unlikely that they initiated the series of killings.

According to Jack Olsen's book on the case, *The Man With the Candy: the Story of The Houston Mass Murders* (Simon and Schuster, 1974), Wayne Henley was already known as the neighborhood drunkard in spite of his young age. He drank himself into a stupor nearly every day. His father was "a troublemaker and wife-beater when he was drunk," suggesting alcoholism in the parent. Young Henley's participation in the mass murders, his reputed public drunkenness, and his father's record of violent behavior while drinking strongly suggest, in my opinion, that Wayne Henley, currently serving six 99-year prison terms for his role in the serial murders, is an alcoholic.

Nothing Olsen says about David Brooks suggests he was an alcoholic.

Olsen says little about the fiendish man who led his teenage accomplices in these awful crimes, but what he does say strongly suggests that Dean Corll, like Gacy and Bundy, was another alcoholic serial killer.

According to a close friend, Corll "began" to drink heavily shortly before he was killed. He admitted to knocking off a bottle of bourbon in one session and was seen downing, one after the other, three strong belts of whiskey. We know that alcoholics frequently hide their drinking from even their closest friends; "sudden" heavy drinking by a man in his thirties is very suspicious. So is another observation, made by the same friend: Corll drank heavily while experiencing stomach pain. Alcohol is a stomach *irritant*. Nonalcoholic drinkers who develop ulcers or inflamed stomach linings soon learn to avoid it. Alcoholics, however, would rather endure even intense pain than go without the substance they crave. Corll also exhibited one other behavioral symptom -- the "geographic cure." In one year, he changed his residence ten times. A final sign of alcoholism: the photograph of Corll on the jacket of Olsen's book shows a man with puffiness under the eyes.

Jeffrey L. Dahmer killed seventeen young men and boys in Milwaukee and kept some of their body parts in his refrigerator. He is, in my opinion, an alcoholic.

Following the 1991 discovery of bodies, and parts of bodies, in his apartment, *The New York Times* reported several clues strongly suggesting alcoholism. A man who had met Dahmer in a bar said he "suffered from problems with alcohol." Dahmer's stepmother said he had been discharged from the Army "because of drinking problems." A former barracks roommate said Dahmer got around the Army's ban on alcohol by rigging a portable bar kit to look like a briefcase. He also said Dahmer would drink until he passed out. According to another soldier, when he was stationed in Germany Dahmer would "get real violent" while drinking. A former classmate said he was already a drinker in high school, guzzling Scotch "in early morning classes."

The F.B.I. believes there may be as many as 500 serial killers on the loose in America. Many of them -- perhaps most -- are alcoholics.

Donald DeFreeze led the Symbionese Liberation Army, the terrorist group that kidnapped Patricia Hearst in 1974. DeFreeze, who raped the 19-year-old Hearst while she was held captive in a cramped closet, was later killed, along with a number of his confederates, in a wild shootout in Los Angeles.

Patricia Hearst provides ample evidence in *Every Secret Thing* (Doubleday & Company, Inc., 1982), that this violent ex-convict (he had cold-bloodedly murdered Marcus Foster, a moderate black leader) was an alcoholic. She saw him get loaded, nearly every day, on cheap plum wine. According to Hearst, *"he was nothing more than a drunk*, playacting the role of the macho revolutionary ... *a strutting egomaniac."* [Emphasis added.]

According to David Horowitz (*Heterodoxy*, March, 1993), Huey Newton, the late leader of the Black Panthers, drank a fifth of cognac daily. Horowitz, who had once been allied with them, says that while commanding the Panthers, Newton ordered the killing of a female bookkeeper for asking too many questions about funds, bull-whipped Panthers who he thought needed discipline, pistol-whipped a middle-aged black tailor, murdered a 17-year-old prostitute (then ordered the attempted murder of a Panther who had witnessed an attempt to kill an eyewitness to the murder of the 17-year-old) and personally whipped and then sodomized fellow-Panther Bobby Seale so violently that "he had to have his anus surgically repaired."

When members of Alcoholics Anonymous refer to themselves as "recover*ing* alcoholics," they are reminding themselves that they can never be *cured* of the disease. If they do not stay with the AA program, they will return to a life of chaos. Unfortunately, not all AA's stick with the program, and of those who leave, some end up committing violent crimes. One man who left AA and subsequently wreaked havoc in the lives of many was Charles E. Dederich.

Dederich joined Alcoholics Anonymous in California in 1956. He soon became an unusually active member who traveled across the state to speak at AA meetings.

Central to the genius of AA's principal founder, Bill Wilson, was his recognition that ego deflation is essential to recovery. He made sure that this idea permeated the program; as already noted, it underlies the famous Twelve Steps. Wilson and other AA pioneers also made sure that no member could use the organization itself as a vehicle for an ego trip. This is one reason for the tradition of anonymity. You can't get famous or powerful as a member, or even an officer, of Alcoholics Anonymous. Unfortunately for him and many others, Charles Dederich thought otherwise.

Dederich not only did not follow the AA Twelve Steps, he actually embarked on a power trip while still in AA, one that was to end, years later, in tragedy.

He formed his own group within AA. Within a short time he invited heroin addicts to join his group and shortly after that -- in 1958 -- led these "alkies and druggies" out of AA and into his own

organization which he named the "Tender Loving Care Club."
Dederich's club was different from AA in several significant ways.
Most importantly for Charles Dederich's ego, unlike AA members,
who use that fellowship only to help themselves and each other to
stop drinking, those who followed him into the "Tender Loving
Care Club" were told to depend on *him* for everything.

The organization was soon managing all aspects of its members
lives, and Chuck Dederich was in command. In time, the alcoholics
who had followed him out of AA complained about Dederich's
methods. His reaction, one he was to repeat over and over again
in coming years, was to simply eject the complaining ex-AA's from
his organization. By then, Dederich had come up with a new name
-- Synanon -- and was rapidly turning this so-called self-help group
into a cult, complete with its own strange rules and with his
megalomaniacal self in supreme command.

Synanon, which got some favorable nationwide publicity for its
success with heroin addicts, flourished. But as is always the case
with the activities of alcoholic power-trippers, the stated objective
of Synanon -- treatment of drug addicts -- was quite different from
its real, hidden, purpose. Its real function was to satisfy an alcoholism-dominated ego -- that of its founder, Charles Dederich.

Dederich expelled the drug addicts in 1968 and directed Synanon
to attract naive members of the middle class. The new recruits
were encouraged to assign all their assets to Synanon and to move
into a Synanon compound.

By 1975, Synanon had become dangerously bizarre. Dederich
required all members -- male and female -- to shave their heads.
By 1977, all men who had been in Synanon for five years -- ex-
cluding Dederich himself -- were required to have vasectomies.
Those who refused to comply were expelled. Women members
who became pregnant were pressured to have abortions. Dederich
ordered all couples, including married couples, to exchange partners.

During this time, Dederich was described by members and ex-
members as "coarse and vicious." Here, for example, is his insight
on childbirth: "I understand it's more like crapping a football than
anything else." But some ex-members report that Dederich was
actually charming and witty. One ex-member called him "the fun-
niest man I ever knew." He was displaying classic alcoholic Jekyll
and Hyde behavior.

He formed a goon squad, called The Imperial Marines, and drilled them in terrorism tactics. Acts of violence were directed against ex-members of Synanon, who were growing in number as the organization rigorously applied its founder's "submit or quit" rule. One ex-member whose wife continued as a follower (and who kept their child inside the Synanon compound) was clubbed by two Synanon goons and nearly killed. His crime? He had hired an attorney to help him recover his own child. Others were viciously beaten. One ex-member, Frances Wynn, filed a civil suit for kidnapping, wrongful imprisonment, brainwashing and torture. She was awarded damages.

Elements of the media, especially *The Light*, a California weekly, started to pay attention to the strange goings-on in Synanon. When *Time* wrote a negative article, Synanon sued. All my information about Dederich is from *The Light on Synanon* (Seaview Books, 1980) by Dave and Cathy Mitchell and Richard Ofshe, the editors and an investigative reporter from *The Light*.

One of Dederich's enemies was Paul Morantz, a California attorney for another ex-member who had won $300,000 in a law suit. Dederich (who had the Nixonian habit of taping his meetings) asked his staff, "When is one of you cowardly people going to go down there and break his legs?" Two of his followers listened and acted. One day in October, 1978, Paul Morantz put his hand in his mailbox and pulled out a rattlesnake. The snake bit him. Morantz survived, and the snake was quickly traced to Synanon.

Dederich was arrested on December 2, 1978 and charged with attempted murder. At the time, he was so drunk he couldn't walk and had to be carried to the police van on a stretcher. His lawyers said he was too drunk to understand the initial trial proceedings. The judge took one look at the horizontal Dederich and agreed. He was booked the next day.

In July 1980, Dederich and two of Synanon's Imperial Marines pleaded "no contest" to the charge of conspiracy to commit murder.

The editorial team from *The Light* says in the book that Dederich did not drink for twenty-two years. Perhaps. Synanon *did* have a strict no-alcohol rule. But there is more to alcoholism than drinking, more to sobriety than abstinence. Because alcoholics develop cross addictions to sedatives in pill form, Dederich could have gulped pills during those twenty-two years. (He also could have limited his booze consumption to periodic benders, out of

sight of others.) But without ego-deflation, even complete abstinence can intensify egomania.

In my opinion, Dederich was either on pills or he was "dry." If
he abstained, he did it with egomania. He power-tripped by
establishing and commanding a violent cult. The power-tripping
enabled him to avoid booze, or at least to limit his drinking (and
perhaps his pill-taking) to the extent that no one noticed it until
1978, twenty years after he walked away from Alcoholics Anonymous, a program based on ego deflation.

Dederich was an alcoholic cult leader whose one known attempt to
take a life ended in failure. Jim Jones, the head of the People's
Temple, led more than 900 men, women, and children to mass suicide in Jonestown, Guyana, in 1978. Jones was addicted to various
prescription drugs. He was also a megalomaniac and, probably, an
alcoholic.

According to Marshall Kilduff and Ron Javers' book *The Suicide
Cult* (Bantam Books, 1978), Jones "constantly popped pills for every
pharmaceutical reason -- to wake up, to stay alert, to go to sleep,
to lighten a mood... " He held all-night meetings, and during them
Jones would keep a small bag full of various pills constantly at his
side. Min Yee and Thomas Layton in *In My Father's House* (Holt,
Rinehart and Winston, 1981) say that near the end he was a
physical wreck who dosed himself with "painkillers, tranquilizers,
and amphetamines" and wore dark glasses to hide the facial damage
brought on by his pill-taking.

Jones went even further than Dederich in demanding abject
submission by members of his cult. He demanded sex with his
female followers and afterwards forced them to announce at public
meetings that they had instigated it. He coerced males into
performing oral sex on him. He had them photographed while so
engaged and used the pictures to keep them under control.

Members of the cult who misbehaved were punished severely.
Adults were forced to stay in a cramped metal box exposed to the
tropical sun. They were fed through a small door. Children were
thrown down wells. Although two adults waited at the bottom of
the well to fish them out before they drowned, the children were
terrified by the experience.

Jones's megalomania led to a catastrophe that shocked the

civilized world. A congressman and others who were visiting Guyana to investigate complaints were murdered. In the aftermath, Jones ordered his hundreds of followers to commit suicide. They did, by drinking poisoned Kool-Aid. Then he killed himself.

Although Jones strictly forbade his followers to drink alcoholic beverages, according to one ex-member, Debbie Layton, the Reverend Jones "reeked of liquor" when he ordered her to join him in bed.

If Jones was addicted to sedatives in pill form, he would be cross-addicted to alcohol. Although many alcoholics use booze as their drug of choice and turn to pill-form sedatives only if alcohol is not available, other addicts develop a reverse relationship. They use sedative pills as the drug of choice, and booze as a fall-back substitute. Oscar Levant, the late pianist-comedian, was addicted to barbiturates, but he would gulp down fifths of whiskey if he couldn't get the sedatives he preferred. Addiction to sedatives in any form would have the same ego-inflating effect as addiction to alcohol.

The psychological effects of his addictions may be the entire explanation for Jim Jones's megalomania and the catastrophe it caused.

Frances Bradshaw Schreuder, a heavy drinker, went on a spectacularly ugly power trip. She persuaded her teenage son Marc to murder her father, the boy's grandfather. Two books have been written about this case, and two television mini-series were made from the books. The books' authors (Shana Alexander and Jonathan Coleman) uncovered many facts about Frances Schreuder, including high tolerance of booze, which are consistent with a diagnosis of alcoholism.

While a student at Bryn Mawr, Frances "was given to inexplicable bouts [with] alcohol." One classmate recalled her high tolerance. "We all knew Frankie had a drinking problem," says another. As an adult, shortly before the murder, she is described as often seeming "drunk or on drugs."

She once ordered a "double-double" at a Manhattan bar, four drinks in one glass. Her constant male companion while she lived in New York and planned the murder is described as an alcoholic. (Alcoholics tend to associate with other alcoholics.) She was extremely abusive to her children, especially to Marc, whom she would lock out of her expensive, roomy New York apartment nearly every night. The boy slept in stairwells. Frances attempted suicide on at least five different occasions. After she was sentenced for arranging the murder of her father, she demanded that her mother smuggle booze into prison and became enraged when she refused.

In their books neither author labels Frances Schreuder an alcoholic (and I shall not do so) but in the television version of the Alexander book the actress portraying Frances Schreuder speculates, in the opening scene, on the possibility that she is an alcoholic.

John Wilkes Booth was an active alcoholic when he assassinated Abraham Lincoln.

The disease was in the family. His father, also an actor, was so addicted to alcohol that he arranged whenever he performed to have an assistant wait for him in the wings, a large glass of brandy in his hand. He'd gulp it down as soon as the curtain dropped. His grandfather was "so often dead drunk" that he couldn't function at his occupation, farming.

Although he was the youngest child of a famous actor and the younger brother of another, John Wilkes Booth had to overcome a certain handicap in his drive to success. He seems to have had little talent. One critic, after watching one performance wrote "Youth may be an excuse for his errors, but it is no excuse for presenting them to the metropolitan audience." Another said that he rendered "some speeches in good voice but his facial expressions remained wooden." But in spite of these unfavorable reviews, John Wilkes Booth was determined to leave the stage as the most famous Booth of all.

The same egotistical drive that forced this young man to ignore suggestions that he might lack the talent of his father and his brother showed in other ways -- he was both a dandy and a Don Juan.

He had a history of violence. In 1860, he got in a drunken brawl in Madison, Indiana, and was stabbed in the face. He once shoved a fellow actor into the orchestra pit in what was supposed to be a mock fight. He threw a book at a prompter who was too slow and smeared lampblack on a fellow actor's face because he didn't like him. On still another occasion he tried to choke his brother-in-law, who had said something he resented.

Despite his great ambitions, his taste for good clothes and complaisant women, Booth consorted often enough with his social inferiors, "stablehands, roustabouts, waterfront loafers" to warrant its mention in books about the assassination. (None of those who wrote about Booth seemed to know that the practice is a power symptom of alcoholism.)

The same desperate ego that drove Booth to hang out with laborers influenced his reaction to the Civil War. Although most Americans are taught that Booth was a Confederate fanatic, he was nothing of the sort. While hundreds of thousands died in the cause he supposedly espoused, he gave it nothing but lip service while earning twenty thousand a year (a fabulous income at the time) in an occupation that gave him plenty of time to chase whores and drink booze. To be a loyal follower of a cause requires a subordination of self, something not within the capability of the alcoholic. Instead of volunteering to serve in the Confederate Army, Booth chose to assign himself a mission of his own choosing.

As for alcoholic drinking, there's an abundance of contemporary reports.

Jack Deery, who ran a bar near one of Booth's favorite theaters, considered him a friend as well as a good customer: "While a steady drinker, I had always found [Booth] to respect the amenities and 'drink square' as we used to say... *he could absorb an astonishing quantity and still retain the bearing of a gentleman... sometimes [he] drank at my bar as much as a quart of brandy in less than two hours."* [Emphasis added.]

Booth's heavy drinking started at an early age. One contemporary noted that by age 18 he had already discovered "the world's most endangering intoxicants -- audience applause, brandy neat, and flattering women."

Booth drank just before the assassination, at a saloon next door to Ford's Theater. He drank enough to lead two actresses, whom he brushed past after shooting the President, to report that he stank of brandy.

An assassin who had organized, as did Booth, simultaneous assaults on several leaders of the Union, would not, after making detailed plans for the murders and for his own escape, go to a saloon and drink so much brandy before he personally undertook the most critical mission -- killing of the President -- that the stench of his breath would become a matter of historical fact. Not unless he was an alcoholic.

Contrary to myth, Abraham Lincoln was not killed by a psychotic, or by a fanatic. He was killed by an egomaniacal actor who was better at seducing women and consuming brandy than he was at undertaking self-sacrificing missions for the Confederacy, his so-called cause. Lincoln was killed by a man who was already so enslaved -- at the age of 26 -- to alcohol that he required an ingestion of his addictive substance before carrying out the most important act of his life. Lincoln was killed because his murder offered an enslaved man an opportunity to prove himself by destroying a man honored by millions. Lincoln was the victim of Booth's alcoholism.

Alcoholism not only drove Booth to assassinate Lincoln. It also cleared the steps leading to the Presidential box of its single guard.

Washington Police Officer John Parker, 34, was further along on his journey to alcoholic oblivion than was the younger assassin. He had been charged with infractions of police department rules no fewer than eight times: using profane language to a grocer, being vile and insolent toward a superior, insulting a woman, abusing a superior, sleeping on a streetcar, being drunk and disorderly in a brothel, sleeping (again) on a streetcar, and (again) using profane language to a woman. One writer on the assassination refers to him as a "drunken good for nothing."

Parker's need for a drink on the night of the assassination was so strong that he deserted his post outside the President's box, left the theater, and went to a bar. When Booth left *his* bar and crept up the stairs leading to the President's box, John Parker wasn't there to challenge him. (Or to stop a bullet, which might have alerted Lincoln and his companions to their great danger.) Abraham Lincoln died because one alcoholic was driven by his disease to commit a despicable murder and another was driven from his post in order to satisfy his craving.

Alcoholic murders seem to fall into two groups: impulsive, senseless killings that occur when the alcoholic is drunk (Richard Speck) and, more rarely, premeditated murder. Certainly Bundy, Gacy, and Dahmer were premeditated murderers, but they acted alone. Sometimes the alcoholic ego entraps nonalcoholic accomplices.

Booth, Dederich, and Schreuder seem to fall into that category.

The impulsive drunken murder occurs when alcohol sets off rage within the alcoholic brain. In their short but excellent book, *Violence and the Brain* (Harper & Row, 1978), Vernon H. Mark, a neurosurgeon, and Frank Ervin, a psychiatrist, have a lot to say about the great capacity of people with damaged brains to get involved in violent destructiveness and the fact that such people are not usually diagnosed. They do not say much about alcoholism, but what they do say is instructive:

> Obviously, individuals who commit violence while acutely intoxicated are behaving, by definition, with a malfunctioning brain... if [a person's] brain is diseased, or malfunctioning, *then his capacity for senseless violence exceeds that of any other animal, for his repertoire of behavior and his lethal abilities surpass those of other species.* [Emphasis added.]

Alcoholics like Speck, and the anonymous men quoted at the beginning of this chapter, probably killed as a result of the *neurological* effect that the ingestion of alcohol had on their *alcoholic* brains. As already mentioned, this probably involves the limbic, or reptilian, brain, the locus of rage-incitement. In most instances, limbic rage is expressed as invective, or by furniture-wrecking or in non-lethal acts of violence. But sometimes it kills.

Other alcoholic murderers -- John Wilkes Booth, John Gacy and (except for his last rampage) Ted Bundy -- kill because of the *psychological* effects of addiction. They kill because their alcoholism-created sick egos perceive murder as a means of shoring up their addiction-plagued self-esteem. Their obsession with power translates into a desire to destroy another human being -- the ultimate power trip.

Most alcoholics, of course, are not killers, but as they say in Alcoholics Anonymous, "Some are sicker than others."

Not all killings are crimes and not all alcoholic killers are murderers. The desperate need to shore up their self-esteem seems to lead some alcoholics to undertake acts of violence that garner the admiration of their contemporaries and decorations from their governments. These are battlefield heroes.

Others have noted the high incidence of alcoholism among former war heroes and attributed the drinking to an attempt to cope with the "stresses and strains" of being a war hero. This is nonsense. Success on the battlefield can no more create an alcoholic than can success in show business. The incidence of alcoholism is high among war heroes for the same reason it is high among movie stars: the alcoholism preceded the courageous behavior that elicited the acclaim and was in fact its root cause.

Youthful alcoholics are usually overachievers, and on the battlefield outstanding achievement requires courage. The alcoholic's need for self-image improvement is greater than most; he may be willing, therefore, to take extraordinary risks to obtain it.

According to Joe McGinniss' *Heroes* (Viking, 1976), Joe R. Hooper, the most decorated U.S. soldier of the Vietnam war, was on a three-day drinking spree while in Washington to receive the Medal of Honor and was "smashed" during the White House ceremony.

In noting the 1971 death of Audie Murphy, an alcoholic and the most decorated American soldier in World War II, *Time* quoted another Medal of Honor winner, "Pappy" Boyington: "Show me a hero and I'll show you a bum." He might have said, "Show me an alcoholic -- a potential bum -- and I'll show you a likely battlefield overachiever -- a hero."*

No consideration of the violence caused by alcoholism can be complete without considering violence against one's self.

It has been estimated by the Committee on Alcoholism of Greater New York that one third of all American suicides are alcoholics. LeClair Bissell, M.D. and Paul W. Haberman in their in-depth study of the alcoholism experience of 407 physicians, attorneys, and other professionals, found that 17 percent of the men and 30 percent of the women had attempted suicide. The AMA, in its *Manual on Alcoholism*, warns of the suicide possibility *during treatment* for alcoholism. Most works on alcoholism mention suicide attempts or suicide gestures as a symptom of the disease.

---

*As I explain in Chapter Ten, Alexander the Great, perhaps the bravest warrior in recorded history, was an alcoholic.

Before suggesting reasons for the high rate of suicide among alcoholics, I need to put to rest a concept held by some psychiatrists and others. This notion might be summarized, "Alcoholics drink because they are trying to kill themselves." (This idea, for some reason, seems especially popular among the British.) Anyone familiar with the behavior of real-life alcoholics will be unable to locate any plausibility in this romantic idea.

Most alcoholics conduct a life-long struggle *against* their addiction. They exert great effort -- and, yes, will power -- to maintain their self-esteem despite the insidiousness of the disease. They usually do not drink continuously, in a manner that could cause death, until many years of addictive drinking have passed. Some *never* reach the stage where they are drunk more than one day in succession. Many do indeed *eventually* die from the results of drinking, but are we to assume that the fatal cirrhosis that develops in the 55-year-old is what the 25-year-old had in mind when he first knocked off a bottle of booze? Or that the airline pilot who succeeds in hiding his drinking from everyone for twenty-five years -- without a single serious accident -- is trying to kill himself?

No, the behavior of any alcoholic, until he reaches the late stage, cannot be reconciled -- even in the most superficial manner -- with any "death wish" theory. Moreover, if they do reach the final awful stage, their addiction is so powerful that they might risk death if they *stop* drinking. Unlike withdrawal from heroin and other narcotics, withdrawal from severe alcohol addiction can be fatal; life-threatening convulsions are possible.

Alcoholics do nonetheless commit suicide in far greater numbers than the general population. I think they do so for three reasons.

First, most alcoholics who kill themselves do it while drinking. According to a study by Aaron T. Beck, *et al*, in the *Quarterly Journal of Studies on Alcohol* (Vol. 37, No.1, 1976), "most alcoholics are intoxicated, and most nonalcoholics are sober when they commit suicide." I have personally witnessed one half-hearted suicide attempt by a drunk alcoholic and have listened to others say they wanted to kill themselves. Like most of the behavior of alcoholics while drinking, these acts are not subject to psychological analysis since they are greatly influenced by the pharmacological effects of a psychoactive substance. Put another way, every binge is an event characterized by heightened risks. At best, and most frequently, the alcoholic and the people near him all go to bed in one piece.

Sometimes, however, someone gets hurt, and sometimes it is the alcoholic.

Another cause of suicide is the depressing effect of the substance itself. According to John Wallace, the "direct negative effects of alcohol are well known... a transient depression that yields to detoxification." It ought not to surprise anyone that among persons who regularly ingest large quantities of a *nonselective general depressant*, suicide (the ultimate expression of depression) occurs more frequently than in the general population.

The third reason why alcoholism causes suicide is withdrawal. Ernest Hemingway, who blew his brains out while a patient at the Mayo Clinc and (apparently) abstaining, may have been the classic example of withdrawal-depression leading to suicide. The poet John Berryman, who killed himself by jumping off a bridge, was for years an in-again, out-again member of Alcoholics Anonymous. He may have been in a withdrawal-induced depression when he killed himself. I have listened to recovered alcoholics tell of serious suicide attempts during withdrawal.

In addition to whatever physiological causes underlay depression during withdrawal, there is also the matter of guilt. Active alcoholics do an excellent job of repressing guilt, not only for their drinking, but for the suffering they cause others. But during the early stages of recovery, alcoholics face responsibility for those acts -- probably for the first time. Some are overwhelmed by remorse and turn to suicide to relieve the pain.

Most alcoholics need help getting through withdrawal. Those who get it in heavy doses, the ones in treatment centers or who follow AA's "ninety-ninety" recommendation (ninety meetings in the first ninety days of abstinence), have the best chance of surviving. Those who attempt withdrawal alone, or with only alcoholism-ignorant professionals to help them, may turn to suicide.

Unfortunately, explanations based on logic and knowledge of alcoholism seem less appealing to many than those based on some romantic notion. For example, the high incidence of alcoholism among successful writers ought to lead us to *expect* a high incidence of suicide among writer-alcoholics. There is such a high incidence, of course. In addition to Hemingway and Berryman, Jack London, Malcolm Lowry, and Hart Crane committed suicide. Eugene O'Neill attempted it. But rather than approaching this problem logically by studying alcoholism, some prefer other, more complicated, analyses.

In *The Savage God: A Study* (Random House, 1971), the author, A. Alvarez, writes at length about the suicide of poet Sylvia Plath -- a friend. Alvarez also looks at suicide in general, civilization's attitudes toward it, and its seeming popularity among writers and artists. He identifies Jackson Pollock as a suicide, mentions Hemingway, and says that Dylan Thomas and Brendan Behan, both well-known alcoholic writers, "drank themselves to death." He quotes several theories about suicide and offers some of his own. However, he does not cite alcoholism as a causative factor.

In the final pages of his book, Alvarez writes about his own attempted suicide. An Englishman teaching at an American college, he had returned home to join his wife and son for Christmas. She had left him weeks earlier and one purpose of the trip, so he tells us, was to try to patch up his marriage.

> We didn't stand a chance. Within hours we were at each other again, and that night I started drinking. Mostly, I'm a social drinker. Like everyone else, I've drunk in my time but it's not really my style; I value my control too highly. This time, however, I went at the bottle with a pure need, as though parched. I drank before I got out of bed, almost before my eyes were open. I continued steadily throughout the morning until, by lunchtime, I had half a bottle of whiskey inside me and was beginning to feel human. Not drunk: that first half-bottle simply brought me to that point of calm where I usually began. Around lunchtime a friend -- also depressed, also drinking -- joined me at the pub and we boozed until closing time. Back home... we kept at it steadily through the afternoon and evening, late into the night. The important thing was not to stop. In this way I got through a bottle of whiskey a day, and a good deal of wine and beer. Yet it had little effect. Toward evening... I suppose I was a little tipsy...

On Christmas morning Alvarez had a shot of whiskey before he got out of bed.

> I remember little of what happened later... in the evening we went out to a smart, subdued dinner party, and on from there, I think to something wilder. But I'm not sure...

Alvarez does remember that very late that night another couple joined them at home, and they were "all very drunk." After that, he remembers nothing at all until he awoke in a hospital -- three days later.

What had happened was that after the other couples left, Alvarez and his wife "had one final, terrible quarrel" which ended when his wife walked out. After she left, he swallowed forty-five sleeping pills.

Unlike Alvarez, when alcoholics attempt suicide they frequently succeed and when they do few attribute their deaths to the disease. Blaming alcoholism for homicide is even rarer. But in spite of this widespread blindness, alcoholism is a major *cause* of both suicide and homicide.

Fortunately, most alcoholics do not kill. Most marry, however, and nearly all abuse their spouses and their children. And as I show in the next chapter, abuse by alcoholic parents can greatly damage the children. Some of their offspring, although not themselves alcoholics, have, as a result of the parent's alcoholism, turned out to be monsters.

9: MURDEROUS SONS

Alcoholism in parents, crime in children.
Louise D. Rabinovitch, M.D.

Although alcoholism is frequently called a family disease, I find that description inadequate. For most families, it is a *catastrophe*. Wives, husbands, and children are all victimized. Subjected to drunken harangues, false accusations, acts of frightening violence, and generally tyrannical behavior, they face difficulties that are, in many ways, more painful and excruciating than those encountered by families of the certifiably insane.

Wild mood swings intensify the suffering. Alcoholics change, without warning, from nice to nasty; from tyrants to sweetly reasonable, charming people who wouldn't hurt a fly. These swings occur regardless of the actions of the family members, adding to their bafflement and delaying their comprehension. If the alcoholic behaved horribly all the time, the family might seek help sooner. Or they could develop earlier an attitude of detachment, an emotional separation that could ease the suffering caused by the outrageous behavior. But the alcoholic manipulates those who live with him, and this capacity to charm adds to the misery. Charm enhances power; it gives the alcoholic the power to hurt as only a loved one can.

Wives and husbands bear the brunt of the abuse. They are often alone with the alcoholic during night-long binges and are the principal target for vileness ranging from petty needling, to accusative harangues, to physical assault, and, possibly, attempts at homicide.

Married as they are to cunning egomaniacs, spouses who attempt to help the alcoholic, or themselves, by turning to professionals may find themselves dangerously out-maneuvered. I once met a recovered alcoholic who, before he sobered up, had his wife committed to a mental institution. Her problem? She was so "crazy" she thought he was an alcoholic! (She was discharged after six months, when the husband joined AA.)

Institutionalization of the nonalcoholic spouse is no longer as easy to accomplish as it once was, but manipulation of professionals is still a problem. According to alcoholism specialist John Wallace, Ph.D.:

Some alcoholics are so skillful... that they manage to pack *their spouses* off to psychiatrists or psychologists for treatment of *their* emotional difficulties. [Emphasis in original.]

Many spouses turn to Al-Anon for help. Veteran Al-Anon members advise newcomers to try detachment, to separate themselves emotionally from the alcoholic. But useful as it is for many, Al-Anon reaches only a small number of those living with alcoholics. Most spouses cope with their enormous problems alone; many never learn that an illness is destroying their lives.

Although spouses can be seriously hurt, they are adults. Many are able to cut their losses; they divorce the drinker. Others learn to live with the disease, doing whatever they can to limit the damage.

But children have few options. Especially when young, children cannot extricate themselves from the harmful parent; they cannot adopt a detached attitude. Because of their greater vulnerability, children are often the most grievously wounded of the alcoholic's many victims.

Ruth Fox was emphatic about the potential for harm: "[the]

enormously damaging effect of parental alcoholism on children has been established beyond doubt." The effects are long reaching:

in analyzing emotionally disturbed nonalcoholic adults, one finds that alcoholism in one of the parents has not infrequently been one of the factors of the neurosis, psychosis, or psychopathic trends for which they seek treatment.

Another alcoholism researcher, Nancy Newell, wrote in "Alcoholism and the Father Image" (*Quarterly Journal of Studies on Alcohol* xi: 92-96, 1950) of the peculiar destructiveness of alcoholic fathers:

the more subtle implications of the alcoholic father differ qualitatively from those of the father who is just rough, unkind, and indifferent. In his periods of sobriety, the alcoholic father frequently is charming, affectionate, understanding, and penitent. He inspires the natural love of his offspring who build therefrom an ideal father image of omnipotence and loving kindness. The disillusionment of a drunken episode is shattering to the frail superego structure of the child. He is forthwith subjected to alternating experiences of exalted hopes and blighted disappointments. He may be compared to the hungry experimental animal which is tempted with food and frustrated by sudden barriers. Such a process may produce convulsions or "nervous breakdown" in the animal. It is surely dangerous to the highly organized human creature who, in the formative period of childhood, is just becoming aware of social and cultural standards, as well as of the interpersonal relationships of his home. It is not surprising that a child thus exposed presents a bewildering array of ambivalence, inconsistencies, antagonisms, and touching overtures of affection.

The damaged child can become a problem to society. Sociologists Sheldon and Eleanor Glueck in *Family, Environment and Delinquency* (Houghton, Mifflin Co., 1962) commented on the relationship of anti-social behavior in children to alcoholism in the father:

Unlike the role of delinquency of the father, which has not been found to contribute to the development of any delinquency-related traits [in offspring], rearing by an alcoholic father has been shown to contribute to the development of the traits of hostility and unconventionality.

... and in the mother:

Excessive indulgence in alcohol was in general found to be more prevalent among the mothers of the delinquents than of the nondelinquents.

Scott C. Guth, M.D., a psychiatrist who directs the alcoholism services at a large mental health center, listed in *The New York Times* some of the awful things alcoholic parents have done to their children, including: "beatings of naked children with horsehair whips, drunken raging fathers holding pistols to the heads of their sons, children hurled bodily against walls... " Many of these brutalized children, in Guth's opinion, grow to be dangerous adults: "When they begin to feel strong enough to take the risk, the rage that is proportionate to their experience of abuse, exploitation, and torture will emerge almost as surely as a falling body obeys Newton's laws... "

One son of a brutal alcoholic father whose actions as an adult confirm Guth's dire prediction: Albert De Salvo, better known as The Boston Strangler. De Salvo murdered thirteen women and sexually assaulted more than a thousand. Some sense of his childhood environment can be gained from this extract of an interview with his brother, Joseph, from Elliot Leyton's *Compulsive Killers: The Story of Modern Multiple Murderers* (New York University Press, 1986):

my father would think nothing of picking up one of us and throwing us against the wall as if we was [sic] no more than a piece of wood. Let me tell you something about myself. When I was 7, maybe 8, I knocked over boxes of huckleberries on a guy's wagon. He told my father and he took me in the house. He disconnected the hose from the washing machine and beat my backside down to my ankles until I was bleeding. That was in the Spring. In the Summer I couldn't understand why he never let me go out of the house or get out of the car when we went to the beach. Know why? Because I still had blue and yellow marks on my legs and he was afraid that if someone saw them he'd go to jail. That's how hard he beat me.

Leyton adds to our understanding of the experiences of the boy who became The Boston Strangler: "[his] violent and alcoholic father subjected him and his mother to savage beatings. [Albert] once watched him break his mother's fingers one by one." The senior De Salvo was arrested five times on charges of assault and battery of his wife. He once *sold* Albert and his sister to a farmer; the children labored on the farm for several months.

Not only was The Boston Strangler himself not an alcoholic, he did not drink at all, not unlike many other children of alcoholics. According to one psychiatrist, he attacked women because he blamed his mother for not stopping the abuse and the beatings.

James Earl Ray, confessed assassin of Martin Luther King, was the son of both an alcoholic mother and an alcoholic father. The mother's alcoholism was cited by Clay Blair, Jr. in *The Strange Case of James Earl Ray (Bantam Books, 1969)*: "At home there was little inspiration for Jimmy Ray. His mother, now burdened with two more infants... had succumbed to that fatal Irish weakness, drink."

In describing the behavior of James Ray, the assassin's father, Blair makes it difficult to believe he was a nonalcoholic. He tells of James Ray's second marriage to a woman named Ruby and the difficulties he had in getting along with his grown children when they visited him and his wife. According to Blair, James Ray, like his wife, also succumbed to the "Irish weakness": "From these occasional damp family gatherings, James turned to hard drinking. He threatened Ruby. Ruby became so frightened that she hid the .22 rifle he used for hunting rabbits." Ruby was awarded a divorce because the assassin's father "used alcoholic beverages to excess."

Contrary to Blair's belief that the father's alcoholism suddenly appeared late in life, I think it likely that it began much earlier, and that both parents of Martin Luther King's killer were alcoholics when he was a child. If the parents behaved typically, the man who shot Martin Luther King was abused by both.

Perry Smith murdered four members of the Clutter family, a crime that was the subject of Truman Capote's *In Cold Blood* (Random House, 1968). Smith grew up as the son of an alcoholic mother. Of the four Smith children, only one, the younger of Perry's two sisters, led a normal life. The other son and the other daughter committed suicide. Perry Smith was hanged for murdering the Clutters.

The existence of a possible drinking problem in the mother of the notorious Charles Manson whose band of "hippies" slaughtered Sharon Tate and four others, was, to my knowledge, mentioned only once -- in *The New York Times* of December 7, 1969. That was shortly after Manson was indicted for the brutal murders. The *Times'* reference in total: "His mother was frequently drunk, he said, and lived with a succession of men." Any further mention of Manson's mother that I came across said she was a prostitute and a teenage mother; the drinking disappeared. Now there is nothing *inherent* in either prostitution or adolescent-motherhood that would interfere with a mother's ability to provide the care, affection and support that all children need. But all alcoholic mothers are flawed mothers, and some (Joan Crawford) are monsters. Manson's mother may have behaved towards the young Charles in the manner vividly described by Fox and Guth. Her alcoholic behavior could have created the monster who ordered the destruction of humans as thoughtlessly as other people change their socks.

John MacDonald, M.D. points out in *The Murderer and His Victim*, "Parental brutality not only generates aggression in the child but also provides a model for future behavior." All of those killed by the small number of killers investigated in this chapter, the victims of The Boston Strangler, the Clutter family, Martin Luther King, Sharon Tate, and Manson's other victims, may have been victims of obscure and forgotten parents whose brutal mistreatment created murderous sons.

Before concluding this chapter with one more case, I need to make it clear that children of alcoholics are not doomed to become psychopaths, sociopaths, or even unhappy misfits. Not all alcoholics are equally abusive. Frequently, the sober spouse is able to offset the effect of the drinker's bad behavior; and some kids, for whatever reason, are simply indestructible. Among the famous, Eleanor Roosevelt, Jacqueline Kennedy Onassis and Ronald Reagan each had an alcoholic father. Carol Burnett and Marlon Brando each had *two* alcoholic parents.

But this book is *about* the damage caused by alcoholism, so I will turn now to the most damaging of all alcoholic parents.

An obscure and forgotten man who lived and died in a European rural backwater may, because he was a brutal alcoholic, have had an enormous impact on human history. Alois Hitler, father of Adolf Hitler, was an alcoholic.

Walter C. Langer, a Freudian psychiatrist, gathered a great deal of evidence indicating a diagnosis of alcoholism in Alois. He wrote his psychiatric portrait of Adolf Hitler during World War II, at the request of William Donovan, founder of the OSS. The analysis was published in book form as *The Mind of Adolf Hitler* (Basic Books Inc., 1972).

Langer advised Donovan that Alois Hitler was a drunkard who had severely mistreated his family. He based his conclusions on information obtained from people who had known Hitler personally and who lived outside Germany during the war, and were thus accessible to Langer.

Langer intensively studied Adolf Hitler's own book, *Mein Kampf*, in which Adolf had written the following description of a "typical" young boy's life in Germany:

Among the five children there is a boy, let us say, of three... When the parents fight almost daily, their brutality leaves nothing to the imagination: then the results of such visual education must slowly but inevitably become apparent to the little one. Those who are not familiar with such conditions can hardly imagine the results, especially when the mutual differences express themselves in the form of *brutal attacks* on the part of the father toward the mother or to *assaults due to drunkenness*. The poor little boy, at the age of six, senses things which would make even a grown-up person shudder... [Emphasis added.]

Hitler, Langer points out, came from a family of five children and "his father liked to spend his spare time in the village tavern where *he sometimes drank so heavily that he had to be brought home by his wife and children.*" [Emphasis added.] In short order, Langer makes a persuasive case for concluding that "Hitler is, in all probability, describing conditions in his own home as a child."

Here's another section of *Mein Kampf* quoted by Langer:

> things end badly when the man from the very start goes his own way and the wife, for the sake of the children, stands up against him. Quarreling and nagging set in, and in the same measure in which the husband becomes estranged from his wife, he becomes familiar with alcohol ... *When he finally comes home... drunk and brutal... then God have mercy on the scenes which follow. I witnessed all of this personally in hundreds of scenes.* [Emphasis added.]

As a boy, Adolf Hitler, according to Langer, had few friends and probably not a single intimate friend. He asks, tellingly, where, if not in his own childhood, Adolf could have witnessed "hundreds" of scenes of drunken brutality? I find Langer's reasoning compelling.

From other corroborating sources, including a nephew of Adolf Hitler who lived in England during the war, Langer was told that Alois Hitler was:

> particularly after he has been drinking,... brutal, unjust, and inconsiderate. He had no respect for anybody and anything... At such times he... played the part of the bully and *whipped his wife and children* who were unable to defend themselves. [Emphasis added.]

In an afterword to Langer's book, Psychiatrist Robert G.L. Waite provides further corroboration, information that was not available during the war:

> New evidence and interviews with neighbors still alive in the 1950's, who knew the Hitler family well in Passau and Leonding, substantiate Langer's professional hunches. Even an old crony and mayor of the village of Leonding admitted that Alois Hitler was "awfully rough" with his wife and "hardly ever spoke a word

to her at home." He concluded with deliberate understatement that "Frau Klara had nothing to smile about."

According to Langer, the father physically abused his children, including little Adolf who was once beaten so severely that he was thought dead.

From other sources, Langer points out that Alois Hitler, when sober, behaved, as do so many alcoholics, with grandiose gestures. He took great care about his appearance. (It is obvious from the context that Langer didn't understand that these are symptoms of alcoholism):

[When sober] he stood very much on his dignity and prided himself on his position in the civil service. Even after he had retired from this service he always insisted on wearing his uniform when he appeared in public. He was scrupulous about his appearance and strode down the village in his most dignified manner. When he spoke to neighbors or acquaintances he did so in a very condescending manner and always demanded that they use his full title when they addressed him. If one of them happened to omit a part of it he would call attention to it.

Langer writes perceptively of the possible effect on the boy who would become the Fuhrer:

His feelings of insecurity would be enhanced inasmuch as he could never predict beforehand how his father would behave or what he could expect from him. The person who should give him love, support, and a feeling of security fills him with anxiety, uneasiness, and uncertainty.

If he had stopped there, Langer's analysis of Adolf Hitler would have been complete. He had produced a convincing portrait of Alois Hitler as a typically unpredictable and abusive alcoholic parent. He had done so unwittingly, however, since he doesn't even consider parental alcoholism as a causative factor. He concludes his book with a weak Freudian-based explanation of Adolf's psyche.

Langer's inadvertent case for Alois's alcoholism is complemented by facts gathered later by Waite, who in his own book, *The Psychopathic God: Adolf Hitler* (Basic Books Inc., 1977), provides additional relevant information.

He tells us that Alois died in a cafe, "while sipping his [daily] *morning* quarter liter of wine." [Emphasis added.]

Waite says that Alois was a womanizer, a heavy smoker, and an arbitrary and ferocious man; all are consistent with alcoholism. He quotes a relative "[He] often beat the dog until... it wet on the floor. He often beat the children, and on occasion... would beat his wife Klara."

Another fact that points to alcoholism in the father was Adolf Hitler's own scant use of alcohol as an adult. He described himself as "almost a complete teetotaler." Why? After all, this is a man who survived four years of combat as a low-ranking soldier in the horrific First World War. He came from a society in which drinking -- and, for young males, frequent drinking to excess -- was not only acceptable, but strongly encouraged. He certainly did not come from a "dry" family. In my opinion, like The Boston Strangler and many other children of alcoholics, Adolf Hitler avoided booze as a reaction to his father's alcoholism.

One of the more intriguing clues to Alois Hitler's alcoholism is his record, described by Waite, of changing his family residence:

> During his twenty-one years of [employment] in Braunau, where Adolf was born, the household was changed at least twelve times; during two years at Passau, the family moved twice; while posted at Linz, Alois moved many times. He had bought attractive property in the neighboring village of Fischlham. This purchase of some nine acres of land allowed Alois to indulge in his favorite pastime of beekeeping; chickens and a cow helped provide for family needs; there were also fruit trees and a lovely view. But after only two years of occupancy Alois sold the place and moved his family to the village of Lambach, where they lived first in the Leingarten Inn, and then in an old mill -- two changes in one year. No financial crisis seems responsible for all these moves. Alois's income was steady, secure and on the rise, and these were peaceful, economically stable times in rural Austria.

Although it's not as extravagant as Beethoven's lifetime record, Alois Hitler's "inexplicable" changes of residence are another vivid example of an alcoholic taking the "geographic cure."

All the information gathered by Langer and Waite convince me:

Alois Hitler, father of one of history's most monstrous individuals, was a brutal alcoholic.

What if Alois Hitler had not been an alcoholic? Would he have been the same brutal father? What if Alois had died when Adolf was an infant, and his mother had remarried a nonalcoholic? What if Adolf Hitler had been spared exposure to parental alcoholism as a child, had not been beaten, or watched his father beat his mother? Would he have become the monster he was? In other words, if it were not for this single case of alcoholism would humanity have been spared World War II, the Holocaust, and the other evils committed by the brutalized child who became Adolf Hitler? These questions are, of course, unanswerable. But some questions, even though unanswerable, are too important not to be asked.

10: ALCOHOLISM REIGNS

The value of a principle is the number of things it will explain.
Ralph Waldo Emerson

There is no date to alcoholism; it was of the past, it is of the present; it will be of the future.
Beverley Nichols

Even if they had no special need for power, a number of alcoholics would inevitably rise to important positions in any society. After all, most are capable of productive work for many years, and they are all surrounded by people who are unaware of its early and mid-stage symptoms. Assuming an equal distribution of innate ability between alcoholics and nonalcoholics, sheer probability would ensure that *some* of the former would end up in seats of power. But if my assertion that alcoholics have an extraordinary need for power is correct, then an exceptional number of them *must* have pushed, elbowed, connived or otherwise managed to climb onto the thrones of the truly powerful.

Because the psycho-pathological pressures that compel alcoholism's victims to seek power do not subside once they acquire it, when they get power they abuse it. After all, authority exercised with a sense of fairness and responsibility would do absolutely nothing for their desperate egos.

Alcoholism is well represented in the executive suites of corporate America. I have personally observed, from within more than one large multinational corporation, powerful executive-alcoholics ruin the careers of many competent subordinates. I have also watched, from a distance, alcoholic CEOs drive large organizations (including a Wall Street brokerage house and a large regional bank) to extinction by their egomaniacal behavior.

One well-known executive who left behind a well-documented record of tyrannical leadership was Henry Ford II, the late Chairman of the Board of Ford Motor Company, an industrial giant founded by his grandfather. Ford reigned for decades as, to quote William J. Hampton in *Business Week* (November 5, 1984), an "alcoholic despot."

Lee Iacocca doesn't call Ford an alcoholic in *Iacocca: An Autobiography* (Bantam Books, 1984). But he gives us more than enough evidence.

When Iacocca reached a level in Ford's hierarchy where he would have frequent contact with the Chairman, Robert MacNamara, then president of the car company, and other executives warned him of Ford's nasty behavior. "Stay away from him," said one, "He'll get drunk, and you'll find yourself in trouble over nothing." Another predicted, "You'll get fired some night when Henry's drunk. He'll call you a wop... it will be over nothing."

According to Victor Lasky's *Never Complain, Never Explain: The Story of Henry Ford II* (Richard Marek, Publishers, 1981), Ford showed the usual high tolerance: "He could drink everything... wine, cognac, Scotch. The amazing thing... was that by nine the next morning he would invariably be in good shape."

He also had the typical alcoholic's superficiality. At one meeting, Iacocca was so touched by Henry's eloquent expression of concern about the plight of Black Americans that he was moved to tears. An hour later, Ford raved to Iacocca: "Those goddamn coons... I hate them. I'm scared of them and I think I'll move to Switzerland, where there just aren't any."

Although a wealthy man, Henry Ford "never spent a dime of his own money" according to Iacocca. He even charged the company for his personal use of his own apartment in London. Eventually, this blatant disregard of normal business rules caused a group of Ford shareholders to sue -- forcing the company's own auditors to investigate. Henry had to write a check for $34,000 to cover funds he had wrongfully pocketed.

According to Iacocca, whenever Ford joined a meeting in progess all the executives would tense; they knew he could fire anyone of them, for no good reason. Many competent executives saw their careers end that precipitously.

He showed the typical penchant for false accusation. He once told Iacocca to fire a certain executive who was, so said Henry Ford, "a fag." Iacocca disagreed, telling his boss that the man was married and a close friend of Iacocca and his wife. Ford insisted: he's a homosexual. Why, asked Iacocca. Because he wears tight pants said the powerful industrialist.

Iacocca protected The Man With Tight Pants; he moved him to an out-of-the-way job, where the chairman wouldn't have to look at his nates. Other executives were not so lucky. He fired a string of Presidents, including, eventually, Iacocca himself. Ernest Breech, the brilliant financial executive who helped the young and inexperienced Henry Ford to introduce modern management controls, was squeezed out. President Arjay Miller, like MacNamara (who left Ford to join the Kennedy Administration) was one of the famous Whiz Kids who helped save the company. Miller was pushed aside without any explanation. His replacement, Bunky Knudsen, lasted nineteen months. According to Iacocca, Ford fired Knudsen, not because his work was inadequate, but because he *dared* to enter the egomaniac's office without knocking!

Henry Ford's campaign against Iacocca was vicious and expensive (to the company, not to him). It included a secret audit of Iacocca's travel and expense accounts and attempts to link him with the Mafia. The three-year investigation, which found nothing, cost the shareholders $2 million. Ford fired, for no legitimate reason, close associates of Iacocca, including several competent executives who later held important positions at Chrysler. (The alcoholic ego is concerned only about itself, not about the welfare of the corporation or its shareholders.)

Ford eventually did fire Iacocca, one of the most successful executives in the history of the automobile industry. When Iacocca demanded an explanation, all Henry Ford could say was, "Well, sometimes you just don't like somebody." Lee Iacocca went on to head Chrysler, and to compete fiercely with Ford.

Henry Ford and other alcoholic heads of corporations inflicted great harm on people unfortunate enough to work for them. But history's most dangerous alcoholics were not industrialists. The catastrophically dangerous ones ruled nations.

The United States has been lucky, so far. Many alcoholics have sought the Presidency, and, by my count, three of them have made it. But our political system limits the damage that an alcoholic President can do. The Republic seems to have survived the three who held that office.

Our three alcoholic presidents: Grant, Pierce, and Andrew Johnson.

In 1854, U.S. Grant was 32 years old and an Army captain. In the words of a biographer, he "took to drink" in that year while stationed in California and resigned his commission. (It is likelier that Grant started to drink while still in his teens.) As a civilian, Grant tried farming but abandoned it because of illness. He failed at various other jobs, including selling real estate. At the age of 38 he took a clerk's job at his father's leather goods store, working under his younger brother who managed the store. There, in the town of Galena, Illinois, Grant drank heavily and was despised by his father and his brothers for it. Everyone thought him a failure.

At the outbreak of the Civil War, he rejoined the Army. He initially led a regiment and, after establishing a record of impressive victories, rose to command the Union Army and to defeat Robert E. Lee. He obviously could not have been drinking as heavily while waging war as he had in Galena. His victories undoubtedly were balm to his ego, probably helping him to limit his alcohol intake. But the record shows that he had some problems with alcohol during the war.

In 1862, a loyal and concerned aide wrote Grant a personal letter, imploring him to stop drinking and to "renew his pledge" of total abstinence. Although some may find it strange that a close associate would resort to written communication, alcoholics are notorious for ignoring oral pleas from those who are sincerely concerned about their drinking; many a modern spouse has resorted to letter-writing to communicate with the drinker.

Grant was a superb horseman. According to some biographers, contemporaries considered him the finest that ever attended West Point. At a time when virtually all young men rode, this was no minor accolade. But in 1863, while participating in a tame military parade, General Grant was so drunk he fell off his horse.

In spite of his record of excessive drinking before and, to a lesser extent, during the war, something extraordinary -- and very fortunate -- happened to Grant. Shortly after the war ended, he stopped drinking and, apparently, abstained from alcohol for the rest of his life. No one, for instance, ever saw him imbibe while he was President.

Because Grant didn't sink into chronic inebriation in middle age, and indeed seems to have achieved true sobriety, most of his biographers (none that I read exhibit any knowledge of the disease) reject the suggestion that he was an alcoholic. Recoveries from alcoholism in the pre-AA nineteenth century *were* rare, but they were not unknown. Actually, Grant's total abstinence after the war is itself consistent with a diagnosis of alcoholism. If he had been a nonalcoholic heavy drinker, he could have cut down on his consumption -- not eliminated it.

Rare as it was, Grant was not the only famous nineteenth century American who managed self-recovery from alcoholism. Sam Houston did it too.

Houston had been Chief Magistrate of Tennessee when his political and personal life fell apart because of an alcoholic incident. Returning home from a rather damp political gathering, Houston started an argument with his wife and falsely accused her of adultery. Although alcoholics' false accusations of infidelity are now known to be common, such charges were not taken lightly in the upper strata of Nashville's 1829 society. Incensed, his wife left him and, in effect, ended the marriage. Because she was a highly respected member of an influential Tennessee family, her termination of the marriage was a political and social disaster for Houston who came from a more modest background. He resigned as Magistrate, left Nashville, and went to live among the Osage Indians. With the Indians for the next two years, he drank so much they gave him a name in their language meaning "Big Drunk."

In 1831, a delegation of Texans sought out Houston and begged him to take command of the Republic of Texas Army. Although soddenly drunk at the time, Houston accepted. Incredibly, he stopped drinking, led the Texans to victory over the Mexicans, and served as first Governor of the state. Like Grant, he apparently never drank again.

Now for our other two president-alcoholics.

Vice President-elect Andrew Johnson drank heavily at a stag party the night before the inauguration. Before entering the Senate Chamber to take the oath and to deliver his acceptance speech, he spent some time in the anteroom with Hannibal Hamlin, who had served as Vice President during Lincoln's first term. A Boston newspaper, *Commonwealth*, reported what happened (from Milton Lomask's *Andrew Johnson, President on Trial* [Farrar, Straus & Giroux, 1960]):

> There was nothing unusual in his [Johnson's] appearance except that he did not seem in robust health... Conversation proceeded on ordinary topics for a few minutes, when Mr. Johnson asked Mr. Hamlin if he had any liquor in the room, stating that he was sick and nervous... Brandy being indicated, a bottle was bought by one of the pages. It was opened, a tumbler provided, and Mr. Johnson poured it about two-thirds full... When [it was near] twelve... Mr. Hamlin rose, moved to the door near which the Sergeant-at-Arms stood and suggested to Mr. Johnson to come also. The latter got up... said, "Excuse me a moment," and walked hastily back to where the bottle was deposited. Mr. Hamlin saw him... pour as large a quantity as before into the glass and drink it down like water.

The two whoppers under his belt, Johnson lurched into the Senate Chamber. His speech was a disaster. Scheduled to talk for seven minutes, but thoroughly intoxicated by those two huge brandies (and by whatever alcohol remained in his blood from the night before), the new Vice President ignored his prepared script and made a rambling, incoherent speech that lasted more than a half-hour. President Lincoln was mortified.*

Not surprisingly, those who write about Andrew Johnson (including Lomask) avoid suggesting that he had an alcohol problem. The speech disaster was the result, so some claim, of an uncommon reaction to alcohol brought on by malaria. This is nonsense. As any drinking nonalcoholic knows, alcohol has no charm when we are ill.

Indeed, in this single episode, Johnson managed to display *five* symptoms of alcoholism. The quantity consumed was enormous, he gulped it down, drank in the morning, drank after a heavy night of drinking, and he drank at a most inappropriate time, immediately before one of the most important public events of his life.

There were other signs. Johnson had a fist fight while a Senator; his opponents accused him of going on a bender while conducting a presidential swing by train through the Midwest (the not-yet-abstemious Grant joined the President's entourage at one point). One of his political rivals, George Templeton Strong, fully expected him to be impeached for intoxication.

Unlike later biographers, an earlier writer on Johnson seems to have suspected alcoholism. Clifton R. Hall, in *Andrew Johnson, Military Governor of Tennessee* (Princeton University Press, 1916), reports tell-tale signs many years before Johnson came to Washington:

> The habit of indulging in intoxicants, afterwards reputed as Johnson's most conspicuous failing as president, had, of course, been formed long before... it occasionally betrayed him into extravagances of action and expression which did him no credit. Charles A. Dana... reports that the governor opened their first interview by producing a whiskey-bottle and, in his opinion, was *addicted* to taking "more than most gentlemen would have... " [Emphasis added.]

Hall quotes Carl Schurz, another eyewitness of pre-Presidential signs of alcoholism in Johnson:

---

*Perhaps Johnson's drunken performance led to a change in inaugural tradition; Vice Presidents no longer speak at inaugural ceremonies.

I could not rid myself of the impression that beneath his staid and sober exterior there were still some wild fires burning... which might burst to the surface. This impression was strengthened by a singular experience. It happened twice or three times that, when I called upon him, I was told by the attendant that the governor was sick and could not see anybody; then after *a lapse of four or five days*, he would send for me, and I would find him uncommonly natty in his attire and generally *groomed with special care*. He would also wave off any inquiry about his health. When I mentioned the circumstances to one of the most prominent Union men of Nashville, he smiled, and said that the governor had "his infirmities" but was "all right" on the whole. [Emphasis added.]

Schurz, obviously, is implying that Johnson took days off to indulge in benders. The natty appearance also points to alcoholism. Hall quotes another witness, John N. Palmer, on aspects of Johnson's personality consistent with alcoholism:

He was sincere and earnest in his opinions, but his prejudices were violent and often unjust. His personal dislikes were never concealed. Baille Peyton said of him "he hated... a gentleman by instinct." And as for slaves, "Damn the negroes; I am fighting these traitorous aristocrats, their masters."

Andrew Johnson stands as a quasi-hero to many modern Americans, probably because he was impeached but acquitted by a single vote. His modern biographers' rejection of the idea he was an alcoholic says more about their own ignorance and prejudices than it does about Johnson, but his drunken inaugural speech and his earlier behavior while Military Governor of Tennessee convince me that he was an alcoholic.

All three of our alcoholic Presidents held office in the nineteenth century and did not have much opportunity to abuse others while in office. Grant was not personally destructive while President; the scandals that engulfed his Presidency are usually blamed on his corrupt cronies. Moreover, by that time he was apparently a recovered alcoholic, and recovered alcoholics are not usually destructive. But Andrew Johnson didn't abstain from booze while in office, and it's probable that his alcoholism-driven ego played a more important role in his clash with Congress, which lead to the attempted impeachment, than alcoholism-ignorant modern historians realize.

Our third alcoholic President, Franklin Pierce, is relatively obscure, and there is no readily available evidence that he abused the Presidency. His alcoholism continued after he left office, however, and he made a typically alcoholic accusatory speech on July 4, 1863. His target? President Lincoln. His diatribe -- in the midst of the Civil War -- was so venomous that many of his fellow New England townspeople stopped speaking to him.*

That our two drinking alcoholic Presidents (Andrew Johnson and Franklin Pierce) were not very destructive probably says more about the strength of our political system than it does about their potential for abuse. Other nations have not been so fortunate. In other lands, the assumption of power by alcoholics has had catastrophic results.

During the brief 1971 Indo-Pakistan War, Indian radio stations played continuously a parody of a patriotic Pakistani song. The Pakistani song, "War Is Not a Game that Women Can Play," was a dig at Indian Prime Minister Indira Gandhi. The Indian parody, "War Is Not a Game that *Drunkards* Can Play," was aimed squarely at the president of Pakistan, the late Yahya Kahn.

During the war, a Pakistani Army officer was quoted as saying that Khan was "both a drinker and a womanizer." Near the end of his rule, when newly elected Ali Bhutto arrived at the President's House to assume power, Yahya Kahn was on a bender. According to one Pakistani official, he was "far too drunk to say anything about anything to Bhutto."

I twice visited Pakistan during Yahya Kahn's reign and while there I heard many reports of his drinking. I was even introduced to a middle-aged woman, known (so my host whispered in my ear) as "Karachi's Gin Queen," and a drinking companion of the President. President Kahn frequently visited this (obviously) alcoholic woman's apartment. Based on published reports and the Karachi

---

*Abraham Lincoln was particularly unfortunate in his encounters with alcoholics: Pierce maligned him, Parker failed to protect him, Booth shot him, and Johnson succeeded him. (But Grant won the war for him!)

gossip I heard, I concluded that Yahya Kahn was an alcoholic.

I've gone to some length to establish Kahn's alcoholism because it was during his reign that the Pakistani Army committed one of modern history's most infamous atrocities, the Rape of Bangladesh.

It is important to understand that the common soldiers of the Pakistani Army in Bangladesh did not mutiny against their leaders; there was no massive breakdown in discipline to account for the rapes and killings of civilians. On the contrary, there seem to have been few atrocities until after Kahn made a particularly ominous speech. In that speech he said (in paraphrase),* "Our Army has responded with great restraint and self control in spite of severe provocation by our enemies. Now the time has come for them to protect themselves. *I have ordered them to crush the anti-government forces with all necessary means."*

What followed was a massacre. Tens of thousands of civilians were slaughtered and 200,000 to 400,000 Bengali women were raped by Pakistani troops.

We will probably never learn what specific orders this alcoholic President gave to his army. We do know, however, that alcoholics are particularly dangerous when their self-esteem is at stake, and I think it likely that the man whose heavy drinking was the scandal of Karachi gave his personal order for the Bangladesh massacre.

I have identified a number of historically important alcoholic rulers by looking first for records of mass destruction and then for other indications that they were alcoholics. One of recorded history's first alcoholics was Alexander the Great.

Peter Green, a biographer of Alexander, has already identified him as an alcoholic. In defending his book against a reviewer who objected to his deflationary view of Alexander, Green responded in *The New York Times Book Review* (November 29, 1970) in part as follows:

> Alexander... raped the entire Near and Middle East from the Aegean to Pakistan. He became [wealthy] on the proceeds. He murdered a number of his faithful lieutenants, probably connived

---

*I listened to his speech (broadcast in English) in my Karachi hotel room.

at his own father's assassination -- and at the time of his death was planning to carry his trail of conquest into Arabia and the Western Mediterranean.

[I believe] that Alexander [changed] between youth and the *premature* middle age that was descending on him when he died [at age 33]. He turned from an ascetic to an *alcoholic*, from an ambitious local prince to a world-embracing *megalomaniac*, from a man of destiny to a self-proclaimed god. [Emphasis added.]

Arthur Wiegall wrote in his classic *Alexander the Great* (G.P. Putnam's Sons, 1933) that Alexander had high tolerance for alcohol and would frequently fly into rages while drinking. Wiegall asserts that Philip of Macedonia, Alexander's father, was an alcoholic, as have other biographers.

Wiegall describes a monumental drinking episode. It was in honor of an Indian wise man, a member of Alexander's entourage, who had committed ceremonial suicide. He goes on to make a telling association of Alexander's drinking with acts of rage:

Kalanes had begged his friends to make merry that evening at a banquet in honor of his death, and Alexander therefore presided at this function, and both he and his officers were soon intoxicated. In this condition the king proposed a drinking contest, and offered prizes for those who could drink the most, the first prize being won by a certain Promanchos who drank, so it is said, twelve quarts of wine, but died four days later. There is a story that forty-one of the other competitors also died; but the probability, I suppose, is that this number represents the cases of illness rather than actual deaths. Be this as it may, the story reveals Alexander and his Companions as typical Macedonians in their style of drinking: ... swallowing their wine rapidly and in great quantities... as though the sole purpose was to become intoxicated.

Plutarch, it is true, tells us that Alexander, on the whole, drank a good deal less than he was generally reported to have done... yet the stories of his prodigious drinking-bouts recorded by Plutarch himself and others are too circumstantial and too many to be ignored. More than once we read of him... drinking such

quantities that he fell into a death-like stupor; and in a play by
Meander, written not many years after Alexander's death,
reference is made to a man who on a certain occasion performed
"the wonderful feat" of drinking "more than Alexander"... those
who drank with Alexander were determined to need the help of
the god of medicine... from time to time he drank -- as did Philip
and his ancestors before him -- rapidly and deeply, until he was
completely stupefied and paralyzed.

These bouts... were now more frequent, and it was perhaps on
this account that he was at this time more short-tempered and
more severe than ever before. On his return into Persia and
Susiana, he had found that various officials had abused their
power, some thinking that he would never return alive from India;
and he therefore ordered all manner of persons, Greek and
Persian, including several great viceroys, to be put to death. He
lost his temper with one young Persian nobleman named Oxathres
or Oxyartes... and seizing a pike from a soldier, ran him through
with his own hand; and he ordered Abulites to be thrown to his
horses, to be kicked and bitten to death by them. In behaving in
this savage manner, however, he did not reveal an aspect of
himself new to his subjects, and there is nothing to support the
usual view that he was now insane or bordering on insanity; the
Alexander who killed Oxyartes is obviously the same who killed
Klietes; the Alexander who threw Abulites to the horses is the
same who dragged the dying Governor of Gaza tied by the heels
to his chariot, or who ordered Bessos to be torn asunder. There
had always been this strain of cruelty and savagery in his nature.

Alexander murdered others who were close to him, including
Parmenion, who had served Philip as second in command, and,
later, in that same capacity for him. Parmenion had strongly supported Alexander's bid for the Macedonian crown following the
murder of Philip but Alexander had him killed anyway. It was a
crime, according to W.W. Tarn, that left "a deep stain on Alexander's reputation." Alexander ordered several generals, including
Cleander and Sitalces, to do the actual killing. Later, he had *them*
executed.

I think Peter Green is right. Although he lived nearly three thousand years ago, enough evidence has survived to conclude that

Alexander the Great was an alcoholic. Moreover, alcoholism explains why this prototypical young overachiever conquered much of the known world. The same alcoholism-created egotism that led him to murder trusting subordinates, and perhaps his father, also drove Alexander to conquer the world. This disease makes its victims think they are gods.

Henry the Eighth, King of England, founder of the Church of England, executioner of four wives, and, like Alexander, murderer of many trusting courtiers, was an alcoholic.

The story of Henry's divorce from Catherine of Aragon and his break with the Church of Rome is too involved to recount here.* Besides, some of the details of putative alcoholic rulers' lives are more interesting, for my purposes, than are those that fascinate traditional historians. There is, for example, Henry's reaction to the news that Catherine, his wife for twenty-seven years, had died. J.J. Scarisbrick, in *Henry VIII* (University of California Press, 1969), tells us that he dressed himself "from head to toe in exultant yellow [and] celebrated the event with Mass, a banquet, dancing, and jousting."

Although Catherine, his first wife, died of natural causes, Henry had her replacement, Anne Boleyn, beheaded. Before ordering her execution, he vilified Anne, claiming she not only had sex with several courtiers, but with her own brother. Henry later talked of her having committed adultery with a hundred men. He exulted in her fall, which was a product of that classic alcoholic tactic, the false accusation. According to historian A.L. Rouse, Henry simply framed Anne.

Henry betrothed Jane Seymour the day after Anne Boleyn's execution. She died in childbirth, and Henry VIII, typically, exhibited no grief.

Anne of Cleaves, his fourth wife, survived. Henry found her unattractive; the marriage was unconsummated. The fifth wife, Catherine Howard, was beheaded as an adulteress. Henry did the

---

*It is worth noting, however, that since many alcoholics tend to reject the religion in which they were raised, the Church of England may hold the unique distinction of having been founded by a disease.

expected: he hosted a large banquet within a week of her execution.
Catherine Parr, his last (and luckiest) wife, outlived him, but not
before she had a close call. She was the intended victim of a
maneuver by certain cunning and ambitious men of the type usually
found near megalomaniacal rulers. She had made the mistake of
arguing religion with Henry. Two of his ministers drafted a warrant for her arrest, and certain beheading, which the King signed.
Fortunately for Catherine, Henry either forgave her, forgot about
his participation in the plot, or (it's possible) simply had an
alcoholic blackout. In any event, he cancelled the warrant.

Henry displayed the dangerous wackiness that persons who've
been closely involved with an alcoholic will recognize. In July of
1545, he ordered a woman burned at the stake for denouncing the
Mass as a valid religious service. A month later, he asked the King
of France to help him with abolishment of the Mass! He had
burned to death three loyal *Protestant* preachers (Barnes, Jerome,
and Garret); they were burned as heretics, which they certainly
were not.

It was nearly as risky to serve in Henry's court as it was to marry
him. Three Thomases -- Wolsey, More, and Cromwell -- did much
to transform England into a powerful state. All were condemned
to death. (Wolsey died before the scheduled execution.) The loyal
Duke of Norfolk escaped execution only because Henry died first.

In 1541, Henry suddenly ordered the execution of the Countess
of Salisbury. The old woman was completely bewildered by the
death sentence, for she hadn't been accused of anything. Nonetheless, she was condemned, and suffered a horrific death. The
executioner, new to the job, failed to sever her neck with the first
blow. He then panicked and rained down blows on the poor
woman's head, neck, and back until, finally and horribly, she died.
Biographer Jasper Ridley sees this murder as one of Henry's worst.
Henry "had slain a most innocent woman, related to him in blood,
aged, and feeble, famous for her virtue -- a woman whom he had
once venerated as a mother." Just the sort an alcoholic despot
would enjoy killing.

According to Scarisbrick, Henry was capable of facile charm, "but,
easily and unpredictably, his great charm could turn into anger and
shouting." He was "highly-strung and unstable, hypochondriac."
Hypochondria is prevalent in alcoholics.

Another historian, Bruce, wrote, "At 44, he was greatly altered from the man [of a few years earlier]... not only in outward appearance -- his increased girth, the shrinking of his eyes to points of cunning in the fullness of his face... but also in character... he had emerged a megalomaniac." The personality change and the small eyes are both compatible with a diagnosis of alcoholism. Holbein's famous portrait of Henry clearly shows puffiness under the eyes.

Biographers mention another important physical sign consistent with alcoholism: premature aging.

In his *Henry VIII, A Difficult Patient* (Christopher Johnson, 1952), Arthur MacNalty wrote, "disease warped Henry's mind, made him uncontrollable in his rages, irritable, cruel, and treacherous, but to the last day of his life it never prevented him from riding [sic] England." MacNalty doesn't identify the disease, but alcoholism is compatible with all these behavior patterns, including, as with many present-day alcoholics, the ability to function to the very end. Mac-Nalty, no doubt inadvertently (he doesn't consider the alcoholism possibility), fingers another alcoholic personality trait: he entitled one chapter of his book, "King Jekyll and King Hyde."

MacNalty also reports that Henry "drank too much, although he was never reported 'being in his cups' or intoxicated." Clearly, this implies high tolerance. He drank wine and ale, and is said to have liked gin "marvelously well." That Henry may have liked gin is not important -- lots of nonalcoholics like it too; what is important is that people noticed both his fondness for alcohol and his apparent tolerance for it.

Jasper Ridley, after writing that Henry drank "enormous quantities," goes on to say "intemperate eating and drinking made him irascible and unpredictable." Belligerence while drinking is a sure sign of alcoholism.

Ridley called Henry a "Tudor Stalin," a most apt comparison. But he could just have well compared him to a contemporary. He shared a number of traits with Ivan the Terrible, the first Czar of Russia.

A monster by the standards of any age, Ivan inflicted unspeakable horrors upon his subjects. To give an idea of his awfulness, I will briefly describe some of his atrocities.

At one point during his reign, Ivan came to suspect that the citizens of Novgorod were no longer loyal to him. He moved on the city with an armed force, surrounded it with troops, and then entered it with an overpowering force of thousands. The Czar and his army met no resistance from the terrified civilian population. Jules Koslow describes what happened in *Ivan the Terrible* (Hill & Wang, 1961):

The next day the punishment of Novgorod began in earnest. A thousand or more inhabitants each day were executed, many of them in full view of Ivan and his son, who sat on a platform especially constructed for the occasion. Before them various diabolical instruments of torture and death, many of them ingenious inventions. The barbarity was almost unbelievable. Wives were forced to witness the quartering of their husbands; husbands were forced to see their wives roasted alive; babes in arms were put on execution blocks together with their mothers.

However, the formal executions proved too slow, and soon they were supplemented by mass drownings in the Volkhov River. The method was to tie a number of people to sleighs, and then run them into the river. Oprichina equipped with long poles stood on bridges or were deployed in boats to push under water any victim who managed to break his fetters. Other Oprichina stood on the banks farther downstream and shot those who tried... to make an escape.

After killing from 15,000 to 70,000 citizens (the estimates vary that widely), Ivan decided that too much was enough, and had the few remaining survivors assembled in front of him. Koslow quotes Ivan's incredible speech:

Men of Novgorod, surviving through the grace of the Almighty Lord God and the spotless Mother of God and all the saints, pray for our God-fearing rule as Czar, for our sons Ivan and Feodor, and for our enemies and adversaries, visible and invisible. But may God judge him who has betrayed us and you... May all the blood that has been shed fall upon them, and may the traitors be held accountable for it. But as for you, lament no more over all this, but live thankfully in this city.

By talking in this sanctimonious manner to the handful of survivors of the slaughter, the monster displayed the typical alcoholic ability to disconnect from the results of his own destructiveness. Ivan continued in this frame of mind and actually returned to Novgorod -- for his honeymoon! The surviving residents were, understandably, terrified when they learned that the ogre was coming back, but he did them no harm on the return visit.

Like Alexander and Henry VIII, Ivan turned on those whom he had used as instruments of destruction. The Oprichina, the gang of thugs who had helped him destroy Novgorod and many other "enemies" inside Russia, was itself later eliminated in mass public executions. Although they were as horrific as the Novgorod atrocities, the murders of the Oprichina did have a prelude of macabre humor. Ivan's reputation by this time was so fearsome that when he arrived in Red Square, the scene of the planned horror show, he found no one there: no audience awaited the coming spectacle. He then drove through the streets of Moscow, imploring his cowed subjects to come out to see the show. He shouted at the house fronts that they had nothing to fear, that they should come quickly so that the fun could begin.

When the citizens of Moscow finally emerged from behind their curtains, they witnessed a display of unspeakable cruelty. The difference this time is that all the victims had been close associates of Ivan. Prince Ivan Viskovaty, the Czar's chancellor, was strung up by his feet and cut into little pieces. Founikov, Ivan's Treasurer, "... was placed repeatedly in iced water and then in boiling water until his skin 'came off him like an eel's.'" Others were roasted alive. Among the victims was Basmanov who had been the Czar's favorite. Ivan forced his son Feodor Basmanov to murder the father, promising to spare the son's life if he did so. Then, to the amusement of his immediate entourage, he told Feodor that since he had committed parricide, he too would be executed.

After a full day of torture and murder of men, Ivan and his son turned their attention to the women. Koslow describes what they did:

> Ivan and his son went to the home of Viskovaty where Ivan had his widow tortured until she told him where the family treasure was hidden. Then he ravished her. The executed man's 15-year-old daughter was given to the Czarevich... Ivan and his son paid

similar visits to the home of others who had been executed. Men were sent to other homes to seize treasure [and] violate wives and daughters of the dead... As a climax to the day's events, Ivan ordered eighty widows of the executed... to be drowned.

After the murders and rapes and after ordering that the corpses be left in the street to rot, Ivan gave much of the money stolen from the dead to the church, and spent many days in fervent prayer.

He tortured and murdered throughout his reign. He enjoyed visiting the dungeons to watch his victims suffer. At alcohol-drenched banquets, he would set ferocious bears loose on human prisoners. He took to carrying a pointed staff and would stab at anyone who annoyed him. His murders became petty and habitual.

Ivan had seven wives. Upon the death of Anastasia, he accused two friends of killing her with witchcraft and had them imprisoned. He banished his fourth wife to a nunnery and murdered her entire family. He insisted that another wife had been poisoned, but was unmoved and unconcerned at her funeral. His unluckiest bride was Maria Dolgorukaya who made the mistake of telling Ivan she was a virgin. When Ivan discovered that she was not, he had the young woman "bound in a carriage and drawn by galloping horses to the river, where she was drowned."

I've already mentioned Ivan's lack of remorse for his murders, so it shouldn't surprise us that he was unmoved when his wives died. One death did effect him enormously, however. Ivan murdered his own son. The reason? His son's wife was wearing two petticoats instead of three. He struck his daughter-in-law, who was pregnant at the time, so violently that she miscarried. That night while his son was berating Ivan for his mad attack on his pregnant wife, Ivan lost his temper and stabbed him with his pike.

Ivan's putative grief over his son's death may actually have been remorse for having killed the only male heir to the throne over a silly argument. (His other son was an idiot). Ivan's twisted ego enabled him to torture and kill, without remorse, thousands, including persons close to him. He buried wives without showing grief. But by killing his only heir, Ivan hurt his own ego; he appeared monumentally foolish. Grief is out of character for an alcoholic, and Ivan's reaction was probably nothing of the sort.

The magnitude of Ivan's murders, the serial nature of his destruction, and the abuse of relatives (he had a father-in-law tortured, a sister-in-law murdered) are strong reasons to suspect alcoholism-created egomania. His biographers note the continuation of terror long past the point where it could be even remotely justified by power-seeking or power-retention. He killed those who were "not only loyal, but abject," and he became convinced of their guilt after he destroyed them.

Although much different in the degree of destruction, the lists of Ivan's victims (and Henry VIII's and Alexander's) are conceptually no different from the lists of Hemingway's victims, or Sinclair Lewis's, or Joe McCarthy's. Yesterday's victim can be vilified for the sake of ego inflation, but the ego continues to be battered by addiction. To compensate, the ego demands fresh blood -- especially innocents'.

Now for Ivan's drinking. One biographer, Henri Troyat, in *Ivan the Terrible* (Berkley Books, 1986), says that when Ivan was merely 17, "It was whispered that he drank too much and that alcohol was shattering his nerves... " His teenage drinking must have been spectacular, for Ivan, after all, lived in a country where "drunkenness was rampant at every social level." Troyat says that the middle-aged Ivan enjoyed the company of his son: "The two of them had long been united by *love of wine*, debauchery, and blood." [Emphasis added.] To Troyat, Ivan was "a heavy drinker."

The record shows Ivan became more furious as he got older. Koslow says "his unbridled temper, his moodiness, his self-pity, his maddening suspiciousness, his impulsiveness, and his lack of patience [all intensified with age.] His appetites, too, grew with the years... he ate to the bursting point, *drank himself into insensibility*, watched scenes of torture... and wallowed in sexual excess." [Emphasis added.]

According to Troyat, Ivan, like most alcoholics, was a hypochondriac.

Three biographers (Graham, Troyat, and Koslow) say Ivan aged prematurely. This, from Troyat: "According to all witnesses, the 34-year-old Czar had the appearance of an old man." He attributes the aging in part to "drinking bouts."

The physical signs, the heavy drinking throughout his adult life, and the years of serial destruction of innocents -- by a man who, according to his biographers, was intelligent and comparatively well-educated -- clinches it for me; Ivan was Terrible because Ivan was Alcoholic.

The case for alcoholism in another despotic Czar -- Peter the Great -- is as strong as that for Ivan.

Peter murdered *his* son, Alexis. The youthful Alexis had fled to Prussia but was enticed back to Russia when Peter solemnly promised that he would not be charged for alleged pretensions to the throne. But once Alexis was back under his father's control, Peter had a number of his son's friends seized. Tortured, all confessed to conspiracy against Peter. Were these false accusations? According to Robert K. Massie, the answer is yes: "The investigators were dealing with friends of Alexis, not with conspirators." Most of the unfortunates were executed, some by methods as horrific as any administered by Ivan.

Although Peter had promised Alexis immunity for his cooperation with the investigation, he reneged on the agreement. Alexis was arrested and flogged with the knout. A fiendish instrument which is soaked in milk to ensure maximum damage to the flesh, the knout inflicted horrible suffering on its victims. According to Troyat, Peter himself administered the whipping. Alexis died of his wounds.

The day after his son died was a public holiday, and Peter not only did not cancel the scheduled festivities but enthusiastically joined in. As reported by Troyat, "Peter was full of good spirits at the banquet table." Such inhuman reactions to the death of a child are typical of alcoholics. (Unlike Ivan, Peter had another male heir. Alexis's death did no damage to his ego.) Peter's lifelong hatred of his son, the false accusations against Alexis's friends, and his recorded nasty treatment of his first wife are all consistent with the serial destruction found in the lives of all alcoholics.

Was Peter's megalomania accompanied by alcoholic-style drinking? The answer, again, is a resounding yes. He certainly had exceptional tolerance for alcohol. The British General, Charles George Gordon, who visited Peter's court, noted that he was none the worse for wear for his excessive drinking. Massie (who, like most historians, evidences no knowledge of alcoholism) writes in his biography: "He could drink all night with his comrades and then, while they snored in drunken slumber, rise at dawn and leave them to begin work... Few could match his pace."

Peter had a fierce temper that sometimes led to violence at the banquet table. He and a small group of armed guards once attacked and murdered four priests whose religious beliefs offended him. He had been drinking.

On another occasion, he forced an official who disliked Hungarian wine to drink so much of it that he nearly died. Another time he forcibly kept a party of courtiers on board a ship, telling his guards that no one could leave until they were drunk. Bullying others to drink excessively is a favorite alcoholic ploy; even present-day alcoholics pressure others to drink more than they want. But as Czar of Russia, Peter could do more than pressure his guests.

Peter was involved in other scenes of drunken violence: "The feast lasted for ten hours... *The Emperor seemed especially disposed to drink...* they wept, embraced, and kissed... and soon passed to quarrels and blows." [Emphasis added.]

He had alcoholic offspring. His son Alexis had an "inclination to drunkenness." His wife on one occasion ascribed an illness of Alexis's to "the great quantity of brandy which he drinks daily, for he is usually drunk." His daughter Elizabeth developed "an unfortunate habit of strong drink which brought [her] to an untimely end." If vulnerability to alcoholism is hereditary, its existence in offspring is confirming evidence in a parent whose own behavior is suspect.

There is no doubt in my mind. Peter the Great was an alcoholic.

Although traditional historians are more interested in the battles, the conquests, the conspiracies, and other *results* of individuals' behavior, not its *cause*, some half-hearted attempts have made to ascribe the irrational destructiveness of the four tyrants in this chapter to illness. Ivan, we are told, may have been syphilitic. Henry once fell from a horse and may have damaged his brain. Peter was afflicted with digestive problems. Alexander suffered from exhaustion. None of these afflictions or conditions, however, are known to cause the patterns of destruction established by these tyrants, or cause them to drink enormously. Only alcoholism fits.

The transformation of a creative, popular young leader into a middle-aged megalomaniac who destroys innocent underlings is an *unnatural* development. The tendency to destroy others, frequently through false accusations, existed in these four monsters to a phenomenal degree. This is a compulsion highly indicative of alcoholism. Adolf Hitler, evil as he was, and sick as he may have been, did *not* engage in capricious destruction of close associates. Neither did Napoleon, nor Lenin, nor Mao. We have no reason to suspect that those tough national leaders were alcoholics. There was, however, a twentieth-century leader whose horrible reign fits the pattern, a man whose alcoholism modern historians have missed, or ignored as irrelevant. My research and analysis have led me to conclude that Joseph Stalin -- the most murderous person who ever lived -- was an active alcoholic during his entire adult life. Because of the wealth of information I have gathered, and the significance of my conclusion, I devote an entire chapter to this "supreme" alcoholic.

11: JOSEPH STALIN, SUPREME ALCOHOLIC

The Soviet Union passed through a serious disease and lost many
of its finest sons and daughters.
                                                    Roy A. Medvedev

Cunningly inventing calumnies, you call the faithful traitors, you
call Christians sorcerers; in your eyes virtues are vices, light is only
darkness; and wherein had these worthy protectors of Russia offended you?
                                                    Andrei Kurbsky,
                                        in a letter to Ivan the Terrible

In all of human history, no human being caused more suffering
than Joseph Stalin. As the Marxist historian Roy A. Medvedev
said, "Not one of the tyrants and despots of the past persecuted and
destroyed so many of his compatriots." He killed about twenty-five
million.* Other millions spent many years in brutal penal camps.

---

*Even this generally accepted estimate may be too low. Feodor Volkov, a
respected Soviet academician, recently claimed that the total deaths from Stalin's
terror may have been as high as fifty million.

Theories abound for the cause of Stalin's ruthless and, most often, senseless killings, but to my knowledge no one has yet advanced the idea that alcoholism was the root cause.* But I am convinced that anyone knowledgeable about alcoholism who studies his biographies as I have will agree with my conclusion: Stalin was an alcoholic and it was his alcoholism-induced megalomania that drove him to murder millions.

Since 1956, when Nikita Khrushchev unmasked Stalin as the architect of the terror, a number of books have been published that delineate the slaughter and amplify his role in it. Two of the best are Robert Conquest's *The Great Terror* (The Macmillan Company, 1968) and Medvedev's *Let History Judge* (Alfred A. Knopf, 1971). These two historians provide massive documentation of Stalin's long war against his own people. Their works and others, especially the two books written by Stalin's daughter, Svetlana, make Stalin comprehensible; they contain convincing evidence of alcoholism. But before we turn to the *other* evidence of his alcoholism, let us look first at his unbelievable record of serial destruction.

Robert Conquest calls the assassination in 1934 of Sergei Kirov "The Crime of the Century":

Over the next four years, hundreds of Russians, including the most prominent political leaders of the Revolution, were shot for direct responsibility and -- literally -- millions of others went to their deaths for the complicity in one or the another part of the vast conspiracy which allegedly lay behind it. Kirov's death, in fact, was the keystone of the entire edifice of terror and suffering...

Alexander Orlov, an early defector from the NKVD (the predecessor to the KGB), was the first to publicly blame Stalin for Kirov's murder. Khrushchev, in his 1956 secret speech, insinuated that Stalin was guilty. Medvedev says that Stalin's guilt is "almost proved." Conquest, in *Stalin and the Kirov Murder* (Oxford

---

*Which is not to say others have not labeled him an alcoholic. As will be explained shortly, some important historical figures have done exactly that.

University Press, 1989), marshals convincing evidence of his culpability.

Kirov, a well-liked Communist and a Soviet patriot, was soon followed to the grave by hundreds, thousands, and eventually millions of Soviet citizens.

It is difficult to comprehend the scope of Stalin's murderous rampage against his own people. However, we can get some sense of the enormity of his crimes by listing the various headings from the index of Medvedev's book under the heading "repression":

In Agency for Anti-Aircraft Defense, in Albania, in Armenia, arrest of close relatives of Stalin's aides and "enemies," in aviation industry, in Azerbaijan, in Kazakhstan, of Komosol officials, in Leningrad, in literary groups, of livestock state farms, of members of Council of People's Commissars, of the military, in military academies, of naval officers, of obkom secretaries, among officials of Jewish origin, among officials of NKVD in Ossetia, of painters, actors, musicians, architects, and film people, of philosophers, in Poland, in railroad industry, in Roumania, in scientific fields, in socialistic countries, in Tadzhikistan, in Tartar Republic, of trade unions officials, in Transcaucasia, in Turkmenia, in the Ukraine, in Uzbekistan, during war and immediately after, in [the] Yugoslavia Communist Party.

That is a list of the organizations, Republics, professions, and so forth. To list the names of twenty-five million *individuals* at the rate of one hundred names per page (about as many as would fit comfortably on the page of this book) would require one-quarter million pages. If those pages were bound in books of four hundred pages each, we would need six hundred twenty-five books to list the names. Just the names.

The numbers are one matter. Another is the *type* of person attacked by Stalin. By 1934, the year of the Kirov murder, Stalin had been in complete control of the Soviet Union for more than five years. Those Communists who had competed against him in the past for political leadership had accepted defeat, or, in the case of Trotsky, were in impotent exile. The peasants who had resisted collectivization of their farms had already been crushed by direct repression or by starvation in a Stalin-engineered famine. By the time the terror began, in other words, there was no reason for it.

No political reason. And because there were no real enemies, the casualty lists were comprised of people who, with very few exceptions, were completely innocent of the charges made against them.

The trial of Bukharin, to cite a paradigmatic example, described by Katkov as "the most remarkable of such cases of legal coercion," saw a "trusted supporter of the supreme ruler [Stalin] and the 'favorite son of the Party' [transformed] into... a plotter, counter-revolutionary, traitor, spy, wrecker, and assassin." Bukharin was charged with nothing less than attempting to murder Lenin. At the close of his trial, some spectators thought they saw Stalin himself "peering out from behind the black glass of a small window, high under the ceiling of the courtroom" as the innocent Bukharin was sentenced to death. (Like many others he was rehabilitated, posthumously, by the Soviet government long after Stalin's death.)

Stalin wiped out the Old Bolsheviks, the founding fathers of the Soviet Union. These men, all patriots, were charged with heinous crimes against the State, tried, and sentenced to death. They were either shot straightaway, or sent to penal camps where they perished. Of all the Old Bolsheviks, only Molotov survived.

He attacked the Communist Party root and branch. When the Eighteenth Party Congress met in 1939, only 2 percent of the rank and file delegates who had attended the 1934 meeting were present. The secret police had arrested the others for "counter-revolutionary crimes." According to Medvedev, the carnage was "pitiless... of people who had done the main work of the Revolution from the days of the underground struggle, through the insurrection and the Civil War, the restoration of the shattered economy and the great upbuilding of the early thirties. [It was] the most frightful act in the tragedy of the thirties." Middle level party officials were arrested and replaced. Then the secret police arrested the new leaders. Sometimes only the fourth or fifth replacement survived. They perished, not because they were incompetent, or because they opposed Stalin. They were killed for crimes they did not commit.

The Red Army was assaulted, ripped apart, and greatly weakened by Stalin. The damage he did to the military, just prior to World War II, was nearly fatal to the nation. According to Conquest, the purge destroyed three of the five marshals, fourteen out of sixteen Army Commanders, eight out of eight Admirals, sixty out of sixty-seven Corps Commanders, 136 of the 199 Divisional Commanders, and 221 of the 397 Brigade Commanders. About one half the officer corps -- thirty-five thousand -- were shot or imprisoned. Again, this was no purge of traitors, or even of alleged incompetents. These officers, experienced leaders and Soviet patriots, were shot, on Stalin's orders, as spies and conspirators.

He accused the managers and technicians who struggled to build the industrial power of Russia of sabotage and "wrecking." Not accusations of incompetency, which might have had some basis in fact, but charges of crimes so bizarre as to be unimaginable. One official, for example, was charged with placing nails in butter in order to poison the Soviet masses.

There were many such accusations and, following brutal interrogation, admissions to absurdities. A female ceramist painted swastikas in the pattern of tea cups. A Jewish engineer designed a plant in the shape of a swastika. Another ceramist made ash trays shaped like the Star of David. A doctor injected patients with venereal disease. A common laborer confessed, after rigorous interrogation, that he tried to blow up a bridge with arsenic, which cannot explode. A frumpy charwoman confessed to seducing foreign diplomats. One man was even sentenced for murdering himself. The secret police charged he had murdered the wrongful holder of his identity papers. The defendant produced a number of witnesses who knew him, but the witnesses were thrown out of court and the man was sentenced -- for killing himself!

After signing a nonaggression pact with Hitler, Stalin ordered the NKVD to turn over hundreds of German *Communists* to the Gestapo! Many were Jews; some had fought the Nazis in street battles in the early thirties. All were loyal Communists, and all perished in the hands of Nazis.

An outstanding physician, Dimitry Pletnev, perhaps the most honored medical man in the Soviet Union, who was *66 years old at the time*, was publicly accused of raping a female patient. It was no random accusation. Pletnev had been set up by a NKVD agent who said he bit her breast and then raped her. The charge was used to force the doctor to admit to a murder -- of which he was innocent. He perished in a penal camp.

Stalin did not limit his attacks to strangers or to political associates. Close friends and even members of his own family were destroyed.

He had shot: Jan Sten, who had been his tutor for three years;

his bodyguard and drinking companion; his brother-in-law; Abel Yenukidze, who had been his closest friend and best man at his wedding.

He sent to prison: the wife of Kalinin, who, as President of the Soviet Union, was the official Chief of State; the wife of Molotov, his slavishly loyal Foreign Minister; the two sons of Anatole Mikoyan, another loyal Politburo member; the wife of Poskrebyshev, the head of his personal secretariat for more than twenty years; the man who had been his personal physician for twenty years; his dead wife's sisters-in-law who had sent Stalin food parcels when he was exiled by the Czarist government. All were falsely accused of various anti-State activities, imprisoned or liquidated.

The wives of those arrested were routinely imprisoned. He changed the law to make children as young as 12 subject to adult penalties. Survivors report seeing children as young as 9 in prison camps.

The methods were as absurd as the charges. Yagoda, head of the NKVD, would telegraph a provincial subordinate telling him to eliminate *ten thousand* "enemies of the people" and to wire his confirmation once the executions had been carried out. If there weren't enough prisoners on hand to meet the assigned quota, the local NKVD would round up assorted priests, veterans of the White Army, and other innocents to fill their quota.

Confessions were demanded of all. These were obtained by inhumane methods, including torture, which was *officially* approved by Stalin in 1937. Another method of coercion was the merciless use of hostages. Even men who knew they were doomed, whether they confessed or not, would capitulate and sign confessions -- *false* confessions -- when told that their families would also be killed if they did not cooperate. Usually, it made no difference. The families were rounded up after the father had been executed, even if he had confessed.

By the end of 1938, *5 percent of the entire population was under arrest.* One out of twenty. And those arrested were concentrated in the elite: members of the Communist Party, the Army officer corps, industrial leaders, technicians, and artists. By that time, one hundred thousand people -- equal to seven Army divisions -- were employed in interrogation activities. Penal camps and prisons were loaded to the breaking point.

Joseph Stalin personally directed the secret police and approved virtually all executions. He signed the execution lists and followed individual cases closely. During the early days of World War II, when his nation faced defeat by Hitler's invading army, two officials meekly approached Stalin and asked if it might be possible to release the Deputy Minister of Aviation. This specialist in air defense was needed, they implored him, to protect the nation against the German attack. Stalin, the dictator of a nation reeling from Hitler's onslaught, immediately recognized the man's name and rattled off his status as a prisoner: "He's been arrested for forty days and hasn't signed a confession." His country was on the brink of military catastrophe, but Joseph Stalin was up-to-the-minute on the status of an obscure prisoner!

Although the terror that began with the Kirov assassination had abated by 1938, it never really ended. He killed some during the war and more afterward, twenty years after he had assumed supreme, unchallenged power. Indeed, he was on the threshold of a new wave of repression when he died in 1953.

"Zachto?" Why? That was the question screamed by Yakov Livshits, just prior to his execution in 1937. The same word -- *Zachto?* -- was carved in the walls of countless cells by Stalin's prisoners. Why?

Could Stalin have murdered twenty-five million of his own countrymen for some *rational* reason? To save his nation? The revolution? His own skin?

There are very few rational reasons that have even superficial plausibility, and all of them fall to pieces under critical analysis. Medvedev makes it clear that the *official* explanations at the time -- that there were huge internal conspiracies aimed at destroying the Soviet Union -- didn't survive the collapse of the Axis powers. If large numbers of Soviet officials and Red Army officers -- tens or even hundreds of thousands -- had been agents of Germany and Japan, as they had confessed, the archives of the defeated nations would have held *some* evidence of this incredible development, or some of the surviving Nazi or Japanese officials would have divulged the secret to the conquering allies. But no evidence was ever found, and no one in Germany or Japan ever confessed. The charges were false; the crimes never occurred.

The Khrushchev speech and subsequent developments -- especially in the Gorbachev era -- publicly exonerated many of the better-known victims. But the charges had always been wildly implausible. Army officers were accused of plotting to reduce military strength; avid communist revolutionaries were really capitalists at heart. Engineers and managers supposedly spent their days scheming to destroy the industrial strength of the motherland; Jews were secret Nazi sympathizers and Nazi spies. Those were the official reasons for the purges. They defy logic and are simply unworthy of serious consideration as a candidate for a response to the question, *"Zachto?"*

Somewhat less implausible, but implausible nonetheless, is the idea that Stalin was eliminating competition. This theory *might* hold water for purges directed at people like Zinoviev, who had opposed him in the past, or others who, as late as 1933 or 1934, voiced disagreement with some of his policies. But even here the theory is weak. Stalin was in complete control of the Soviet Union *before* the terror began. The totality of his command was made clear at the Party Congress of 1934. Former oppositionists, such as Zinoviev, took the platform and unequivocally and effusively praised Stalin and his policies and abused his enemies, particularly the exiled Trotsky. Zinoviev's abject surrender did him no good; he was one of the earliest murder victims.

Even if *some* of his victims had been former contenders for power or even potential future threats to his position, the "eliminate-the-competition" hypothesis cannot possibly explain the killing of slavish Stalinists, faithful bodyguards, harmless artists, doctors, schoolteachers, and common laborers. Stalin had, at most, a dozen *potential* replacements and each of them had, perhaps, a few hundred supporters. One or two thousand deaths could have been attributable to the cold-blooded elimination of competition -- real or imagined. But when the toll mounts into the hundreds of thousands, and then into the millions, the notion that Stalin was, somehow or other, killing to protect himself falls apart.

There is yet another reason to reject the proposition that Stalin murdered to eliminate competition. Robert Conquest notes the serious discrepancy between Stalin's slow movement against his so-called enemies and Adolf Hitler's crushing swiftness in destroying the threat presented by Ernst Roehm and the S.A. in the summer of 1934 (virtually in one night) and the German dictator's quick and brutal handling of the generals who tried to assassinate him during the war. In contrast, Stalin's accusation that many had conspired to murder him -- a charge made repeatedly against assorted batches of "enemies of the people" -- was followed by a process which can only be described as languid. The arrests, the interrogations, and the show trials consumed many months. If Stalin was really facing gangs of tough ex-revolutionaries and military officers who were out to kill him, why didn't he simply have them shot straightaway? His loyal subjects would have applauded swift brutal justice. But he didn't act with dispatch and his apparent delight in the *process* of destruction must be explained.

There's another conceivable rational explanation for the elimination of twenty-five million people. In the aftermath of any revolution (so an advocate of this notion might say), there is an inevitable period of upheaval when many people, even the innocent, are destroyed. Stalin's purges might be compared to the Reign of Terror that followed the French Revolution.

Russia indeed had its Reign of Terror during and after the revolution. It occurred when "class enemies" of the Bolsheviks were terrorized, and it had as its climactic act the execution of the ruling Romanov family in 1918. But that period of terror, which had a certain evil rationality within the context of the revolutionary struggle, was long past when Stalin started his rampage in the 1930's. The Soviet Union was a fact. The collectivization of the country's agriculture was a fact. The defeat of the White Army was a fact.

The Soviet Union of 1934 was in the midst of a nationwide burst of creative activity and growth. The huge and struggling country was determined to show the world that it could build a modern industrial state in accordance with Marxist principles. The times cried out for laborious but glorious effort to build a great nation. Such efforts require a government that gave the people the means of accomplishing those objectives. Not merely propagandistic exhortations, five year plans and quotas, but the material and, above all, the human wherewithal demanded by the great undertaking. Nation-building requires enormous numbers of worker-years of effort from all citizens at every level of society.

But to help build his nation, Stalin killed twenty-five million potential contributors and kept eight million locked up. (That was the level reached at the end of 1938.) He had one hundred thousand police engaged in questioning suspects and producing nothing but absurd confessions. He gutted the ranks of the professionals and technicians so necessary to the development of any nation. Medvedev documents Stalin's decimation of Soviet science and the technological disciplines with his zany charges of spying and wrecking in all fields: agronomy, genetics, medical research, linguistics, aviation, armament design, hydroelectric engineering, fertilizer production, and so forth. Plant managers, railway technicians, and others needed for the building of infrastructure were deliberately not made available to the nation by imprisonment or death. Great strides forward *were* made during the thirty years of Stalin's rule, but they were made *in spite of* the efforts of the "Great Wrecker" himself. The man who was in total control of the nation behaved in a way totally inconsistent with any desire to build a nation. The irrevocable loss of the labor of those twenty-five million left a shortfall in Soviet development, one that remains today in Russia and in the other successor states to the Soviet Union.

The loss to Stalin's terror of essential military leaders nearly cost the Soviet Union its very existence.

In 1937-1938, the Soviet Union was preparing for an *unavoidable* war with the fascist countries, which had already begun their aggression in Spain, Abyssinia, and China. Sparing neither energy nor goods, the Soviet people strengthened the defenses of their country, nourishing the Red Army like a favored child. [Emphasis added.]

That is how Medvedev sets the scene for his description of Stalin's incredible assault on the military cadres of the Soviet Union, an assault that eliminated, on the eve of the great war against Nazi Germany, tens of thousands of officers. Never before, "did the officer staff of *any* army suffer much great losses in *any* way as the Soviet Army suffered in this time of peace." [Emphasis added.] No *enemy* during *any* war killed as many commanders as did Stalin.

The Soviet people soon paid for that destruction with untold casualties. Not only was the early course of the war affected by the deaths in 1938 of the finest military leaders and the great demoralization that followed, but it is possible that the invasion itself might not have occurred if Hitler hadn't known -- and post war investigations determined that he indeed knew -- that Stalin had eliminated all his first rank commanders.

In summing up then, Stalin's repressions cost the Soviet Union enormous casualties in the early years of the war and hundreds of millions of worker-years of labor. In the end, Stalin's regime left a legacy of tragedy and guilt whose scars -- social, psychological, and economic -- are still evident.

Why? What ghastly irrationality ruled Joseph Stalin?

Medvedev examines the question of motivation at some length and concludes that, although he displayed many symptoms of "paranoia," Stalin's actions "were not the products of fear or deception; they were the well-calculated moves of a man determined to stop at nothing to reach his goal." He rules out paranoia as a cause for Stalin's behavior because of what Medvedev calls his "great self control." Stalin not only imprisoned the wives of Molotov and Kalinin, the sons of Mikoyan, and close relatives of other aides, but he then continued to meet daily -- socially, as well as officially -- with these men. As Medvedev shrewdly points out, this is not the behavior of a paranoid, of someone who sees threats everywhere. Stalin showed pure *contempt* for his underlings -- not fear. Contempt for those you destroy is not the mark of a frightened paranoid.

Medvedev mentions something else about Stalin that contradicts the paranoia theory. When it came to deciding who was to live or to die, or who was to be imprisoned or set free, Joseph Stalin was simply capricious. He describes the case of Kavtardze, an old comrade of Stalin's. Following his arrest on (naturally) trumped up charges, Kavtardze wrote to his old friend -- claiming innocence. Stalin, who was usually deaf to such pleas from old pals, ordered Kavtardze released. But his release was not only unusual, it was also temporary. A few years later, he and his wife were arrested, tortured, and sentenced to death. Then, after spending months in a "death cell," Kavtardze was suddenly taken to Beria, then head of the NKVD. His wife, who had been in another camp, was already in Beria's office. The two of them were released, again. Still later, the couple invited Joseph Stalin to their Moscow apartment for dinner. At one point Stalin took Kavtardze's arm, waved his index finger under his chin, and said, "And still you wanted to kill me." Medvedev tries to fit this incident, which he says some might ascribe to paranoia, into his own analysis by saying Stalin, of course, knew that Kavtardze never tried to kill him.

Medvedev is right about Stalin not being paranoid, but he is right for the wrong reason. By that time Stalin may have convinced himself that Kavtardze was guilty, but this had nothing to do with paranoia and everything to do with alcoholism.

I have heard many recovered alcoholics at Alcoholics Anonymous meetings say that they not only became habitual liars during their drinking years but that their lies became so entangled with reality that they often convinced themselves that the lies were true. Alcoholics are *damned good* liars, a simple fact that can be greatly underestimated in judging the damage they do, and in understanding what makes them tick.

Joe McCarthy convinced millions that he was a sincere, honest anti-communist. He may have even believed it himself. After completing his malignantly accusatory play, *Long Day's Journey Into Night*, Eugene O'Neill called it "an act of honesty and love." Stalin appears to have had the same weird capacity for *self*-deception. It was, I am convinced, this strange ability of alcoholics to accept their own lies (or their inability to know what is true), that led Stalin to *believe* that poor, terrified Kavtardze had actually conspired to kill him.

This is not paranoia. It is something simpler, and simpler ideas are often more difficult to understand. The alcoholic begins by deliberately lying. But the lie eventually becomes more acceptable to him -- both at a conscious and at an unconscious level -- than reality. Once a false accusation is made (and in Stalin's case, the deadly wheels of Soviet justice set in motion), it becomes impossible for the alcoholic to admit -- at any level -- the truth: that the accused was innocent. For permanently fastened to the statement "I know X is innocent" is its corollary, "And I am unspeakably evil for having accused X." The alcoholic cannot admit to such evilness, *especially* to himself.* He has no choice. The truth *must* be repressed. The lie *becomes* the truth.

Medvedev makes another telling point against the paranoia hypothesis when he points out, "A man suffering from a persecution mania would not, after destroying thousands of devoted Party

---

*As noted in Chapter Eight, self-acknowledgement of past evil behavior does occur if and when the alcoholic achieves sobriety; it is one reason why suicide is a risk in early recovery.

leaders, have replaced them with men with such murky political records as Beria and Alakumov." He also points out that Vyshinsky, Stalin's favorite prosecutor, had served under Kerensky, the last non-Communist leader of Russia, and while in that position had ordered the arrest of Bolsheviks. Why would a man possessed, supposedly, of paranoiac fears choose a former enemy of the Bolsheviks to be his chief prosecutor in the purge trials? His promotion of the infamous Beria (who, once Stalin died, was summarily liquidated by his fearful Politburo comrades), is strong evidence of the lack of paranoiac fear in Stalin.

The late Harrison E. Salisbury, in reviewing Medvedev's book in *The New York Times,* accepted these arguments against paranoia, but rejected the claim that Stalin was simply power hungry:

> Medvedev is weakest in his belief that Stalin was not mad... surely the answer lies deeper [than politics] since... Stalin was already so powerful at the onset of the 1930's that he could not have been overthrown... the mass killings and the mass purges began after Stalin was all powerful... [the answer] is to be found in the realm of psychiatry rather than politics.

The riddle then is this: Why did a man who was *not* paranoid, but obviously power-hungry, murder millions of his loyal subjects *after* he had achieved supreme power?

The answer to the riddle, of course, is that Stalin was an alcoholic. Alcoholism explains his massacres. Twenty-five million died because they were ruled by an agent of alcoholism, not for any "rational" reason, and not because Joseph Stalin was paranoid, or "insane," in any conventional sense of that word. As ruler of the Soviet Union, he had at his command a large organization of rabid co-religionists, devout Marxists, many of whom were willing to confess to crimes they did not commit and indeed could not have committed. Some could accept the death penalty for those uncommitted crimes and shout "Long live Stalin!" even as the bullets ripped into their bodies. Stalin had a pliable population at his feet (all of them products of a culture influenced in no small way by the reigns of the alcoholic Czars Ivan and Peter) and a force of brutal secret police at his command. Stalin had virtually unlimited power.

And alcoholism had Stalin.

All alcoholics exist in situations, and Stalin's situation was fatal for millions. He could exploit, almost without limit, the alcoholic's compulsive need to tear down others. All alcoholics stretch, sometimes to the breaking point, the rules and restraints that society places on their demented egos. As a Marxist dictator, Stalin had virtually no restraints. He brought to the seat of totalitarian power not only the alcoholic's need to destroy and the typical amorality, but the craftiness and the cunning that are enhanced by the disease. He had complete control over people inured to tyranny by centuries of autocratic, often despotic, rule. He had at the disposal of his alcoholism-hounded ego the most powerful and ruthless army of thugs ever assembled.

Stalinism was alcoholism run rampant. Instead of a wife and children to browbeat and terrorize, he had an empire. He could do more than insult his victims, or physically assault them, or ridicule them in a novel or in a play; he could *liquidate* them. Of course he still made them appear as fools or knaves, cursing them with labels like "wrecker," "spy," and "imperialistic tool" -- terms as opprobrious within the context of the Soviet Union of the nineteen-thirties as was John Nichols' curse of "syphilitic" in Victorian England. But after demeaning his victims in the worst possible manner, Stalin could kill them with impunity and with little fear of retribution. It was the *situation* he was in that made this single case of alcoholism a cataclysmic disaster. Without that political power, his alcoholic destruction would have been borne solely by his family. In fact, they had the usual dose of alcoholic woe.

In *Khrushchev Remembers* (Little, Brown and Company, 1970), Nikita Khrushchev described a scene between Stalin and his daughter:

> [Svetlana] found herself in the middle of a flock of people older than she, to put it mildly. As soon as the sober young woman arrived, Stalin made her dance. I could see she was tired. She barely moved while dancing. She danced for a short time and tried to stop, but her father still insisted. She went over and stood next to the record player leaning a shoulder against the wall. Stalin came over to her, and I joined them. We stood

there together. *Stalin was lurching about.* He said, "Well, go on, Svetlana, dance!"

She said, "I've already danced, Papa, I'm tired." With that, Stalin grabbed her by the forelock of her hair with his fist and pulled. I could see her face turning red and the tears welling up in her eyes. I felt so sorry for Svetlana. He pulled harder and dragged her back onto the dance floor. [Emphasis added.]

In her own book, *Twenty Letters to a Friend* (Harper & Row, 1967), Svetlana recalled Stalin's chilling behavior toward his eldest son, Yakov.

The son of his first wife, who had died of natural causes, Yakov got along well with everyone including his stepsister, Svetlana, who wrote about him with obvious affection. He was close to his stepmother, Nadya, who was "tender and affectionate with him," and with his stepmother's parents. He did not, however, get along with his father. In Stalin's eyes, his first born son could do nothing right. He "disapproved of his marriage, of how he was doing in his studies, and of his character." His father's mistreatment, according to Svetlana, drove Yakov to attempt suicide in the late 1920's:

In despair over the attitude of my father, who wouldn't have anything to do with him, Yakov went to the kitchen of our Kremlin apartment and shot himself. Luckily he was only wounded. My father used to make fun of him and sneer, "Ha! He couldn't even shoot straight!" My mother was horrified.

Svetlana is convinced Stalin finally succeeded in driving his son to suicide. Yakov had been captured by the Germans (as were millions of poorly-led Soviet soldiers) during World War II. This fact was known at the time in the West, where it was published, but the news had been withheld from the Soviet people. A Western journalist asked Stalin about his son and was told (by the man who had killed more patriotic Red Army officers than Hitler's armed forces ever would), "there are no Russian prisoners of war, only Russian traitors, and we shall do away with them when the war is over." When the journalist persisted and asked about Yakov, who was a front-line officer, Stalin, who never even visited the front during the war, said, "I have no son called Yakov."

Svetlana was later told by a soldier who had been in the same prison camp that Stalin's words, which had been reported in the Western press, were broadcast by the Germans over the camp's loudspeakers. On that very day, Yakov threw himself on the electrified fence surrounding the camp and perished.

Stalin rejected each of his children at critical times in their early years. When his first wife died, Stalin abandoned Yakov. He would have been put in an orphanage if it were not for some kindly neighbors who took him in. And upon the death of his second wife, Stalin established himself in a bachelor's apartment in the Kremlin -- leaving his young children to live with his wife's relatives. According to Svetlana, the older Stalin showed no interest in his grandchildren.

He bullied and abused his wives. Alexander Orlov reports that Stalin's first wife (Katherine Svanidize) was a gentle and deeply religious woman who "according to the Old Bolsheviks, Stalin bitterly mistreated." Orlov wrote that it was no secret that Stalin abused his second wife, Nadya Alliluyeva. He used to humiliate her in the presence of guests at dinner or at drinking parties:

> When she tried to hint timidly that he should stop the taunting [this] merely brought about an angry response from Stalin and at times *when he was drunk he resorted to the choicest kind of Russian-mother type of swearing.* [Emphasis added.]

According to Svetlana, her mother often thought of leaving Stalin because he was "callous and harsh and inconsiderate of her feelings."

Nadya, like Stalin's oldest son, committed suicide. What is known of the actual event has the tell-tale mark of alcoholic abuse.

Stalin had once again humiliated his wife. Khrushchev said Stalin had publicly accused her of infidelity, the favorite false accusation of married alcoholics. Conquest retails a version in which Stalin threw a lit cigarette at her. Svetlana says her father "merely said to her, 'Hey you! Have a drink!'" whereupon Nadya screamed, "Don't you dare 'Hey you' me!" and ran from the table. Svetlana believed the incident was the "last straw" for the woman who had often been humiliated by her husband.

Another possible factor in the suicide was adultery. Recently published Khrushchev memoirs report that a bodyguard had inadvertently told Nadya that Stalin was spending the night with another woman.

Although there were reports that Stalin was grief-striken by his wife's suicide, these were false. Conquest labels as "myth" stories of Stalin's frequent visits to her grave. Other facts suggest the absence of grief: not only did he abandon her suddenly-motherless young children to the care of others, he had her sister and the widow of her brother imprisoned in the 1940's.

Svetlana was often treated badly by her father. He broke up her romance with Alexei Kapler and sent the young man to Siberia. He called Svetlana a "parasite" in front of a group of sycophants. Another time, he accused her of anti-Soviet behavior. Once, as a schoolgirl, she sent him her photograph as a present for his birthday. He sent it back with an angry letter telling her, "You have an insolent expression on your face."

In addition to the typical abuse of his family, there are other signs pointing to alcoholism. He was a Georgian, and Georgians were reputedly the heaviest drinkers in the Soviet Union. Leon Trotsky, in his *Stalin: An Appraisal of the Man and His Influence* (Grosset & Dunlap, 1941), quoted an old Russian encyclopedia: "There is scarcely another people in the world who drink as much wine as the Georgians."

Trotsky, incidentally, mentions two *ludicrous* reasons for suspecting "alcoholic heredity on his father's side": Stalin had two toes grown together, and he had cachexia (emaciation) of the left arm. There is no support in medical literature for Trotsky's notion that these conditions have anything to do with alcoholism. But, more important, one must ask *why* Trotsky, who had spent enough time with Stalin to know his personal habits, suggested that he had inherited the ability to become an alcoholic? His wacky assertions suggest to me that he had seen Stalin consume a lot of alcohol. In any event, there is enough other evidence to conclude that Trotsky was right about Stalin's father.

Khrushchev quotes Stalin as saying his father used to sell his belt for drinking money and "a Georgian has to be in desperate straits before he will sell his belt." Stalin told Khrushchev and others, "My father sold his belt a number of times, and when I was still in the cradle, he used to dip his finger in a glass of wine and let me suck on it. He was teaching me to drink even when I was still in the cradle!" According to Svetlana and others, her grandfather was killed in a drunken brawl.

His father was not the only blood relative afflicted with alcoholism. His son, Vasily, became, as a young man, a flagrant late-stage alcoholic who was committed, more than once, to a drying out facility after his father died.

At first glance, the life of Vasily Stalin seems to be in such contrast to that of Joseph that suggesting the two of them shared a disease in common seems implausible. Joseph lived to be 73; Vasily died at 41. Some Westerners who met Stalin claim they never saw him take a drink; Vasily was continually drunk in public. Vasily was a has-been (or a never-was) at 24, kicked out of an important military post by his father; Joseph Stalin remained in power until his death. Vasily, unlike his seemingly austere father, used his position to gain personal favors and material wealth. He had a huge dacha, complete with a staff of servants, stables, and kennels. According to his sister, "Everything was given him, and he was given everything he wanted."

But there were important similarities. According to Svetlana, Vasily not only engaged in intrigues, but "anyone who'd fallen out of favor with him was kicked out of his path and even went to jail." When his father died, "There was no one he didn't blame. He accused the government, the doctors, and everybody in sight of using the wrong treatment... and failing to give him a proper funeral." Vasily was married three times and was living with another woman when he died. He was estranged, intermittently, from his children. Joseph Stalin had eight grandchildren, but only allowed three of them to be introduced to him. Although Georgians generally adore children, Joseph Stalin did not.

Another interesting point is that Vasily Stalin seems to have genuinely liked his father. Alcoholics often hate their *non*alcoholic parents as is clear from the biographies and the works of O'Neill, Hemingway and Tennessee Williams. In Williams' case, dislike of the nonalcoholic mother was matched by affection for the alcoholic father -- despite the fact that the father had abandoned the family when Tennessee was a child. The same sort of affection seemed to have flowed from the alcoholic Vasily to the alcoholic Joseph, despite reports that the father had beat Vasily's mother.

Conquest notes that all who knew him described Vasily with contempt, as a semi-literate drunkard who behaved like "a beastly pampered schoolboy let out into the world for the first time." But there is no doubt that of his three children, Vasily was the one Joseph liked the most once they were adults. And once he was an adult, Vasily was an alcoholic.

After his father died, Vasily was arrested, accused of intriguing and causing the wrongful imprisonment and deaths of others. Although he was sentenced to eight years imprisonment, he was released earlier on his promise "to live in peace." His attempts to do so failed, and he was soon drinking heavily. He was incarcerated again, and released again. Then he died -- of alcoholism.

Turning now to the question of whether Joseph Stalin had a high tolerance for alcohol, there are many significant accounts.

Thaddeus Wittlin reports that in 1921, while visiting Tiflis in his native Georgia, Stalin emptied, with no reported drunkenness, a "khanty" -- a goblet, made from a large buffalo horn, with a capacity of three or four bottles of wine.

Years later, when Stalin was the supreme ruler of the Soviet Union, he held court nightly at interminable dinners that usualy turned into drinking bouts. Khrushchev recalls that Beria, Malenkov, and Mikoyan arranged with the waitresses to have colored water poured in their glasses instead of wine; they couldn't keep up with Stalin. (In nonalcoholics, tolerance decreases with age; senior citizens can't handle liquor as well as younger adults. But when the older man is an alcoholic, this general rule doesn't apply. Joseph Stalin, 60 years old in 1939, was older than the men who resorted to dangerous subterfuge to avoid drinking at his pace.)

Conquest says Stalin "did not like non-drinkers" around him, and was in the habit of pressing others to drink to excess. Alcoholics are notorious for "pushing" alcohol on others.

During these dinners, Stalin would frequently reminisce about his youthful adventures. Khrushchev has passed along one such tale which gives us another strong indication of high tolerance for alcohol:

The talk helped to explain why he drank so much. He was [arrested and] sent somewhere in Vologda Province. Many political and criminal convicts were sent there. Stalin used to say, "There were some nice fellows among the criminal convicts during my first exile. I hung around mostly with criminals, I remember we used to stop at saloons in town. We'd see who among us had a ruble or two. Then we'd hold our money up to the window and drink up every kopek we had. One day I would pay; the next day someone else would pay, and so on, in turn. These criminals were nice salt of the earth fellows. But there were lots of rats among the political convicts. They once organized a comrade's court and put me on trial for drinking with criminal convicts, which they charged was an offense."

I don't know what kind of sentence this comrade's court passed on Stalin. No one ever dared ask him. We just exchanged glances. Only afterward would we exchange remarks such as, "You see, even in his youth he was inclined to drink too much. It's probably inherited."

Nikita Khrushchev was no abstainer from alcohol; while Premier he occasionally got tipsy in public, including a publicized episode during a New York visit. The fact that he was not an intolerant teetotaler adds great credibility to his blatant assertion that Joseph Stalin had a drinking problem.

Stalin could be a most difficult host at those dinners. Khrushchev says that the guests had to "walk on eggs," lest they incur the wrath of the mass murderer.

He enjoyed ridiculing others, a common alcoholic trait. Once he told Khrushchev to dance the Gopak, the strenuous Ukrainian folk dance performed from a deep knee-bend position. The fat future Premier of the Soviet Union had no choice. He squatted on his haunches and kicked out his legs, which he says was not easy. But as he later told Mikoyan, "When Stalin says dance, a wise man dances." Some male underlings even danced arm-in-arm with each other when Stalin, for his amusement, would crank up a Victrola and order them to waltz with each other.

Medvedev reports several incidences of similarly sadistic behavior at social events. Pushing guests into the pond at his dacha was a favorite trick. Another was to ask a guest to make a toast and then slip a piece of cake on to his chair while he was standing. These victims got off easy compared with his personal secretary, Poskrebyshev. To welcome in one New Year, Stalin summoned Poskrebyshev to his table and told him to extend his hands. He then placed rolled up pieces of paper between Poskrebyshev's fingers and lit them, as if they were New Year's candles. Stalin roared with laughter as the "candles" burned all the way down and his loyal secretary writhed in pain.*

Khrushchev gives a sense of the pervasive threat that hung over these drinking sessions:

> These dinners were frightful. We would get home from them early in the morning, just in time for breakfast, and then we'd have to go to work. During the day I usually tried to take a nap in my lunch hour because there was always a risk that if you didn't take a nap and Stalin invited you to dinner, you might get sleepy at the table; and those who got sleepy at Stalin's table could come to a bad end.

This again suggests high tolerance. If Stalin drank as much as (or more than) his guests and they became sedated, while he did not, then something was wrong -- with *him*.

Another witness to Stalin's spectacular tolerance was Charles de Gaulle, who wrote at length in *Salvation* (Simon & Schuster, 1960) of an all night affair in wartime Moscow hosted by the Soviet dictator. Stalin served himself copiously from a bottle of Crimean wine that was frequently replaced by attentive waiters. He proposed toasts to de Gaulle, the United States, Roosevelt, Britain, Churchill, Bidault, Juin, and the French Army. "Thirty times Stalin stood up to drink to the health of those Russians present." At one point, de Gaulle retired to his quarters while second-rank French and Russian officials hammered out details of an agreement between the two governments. While de Gaulle slept, Stalin, who was then in his sixties, stayed on, passing through the salons to chat and drink with one man or another. Finally, at four o'clock in the morning, the negotiations were completed, and de Gaulle was awakened by an aide. He returned to the banquet hall. When he entered he was greeted by Stalin -- who immediately proposed another toast!

The strange hours kept by Stalin -- he usually didn't go to bed until four in the morning, or later -- have been attributed, by

---

*Another humiliation imposed on Poskrebyshev: Stalin forced him to sign the papers that sent his own wife to the gulag.

others, to his revolutionary activities. This silly idea says that while he was a revolutionary he had to elude the Czar's secret police, so he got in the habit of sleeping during the day and moving about at night. The young Stalin supposedly liked those hours so much he permanently adopted them for the rest of his life.

A likelier explanation is that Stalin kept the hours he did because his addiction wouldn't let him do otherwise. Alcoholics are not sedated by normal amounts of alcohol. Both the alcoholic Dorothy Parker and the alcoholic Tallulah Bankhead would frequently host drawn-out "dinner parties," which were nothing more than thinly-disguised binges arranged by the alcoholic hostesses. The alcoholic James Thurber was remembered by his close friend, Robert Coates, as a "noctambule," a person who reversed the normal working-sleeping habit. Alcoholics are notorious night people. Caught in the trap of a binge -- where one drink raises tension that can only be relieved by another drink -- the alcoholic is wide awake. If an alcoholic has consumed, say, a dozen drinks by midnight, his system is screaming for *more*. He is *up*. The nonalcoholic would be drowsy and ready for bed, but the alcoholic *cannot* sleep. Stalin stayed up drinking for the same reason alcoholics Parker, Bankhead, Thurber, and millions of obscure alcoholics did: he *had* to ingest a large volume of alcohol before he could call it a night.

Anyone who has survived the hell of a long night's drinking session with an alcoholic has to wonder how many death orders Stalin signed while drinking. Perhaps on many of those nights, with alcohol drenching the part of his brain that controls hostility, Stalin would issue arrest and execution orders to the secret police. This alcohol addict, after all, had no wife to terrorize, not after 1932, and he saw little of his children. With no family to abuse, he could vent his alcoholic rage on an entire nation. Instead of false accusations of spousal infidelity, this alcoholic could take his pick among millions of loyal citizens and hang all sorts of vicious false accusations on them, and then order them imprisoned or shot.

Stalin reflected typical alcoholic emotional shallowness. He didn't even attend his mother's funeral.

Perhaps nothing says more about Stalin's shallowness than his working on day-to-day matters with Mikoyan while Mikoyan's two sons were in penal camps, and with Molotov, Kalinin, and Poskre-byshev while their wives were incarcerated. All alcoholics have this maddening inability to *connect* with the effects of their abusiveness. They are actually puzzled when others react to their bad behavior. Joe McCarthy once ran into Dean Acheson on an elevator. He was astonished when Acheson -- the Secretary of State whom he had labeled a pro-Soviet tool -- did not respond to his cheery, "Hi, Dean!" Another time, McCarthy met a former friend, an ex-government employee whose career he had ruined with a false accusation. He walked up to this man and accused him of avoiding the McCarthys. "Jeanie [Mrs. McCarthy] was talking about you the other night. How come we never see you? What the hell are you trying to do -- *avoid* us?"

Although he was far more destructive than McCarthy, Stalin's continued official and social contacts with men whose families he had imprisoned has the same alcoholic "smell" about it.

Another clue pointing to Stalin's alcoholism is reported by Svetlana. She heard her father agreeing to the proposal that Alexei Kuznetsov be invited to a particular dinner. When Kuznetsov arrived he went to pay his respects to Stalin who told him, coldly, "I didn't summon you." Poor Kuznetsov was obliged to leave. We have no way of knowing, of course, but perhaps Stalin didn't remember inviting his guest because he had a blackout. Kuznetsov, by the way, was later arrested and shot.

According to Medvedev, Stalin often showed a marked neglect of affairs of state. Once, while presiding over a meeting of the Council of Ministers, which was about to review nothing less than the yearly plan for the entire Soviet economy, Stalin picked up the bundle of papers and said, "Here is the plan. Who's against it?" When all the ministers met his question with silence, the leader of the Soviet Union said, "Then we accept it. Let's go and see a movie." This is typical alcoholic contempt for rules.

He showed contempt for authority long before he commanded the entire Soviet Union. In 1918, during the Civil War, he ignored the chain of command and took charge of a military operation in Southern Russia. The operation turned out badly and cost many lives, the result, mainly, of his insubordination.

Although he was seldom photographed smoking anything other than a pipe, Stalin was described (by Roosevelt's colleague, Harry Hopkins) as a chain smoker of cigarettes. (He later quit smoking, which is unusual for alcoholics but not unknown.)

Like other alcoholics, Stalin seems to have aged quickly. In 1930, Eugene Lyons, an American journalist who had a rare interview with Stalin, reported that he "seemed to me older than his fifty-one years." Medvedev mentions one old acquaintance who thought Stalin had aged twenty years in eight.

Lord Beaverbrook, on a visit to Moscow, noticed Stalin abstaining from alcohol at an official dinner. While nonalcoholic drinkers *might* abstain from alcohol occasionally (for health or other reasons), going on the wagon is a confirming symptom.

Both Anthony Eden, the British Foreign Minister, and Anatole Baikaloff, a Russian exile, noted that Stalin had "small" eyes. Photographs taken in his later years show a typical alcoholic's puffiness below the eyes. In newsreels of wartime meetings with Churchill and Roosevelt (which the author recently saw on television), the swelling is so pronounced that Stalin's eyes look like mere slits.

Although he is reported to have thought he had charmed Stalin, Franklin Roosevelt got a hostile reaction from the Russian leader when he told him that Americans had given him the friendly nickname "Uncle Joe." Churchill said, "You could not be certain how he would take things." Alcoholics can be unreasonably resentful of real or imagined slights.

Alcoholics share a notoriously low tolerance for frustration. Stalin meets this requirement. Svetlana gives two examples in *Only One Year* (Harper & Row, 1969):

> I once saw how, having completely lost his temper, he grabbed the telephone with both hands and flung it against the wall; the telephone had been giving a busy signal and he had been in a hurry to put a call through. My nurse said that my father had once thrown a boiled chicken out of a casement window in our apartment in the Kremlin. This was... when... famine reigned in the country.

Alcoholics often exude charm, and Joseph Stalin was no exception. The Yugoslav author, Milovan Djilas, said he had "a rough humor, self-assured, but not entirely without finesse and depth." Medvedev said he could be "the most affable host." Joseph E. Davies, United States Ambassador to Moscow during World War II, commented, in his *Mission to Moscow* (Simon and Schuster,

1941), on Stalin's "sly humor." In a letter to his daughter, Davies painted the following portrait of the man.

> If you can picture a personality that is exactly the opposite to what the most rabid anti-Stalinist anywhere could conceive, then you might picture this man... A child would like to sit on his lap and a dog would sidle up to him.

There was another quality to Stalin, one which we can lose sight of in view of the horrible crimes he committed. It's a characteristic he shared with other alcoholics in this book, including Joseph McCarthy and Huey Long. There is no scientific name for the condition that I'm aware of, so a term like "nutty" will have to do. It was essentially nutty of McCarthy to accuse George C. Marshall of being a tool of the Russians, and to make a big deal about the Army's promotion of an obscure dentist. Long's accusations against James Farley were also weird. Late in *his* life, Stalin accused those two most perfect Stalinoids, Mikoyan and Molotov, of being foreign spies. When he died, plans were in the works to arrest the man who had been his personal secretary for fifteen years. (The infamous Doctor's Plot -- dozens of top Soviet physicians were accused of attempting to murder the Soviet leadership -- also fell apart when the tyrant died.) His elimination of the Old Bolsheviks in the late 1930's was also nutty. It was as if George Washington had accused the signers of the Declaration of Independence of being British agents, then rigged phony treason trials and hanged them all.

According to Khrushchev, Stalin never apologized ("Apologies were alien to his very nature"), a significant fact in view of Khrushchev's long association with the despot. There is no record of him showing any sign of regret or remorse for all the destruction.

Worse than the lack of remorse, Stalin ridiculed some victims after he had them killed. One of his favorite amusements was to have Pauker, his personal NKVD guard -- and a drinking companion -- put on a little comedy show. It was an impression of the last moments of Zinoviev, one of the first high-ranking leaders to be executed. Stalin had gone to Zinoviev's cell during the interrogation process and in a face-to-face meeting personally guaranteed that Zinoviev would not be executed if he signed a confession admitting he had arranged Kirov's murder -- which, we now know, was ordered by Stalin himself. Zinoviev accepted Stalin's offer and signed the false confession. After his trial, when Pauker and the other executioners came to his cell, Zinoviev suddenly realized he was going to be shot -- right there, in his cell. He collapsed, "yelling in a high-pitched voice a desperate appeal to Stalin to keep his word." This awful scene is what Pauker would reenact to amuse his master. As Stalin guffawed, Pauker would get down on the floor and writhe and scream in imitation of Zinoviev's final moments.*

Khrushchev relates a harmless fisherman's tale that Stalin used to tell, and then goes on, "It's hard to say what motivated him. He must have had some sort of inner urge [to lie]. This particular story was an entertaining lie and it didn't do [the nation] any harm, but he often lied in more serious conversations, too." Stalin lied for the same reason Lillian Hellman lied; he was an alcoholic.

The alcoholic's need to lie can encourage some to develop a talent for histrionics. As already noted, some have become rather famous actors. Both George F. Kennan and Milovan Djilas were impressed by Stalin's bent for theatrics.

Alcoholics can take sudden dislikes to people. They can be gratuitously antagonistic, especially when drinking. I've already mentioned the bizarre incident of Hemingway's encounter with Charles Boyer, Jackson Pollock's punching a complete stranger in a bar, and Thomas Wolfe attacking "a grey-faced man." Stalin showed this sign too. He often took sudden and irrational dislikes of people.

At a dinner following a wartime meeting with Churchill, Stalin suddenly accused British General Brooke of a lack of appreciation for the Red Army. This must have been a vivid incident, for Churchill remembered it and included it in his memoirs. Churchill makes it clear that there was no basis for Stalin's attack on Brooke. A similar incident was recalled by Svetlana. At another dinner party, Stalin turned on one of his high ranking underlings, Andrei Zhdanov, who had been silent during dinner, and said, "Look at him, sitting there like Christ, as if nothing were of any concern to

---

*Pauker's final payoff for his obscene mimicking of a doomed man's last moments: a bullet in the head, courtesy of Stalin, who had him executed on, naturally, trumped-up charges. There is no record of how he behaved at the end.

him! There -- Looking at me now as if he were Christ!" Zhdanov had had a number of heart attacks and as the mass murderer ridiculed him, Svetlana thought he might have another.

While he was supposedly an ideologically-pure Bolshevik, Stalin married his first wife at a *religious* ceremony! For sincere Marxists, this was unthinkable. He had never shown any affection for religion after he had left the seminary as a teenager, but there may have been an alcoholic reason for his church wedding. Alcoholics like to break rules, to thumb their noses at authority. What better way to defy the authority of atheistic Marxism than to participate in a church service?

Alcoholics do not like to assume reactive roles to others. Reaction is a subordinating activity, and alcoholics' unwillingness to play subordinate roles is one way their egomania manifests itself. A few years ago, I watched in horror as a high-ranking alcoholic executive overrode the objections of his technical advisors and ordered the release of his pet new product despite its failure to pass the company's quality control tests. Six months later, the product, which was defective, was recalled from customers at a cost of millions of dollars. I'm convinced the man's alcoholic ego pushed him into the decision. He had to prove that he -- not the facts or those technicians who laid them on his desk -- was in charge. (There's no question about this man's alcoholism; he has since died in a drunken fall.)

Stalin made a similar, but far more catastrophic, decision under strikingly similar circumstances. He did absolutely nothing about very precise information from several intelligence sources (including his alcoholic spy, Richard Sorge, in Tokyo*) warning him that Hitler planned to invade in June, 1941. His refusal to heed the many warnings (according to one researcher, they totalled eighty-four!) is a puzzlement to all of Stalin's biographers. But his refusal to listen isn't a mystery if one realizes that to accept the warnings at face value would have put Joseph Stalin in a subordinate position to others. He would have been subordinate to Hitler if he

---

*When Sorge was captured, the Japanese offered to swap him for several Japanese spies held by the Russians. Stalin refused, condemning his own spy to death. Like the unfortunate New York Police Lieutenant Becker, Sorge suffered a horrible execution. Hanged, he lived a full nineteen minutes, slowly strangling to death.

acted defensively to the invasion threat, and he would have been subordinate to those advisors who urged him to act. No healthy leader has a problem reacting intelligently to facts. But Stalin, like that alcoholic executive I once observed, was not healthy. He had an alcoholism-bloated ego. His ego led this alcoholic to reject facts, and the advice of his loyal underlings, and to "trust" Adolf Hitler.

Not only was Stalin capable of destroying, with the power of a state, millions of his fellow citizens, he also resorted to common alcoholic physical abuse of his wife. Litvinov saw him grab Nadya by the throat and shake her. He was reacting with rage to what she had just said, "You are a tormentor, that's what you are! You torment your own son... you torment your wife... you torment the whole Russian people!"

A drinking session with an alcoholic often ends in an ugly scene. In his description of his final meal with Stalin, the last before he died, Khrushchev says it ended with Stalin accompanying his guests to the door and playfully jabbing Khrushchev, who added, significantly, "Dinners at Stalin's didn't always end on such a pleasant note." Most nonalcoholics are almost always in a friendly mood after an evening of good food and drink. Unpleasant behavior while drinking is, according to Mann, one of "the most obvious signs [of alcoholism] to an informed onlooker... "

His behavior immediately before his death, as well as the reactions of his underlings to the circumstances, reek of alcoholism. "As usual," Khrushchev writes, "dinner lasted until around five or six o'clock in the morning. Stalin was pretty drunk after dinner and in very high spirits." Later, Khrushchev and other Soviet leaders were summoned back to his home. Once there, they were told that Stalin had been found by his servants sleeping on the floor. Khrushchev, Malenkov, Beria, and Bulganin decided "it wouldn't be suitable for us to make our presence known while Stalin was in such an unpresentable state." One author, H. Montgomery Hyde, points out that these men thought Stalin was sleeping off the effects of drinking, that the "unpresentable state" they feared was complete drunkenness. I agree with Hyde, and add that if Stalin was not a *habitual* heavy drinker, his sycophants would not have made that assumption. And if he was not capable of rage while drunk, why were they afraid to rouse him?

Throughout his life, until the night of his fatal stroke, Joseph Stalin displayed an extraordinary array of behavior patterns which can be explained only by his alcoholism. Perhaps the most convincing evidence is that of a bender lasting several days, at a time and under circumstances that make it extremely difficult for any informed person to believe that Stalin was a not an alcoholic.

In June 1941, thanks to Stalin's egotistical refusal to heed the many warnings he had received, Hitler's invading armies easily punched through the Red Army's single line of defense. In spite of the compelling logic of defending against a highly mobile attacking force with a defense in depth, Stalin ordered the Red Army to defend every inch of Soviet territory. He had, against the recommendations of his generals (those he hadn't killed), dismantled fortified areas located along the former frontier, the one that existed prior to the Soviet-German annexation of Poland. With this natural secondary defense line abandoned, with most of his troops spread out on the front line, and with the Red Army still suffering from his massacre of its officer corps, the Soviet forces incurred severe defeats. How Stalin reacted to this disaster is most important.

At this time of peril, the leader of the Soviet Union disappeared. Medvedev reports that "No one saw him. He did not appear at the Kremlin. No one heard his voice on the telephone." Having established the most centralized government in modern history, his absence threatened to paralyze the nation. No one else had the power to issue important orders, and his subordinates were too terrified to act. But the records show that he didn't sign a single document for a week and a half, from June 24 to July 2. Stalin's desertion of his post was, according to Medvedev, "an important reason" for the early success of the Nazi invaders.

The explanation for this strange disappearance? Stalin went on a bender. Medvedev writes that "Khrushchev once said Stalin simply drank, and that sounds... like the truth."

So Stalin, the so-called Man of Steel, took to the bottle when faced with a force he could not control -- Hitler's invading hordes. He later regained enough control over his behavior to take command of his government, and his people eventually defeated Hitler, but the fact of his bender stands. Although a fool might say that any national leader faced with the sudden invasion by Hitler's legions would feel like getting drunk, nothing could be further from the truth. The normal response would be to flee or to fight. Only someone with a well-established addiction to alcohol would go on a bender.

Stalin delivered a radio speech to his nation on July 3, 1941. He spoke in a "dull colorless voice... seemed to be ailing and at the end of his strength." And when he paused to drink from a glass of water, observers noticed that his hands were trembling. Alcoholism causes tremors of the hands.

This was not Stalin's only bender. According to Hyde, he was in the habit of suddenly disappearing for days -- even before the war. He would tell his subordinates not to disturb him, then spend several days at his dacha. It is not unusual for some alcoholics to develop periodicity in their benders. These "missing days," including the documented one when Hitler attacked, were probably Stalin's lost weekends.

Just before Stalin's wife, Nadya, committed suicide, she called Svetlana, who was 9 years old at the time, to her room:

> The last time I saw her was on the eve of her death, or at least no more than a day or two before. She called me to her room... and spent a long time talking about what I ought to be like and how I ought to behave. *"Don't touch alcohol!"* she said. *"Never drink wine!"* [Emphasis added.]

Adam B. Ulam concludes in his biography of Stalin that Nadya attributed Stalin's terrible temper to "a hereditary predisposition to alcoholism."*

Stalin's relationships with others bear a strong resemblance to that of identified alcoholics who have been subjects of comprehensive biographies. The strange coincidence of lists of rejected friends in the biographies of Hemingway, Fitzgerald, Sinclair Lewis, and others finds its roaring echo in the monstrous destructiveness of Stalin. And yet, with Stalin, unlike Fitzgerald and Lewis (or his son Vasily), there seems not to have been a final collapse into late-

---

*Professor Ulam relegates Nadya's opinion to a footnote, clearly showing that he doesn't think much of her idea.

stage alcoholism. How can this be? How can an alcoholic live to be 73 years old and die of something else? The explanation lies in the relative efficacy of alcoholic egomania as a defense mechanism. Although alcoholics are all victims of the same disease, they do not all react the same way to their addiction. Some, those who apparently have little ego-inflation capability -- the untalented, the insecure, the economically disadvantaged -- succumb very quickly to the demands of the addiction. They adopt the *self*-destructive patterns of the late-stage alcoholic at an early age; some make it to Skid Row while in their twenties. Stalin's son seems to have been this type. However, most alcoholics have some potential for egocentric accomplishments, to succeed in some field, and to manipulate and malign others. These people do *not* move to Skid Row (literally or figuratively), at least, not as long as they hold on to power. They seem able to postpone the onset of the late stage of alcoholism until they are in their fifties or even later.

Ego-tripping works. It delays progression of the disease. Although in the eyes of his close ally, Roy Cohn, Joe McCarthy "became" an alcoholic after his censure by the Senate, what Cohn really observed was McCarthy's collapse into the late-stage of a disease that got underway many years earlier. Humiliated by the Senate and deprived of the egocentric defense mechanism, his addiction asserted itself with ferocity. The actress Laurette Taylor, on the other hand, was able to push back the years and to actually drink without apparent loss of control upon achieving success and, presumably, great ego satisfaction, from her highly acclaimed, late-life success in *The Glass Menagerie*.

Phenomena that support this idea have been noted in alcoholism literature. Many authorities say that progression of drinking often accelerates following ego-threatening events. Those same events may even threaten to drive long-sober alcoholics back to drink. AA's are aware of this and seek support of fellow members when they experience shattering events such as the loss of a job, death of a loved one or even a geographic relocation.

A vivid example of an alcoholic slowing down progression during a period of high achievement has been reported in *Alcoholism: A Family Illness* (Christopher D. Smithers Foundation, 1969). George Grant (a pseudonym) made *two* dramatic changes in his drinking patterns. A rich man's son, Grant drank heavily until he became an Army officer during World War II; he controlled his drinking out of fear of a court martial. Once discharged from the Army, he went back to alcoholic drinking. Then his father died, and George took the helm of the company his father had founded. He changed once again, this time to a periodic alcoholic -- he only drank during widely spaced benders.

If ego-destructive events (McCarthy's censure) speed up progression of the disease, and if ego-inflating events (Taylor's hit play, George Grant's takeover of a corporation) slow it down, should it surprise us that another alcoholic -- Joseph Stalin -- whose supply of ego-inflating events was virtually unlimited, would not, even at age 73, succumb to late-stage alcoholism? But what happened to Stalin's ability to stave off uncontrollable benders when his ego was mugged by Hitler's powerful forces? He went on a bender!* What would have happened to Stalin if, like McCarthy, he had permanently lost the power to destroy? We'll never know, of course, for the old fraud pulled himself together in 1941 and held omnipotent power until the very end.

Stalin's alcoholism-induced ego-tripping accounts for what Medvedev calls his "great control." It also explains Conquest's perceptive observation that Stalin didn't pounce on his "enemies" like Hitler, but preferred to pick them off slowly -- almost one at a time. Alcoholism and its demands for ego-inflation persist unless, and until, the alcoholic accepts recovery which always includes ego deflation. Without recovery, the alcoholic responds to the pressure of addiction by ego-inflating behavior, including abusiveness. And in the continuum in which alcoholism exists, prior debasements cannot satisfy today's ego demands.

The alcoholic ego is a carnivore. It demands fresh meat. The married alcoholic will use his spouse as a verbal, and sometimes actual, punching bag. But last week's harangue or fight is not going to help the alcoholic the next time the addiction humiliates his ego. So he will start another session of accusation, and later still another, and another, until a lifetime is devoured by outbursts of verbal abuse and violence. But in Stalin's case, since he had the power not only to level false accusations at his subordinates, but to obliterate them, the elimination of, for example, Zinoviev, could

---

*As did Pakistan's President Yahya Kahn when his army was soundly defeated by India.

furnish only temporary relief to the psychic pain created by his alcoholism. Eventually, in spite of the additional satisfaction gained from Pauker's vile imitation of Zinoviev's last moments, new victims were needed. And with totalitarian power at his command, new victims were just a telephone call away. His efficient death machine served Stalin's ego with great numbers of victims over a long period of time.

The reason Stalin personally signed so many execution lists, why he insisted on drawn-out interrogations, why he was destroying loyal Russians throughout the war, and why he was planning, just prior to his death, a new blood bath, was that he *couldn't* stop. Trapped in addiction, his desperate ego-needs didn't go away -- so the deaths never stopped. Stalin was pathologically addicted to the *process* of destruction. Any sudden massacre of all his "enemies," any "Night of the Long Knives," would have left him with no future victims, a prospect as unappealing to an alcoholic as that of drinking up all the booze. The alcoholic drinks to anesthetize himself, and he worries about running out of booze. So he conceals liquor. Stalin subconsciously knew he needed more murders in his future, so he always had victims for the next blood binge stashed away in devilishly clever hiding places: in the upper levels of the bureaucracy, in the Politburo and in his entourage.

Another factor accounting for the slow progression of Stalin's alcoholism: success is a trap. Executive alcoholics cannot drink as much as their addiction demands. Painting and writing are solitary occupations and alcoholics in those fields can maintain a facade of success -- even while indulging in lost weekends. But the alcoholic bank president or senior government official cannot go on week-long benders, or even two-day benders, without risking his job. In Stalin's case, his *life* was at risk.

Once Stalin began his terrorism against Soviet officials, it's not hard to imagine what would have happened if he had many unconcealed, unpredictable, days-long benders such as the one he had when Hitler struck. If Stalin slid into late-stage alcoholism and was constantly inebriated -- incapable of functioning -- Beria, Khrushchev, or others in the Politburo could have seized power. And a successful anti-Stalin coup would --who can doubt it? -- have led to his execution, especially after 1938. Stalin had far more than the typical alcoholic's motivation to fight his addiction. So he limited his drinking to all-night binges and, apparently, to occasional, planned benders at his dacha.

Other alcoholics have avoided the onset of late-stage alcoholism. As the AMA notes in its manual:

> The concept that alcoholics *always* show progressive deterioration as a direct result of drinking really is not valid, and it therefore is not a *requirement* of the definition of alcoholism.

Alcoholism literature is replete with warnings that alcoholics do not live as long as nonalcoholics, but Joseph Stalin didn't die until he was 73. How do I reconcile his age with his disease?

Although alcoholics, *on average*, do indeed die earlier than nonalcoholics, other well-known active alcoholics have survived to ripe old age. In *Famous Women and Alcohol*, Robe expresses her opinion that the following women, all of whom died at either the same age as Stalin, or later, were active alcoholics to the end: Joan Crawford, who died at age 73; Lillian Hellman, 79; Ethel Merman, 76; Dorothy Parker, 74; Louella O. Parsons, 91; and the Duchess of Windsor, 90. Edmund Wilson, the alcoholic writer and critic, lived, and drank, to 79. Stalin's relatively long life is no basis for rejecting the diagnosis of alcoholism.

It is pointless to look for Stalin-like behavior patterns in despotic rulers who were not alcoholics. Of course, there have been many nonalcoholic tyrants, but the alcoholic ruler distinguishes himself from the "run of the mill" despot. I'll mention three characteristics. One is the abuse of close associates and family members, another is the tendency to falsely accuse, and the third, of course, is addictive drinking. Tito and Franco were harsh in their suppression of perceived threats to their power, but neither abused relatives, made up lies about others, or drank addictively.

In order to find Stalinistic behavior in political leaders, we must look to Alexander the Great and Henry VIII, to the Czars Ivan and Peter, and even to Henry Ford II, Huey Long, and Charles Dederich. All of these alcoholics, like Stalin, delighted in humiliating those already at their feet. We can compare him also with Joseph McCarthy, Eugene O'Neill, and Thomas Wolfe, and to any other alcoholic who maligned the innocent. We can also see Stalin in

Ted Bundy, John Gacy, and Jeffrey Dahmer, for he too was a serial killer who debased his victims before and after death. And we can see Stalin in Burgess and Maclean, in Philby, Blunt, and in all other alcoholic traitors, for Stalin betrayed everyone and everything -- especially the very people he ruled.

Stalinistic behavior appears whenever alcoholics get power. The only limits on their perversion of that power are those forced on them by their environment: by other people, and by the situation in which they exist. In all of human history, only one alcoholic had the power to slaughter millions of his innocent countrymen. And that's exactly what Joseph Stalin, an alcoholic, did.

SELECTED BIBLIOGRAPHY

Alexander, Doris. *The Tempering of Eugene O'Neill.* New York: Harcourt Brace & World, 1962.

Alexander, Shana. *Nutcracker: Money, Madness, Murder: A Family Album.* New York: Dell Publishing Co., Inc., 1985.

Alliluyeva, Svetlana. *Twenty Letters to a Friend.* New York: Harper & Row, 1967.

------------------------ *Only One Year.* New York: Harper & Row, 1969.

Altman, Jack and Ziporyn, Marvin, M.D. *Born to Raise Hell: The Untold Story of Richard Speck.* New York: Grove Press, 1967.

Alvarez, A. *The Savage God: A Study.* New York: Random House, 1971.

American Medical Association. *Manual on Alcoholism.* Chicago: American Medical Association, 1968.

Anonymous. *Alcoholics Anonymous.* New York: Alcoholics Anonymous Publishing Company, 1955.

------------ *"A Different First Drink." A.A. Grapevine,* January, 1970.

------------ *Alcoholism: A Family Illness.* The Christopher D. Smithers Foundation, New York, 1969.

------------ *Living With An Alcoholic.* Al-Anon Family Group Headquarters, 1960.

Baker, Carlos. *Ernest Hemingway: A Life Story.* New York: Charles Scribner's Sons, 1969.

Bates, Richard C., M.D. "The Diagnosis of Alcoholism." *Applied Therapeutics,* June, 1965.

Beck, Aaron T., M.D., Weissman, Arlene, M.A. and Kovacs, Maria, PhD. "Alcoholism, Hopelessness and Suicidal Behavior." *Quarterly Journal of Studies on Alcohol,* Vol. 37, No.1, 1976.

Bennetts, Leslie. "A Cooler George C. Scott Stays Busy." *The New York Times,* October 31, 1985.

Berg, A. Scott. *Max Perkins: Editor of Genius*. New York: E.P. Dutton, 1978.

Bernstein, Burton. *Thurber*. New York: Dodd, Mead, 1975.

Bissell, LeClair, M.D. and Haberman, Paul W. *Alcoholism in the Professions*. New York: Oxford University Press, 1984.

Bishop, Jim. *The Day Lincoln Was Shot*. New York: Harper & Brothers, 1955.

Blair, Clay, Jr. *The Strange Case of James Earl Ray*. New York: Bantam Books, 1969.

Blane, Howard T., M.D. *The Personality of the Alcoholic: Guises of Dependency*. New York: Harper & Row, 1968.

Blane, H.T., M.D., Overton, W. F., Jr., M.D., Chafetz, M. E., M.D. "Social Factors in the Diagnosis of Alcoholism." *Quarterly Journal of Studies on Alcohol*, December, 1963.

Block, Marvin A., M.D. *Alcoholism, Its Facets and Phases*. New York: John Day, 1965.

------------------------------- *Alcoholism is a Disease*. New York: The National Council on Alcoholism, 1968.

Blotner, Joseph. *Faulkner, A Biography*. New York: Random House, 1974.

Blum, Howard. *I Pledge Allegiance: The True Story of the Walkers: An American Spy Family*. New York: Simon and Schuster, 1987.

Bortoli, George. *The Death of Stalin*. New York: Praeger Publishers, 1975.

Boyle, Andrew. *The Fourth Man*. New York: The Dial Press, 1979.

Bradshaw, Jon. *Dreams That Money Can Buy*. New York: William Morrow & Company, 1985.

Bruce, Marie Louise. *Anne Boleyn*. New York: Coward, McCann & Geohegan, Inc., 1972.

Brussel, J.A., M.D., *Casebook of A Crime Psychiatrist*. New York: Bernard Geis Associates, 1968.

Burk, John N. *The Life and Works of Beethoven*. New York: Random House, 1943.

Cahill, Tim. *Buried Dreams: Inside the Mind of a Serial Killer*. New York: Bantam Books, 1986.

Capote, Truman. *In Cold Blood*. New York: Random House, 1968.

Cartwright, Frederick F. *Disease and History*. New York: Thomas Y. Crowell Co., 1972.

Catanzaro, Ronald J., ed. *Alcoholism: The Total Treatment Approach*. Springfield: Charles C. Thomas, 1968.

Clarke, Gerald. *Capote: A Biography.* New York: Ballantine Books, 1989.

Chavetz, Morris E., M.D. *Alcoholism and Sobriety.* New York: Oxford University Press, 1962.

Churchill, Winston. *Closing the Ring.* Boston: Houghton Mifflin, 1951.

Coleman, Jonathan. *At Mother's Request.* New York: Pocket Books, 1985.

Conquest, Robert. *The Great Terror: Stalin's Purge of the Thirties.* New York: The Macmillan Company, 1968.

------------------------ *Stalin and the Kirov Murder.* New York: Oxford University Press, 1989.

------------------------ *The Great Terror: A Reassessment.* New York: Oxford University Press, 1990.

------------------------ *Stalin: Breaker of Nations.* New York: Penguin Books, 1991.

Conway, Daniel Moncune. *The Life of Thomas Paine.* New York: G.P. Putnam's Sons, 1908.

Cook, Fred J. *The Nightmare Decade: The Life and Times of Senator Joe McCarthy.* New York: Random House, 1971.

Cookridge, E.H. *The Many Sides of George Blake, Esq.: The Complete Dossier.* Princeton: Brandon/Systems Press, Inc., 1970.

Coolidge, Olivia. *Tom Paine, Revolutionary.* New York: Charles Scribner's Sons, 1969.

Courtney, Marguerite. *Laurette.* New York: Atheneum House, 1968.

Crawford, Christina. *Mommie Dearest.* New York: William Morrow and Company, Inc., 1978.

Criteria Committee, National Council on Alcoholism. "Criteria for the Diagnosis of Alcoholism." *American Journal of Psychiatry,* August, 1972.

Cutter, Henry S.G., Ph.D., *et al.* "Feeling No Pain." *Quarterly Journal of Studies on Alcohol,* March 1976.

Dardis, Tom. *The Thirsty Muse: Alcohol And The American Writer.* New York: Ticknor and Fields, 1989,

Davie, Michael. *The Diaries of Evelyn Waugh.* Boston: Little Brown and Company, 1977.

Davies, Joseph E. *Mission To Moscow.* New York: Simon and Schuster, 1941.

Day, Donald and Ullom, Harry Herbert, eds. *The Autobiography of Sam Houston.* Norman: University of Oklahoma Press, 1954.

Day, Douglas. *Malcolm Lowry*. New York: Oxford University Press, 1975.

De Leon, George. "The Baldness Experiment." *Psychology Today*, October, 1977.

Deedy, John. "Tom Paine Would Drink to New Rochelle." *The New York Times*, April 22, 1973.

De Gaulle, Charles. *Salvation: 1944-1946*. New York: Simon & Schuster, 1960.

Djilas, Milovan. *Conversations With Stalin*. New York: Harcourt, Brace & World, Inc., 1962.

Dorland's Illustrated Medical Dictionary, 24th Edition. Philadelphia: W.B. Saunders Company, 1973.

Elder, Donald. *Ring Lardner*. Garden City: Doubleday, 1956.

Estes, N.J., R.N., M.S., and Heinemann, M.E., R.N., M.A., F.A.A.N., eds. *Alcoholism: Development, Consequences and Interventions*. St. Louis: The C.V. Mosby Company, 1986.

Faulkner, John. *My Brother Bill*. New York: Trident Press, 1963.

Fink, Arthur E. *Causes of Crime: Biological Theories in the United States*. New York: A.S. Barnes & Company, Inc., 1938.

Fitzgibbon, Constantine. *The Life of Dylan Thomas*. Boston: Atlantic, Little, Brown, 1965.

FitzGerald, Kathleen Whalen, Ph.D. *Alcoholism: The Genetic Inheritance*. New York: Doubleday, 1988.

Ford, John C. *Man Takes a Drink*. New York: P.J. Kennedy & Sons, 1955.

Fox, Ruth, M.D. and Lyon, P. *Alcoholism: Its Scope, Cause and Treatment*. New York: Random House, 1955.

Fox, Ruth, M.D. " A Multi-disciplinary Approach to the Treatment of Alcoholism." *American Journal of Psychiatry*, January, 1967.

---------------------- "The Effects of Alcoholism on Children." *Proceedings of the Vth International Congress on Psychotherapy*, New York: Karger, 1963.

Fox, Ruth, M.D., ed. *Alcoholism: Behavioral Research, Therapeutic Approaches*. New York: Springer Publishing Company, 1967.

Frank, Gerold. *The Boston Strangler*. New York: The New American Library, 1966.

Freemantle, Brian. *CIA: The 'Honourable' Company*. London: Michael Joseph/Rainbird, 1983.

Freidel, Frank. "Eleanor and Franklin." *The New York Times*, October 17, 1971.

Friedman, B.H. *Jackson Pollock: Energy Made Visible*. New York: McGraw Hill Book Company, 1972.

Furnas, J.C. *The Late Demon Rum*. London: W.H. Allen, 1965.

Gardner, Virginia. *Friendship and Love: The Life of Louise Bryant*. New York: Horizon Press, 1982.

Gehlen, Reinhard. *The Service: The Memoirs of General Reinhard Gehlen*. New York: World Publishing, 1972.

Gelb, Arthur and Gelb, Barbara. *O'Neill*. New York: Harper & Brothers, 1960.

Gentry, Curt. *Frame-Up: The Incredible Case of Tom Mooney and Warren Billings*. New York: W.W. Norton & Company, Inc., 1967.

Gersher, Martin. *Destroy or Die*. New Rochelle: Arlington House, 1971.

Gitlow, Stanley E., M.D. "A Pharmacological Approach to Alcoholism." *A.A. Grapevine*, October, 1968.

Glueck, Sheldon and Glueck, Eleanor. *Family, Environment and Delinquency*. Boston: Houghton, Mifflin Co., 1962.

Goodwin, Donald W., M.D. "The Alcoholism of F.Scott Fitzgerald" *Journal of the American Medical Association*, April 6, 1970.

--------------------------- *Is Alcoholism Hereditary?* New York: Oxford University Press, 1976.

-------------------------------- *Alcohol And The Writer*. Kansas City: Andrews and McMeel, 1988.

Graham, Steven. *Ivan the Terrible*. New Haven: Yale University Press, 1933.

----------------------- *Peter the Great*. New York: Simon and Schuster, 1929.

Green, Peter. Letter to the Editor. *The New York Times Book Review*, November 29, 1970.

Griffith, Robert. *The Politics of Fear, Second Edition*. Amherst: The University of Massachusetts Press, 1987.

Hackett, Francis. *Henry the VIII*. New York: Liveright, 1957.

Hall, Clifton R. *Andrew Johnson, Military Governor of Tennessee*. Princeton: Princeton University Press, 1916.

Hampton, William J. Review of *Iacocca: An Autobiography*. *Business Week*, November 5, 1984.

Hawthorne, Nathaniel. *Life of Franklin Pierce*. Boston: Ticknor, Reed and Fields, 1852.

Hearst, Patricia Campbell with Alvin Moscow. *Every Secret Thing*. Garden City: Doubleday & Company, Inc., 1982.

Hemingway, Leicester. *My Brother, Ernest Hemingway*. New York: World Publishing Company, 1962.

Hesseltine, William B. *Ulysses S. Grant, Politician*. New York: Frederick Unger Publishing Co., 1957.

Hingley, Ronald. *Joseph Stalin: Man and Legend*. London: Hutchinson of London, 1974.

Hoffman, Daniel. *Poe Poe Poe Poe Poe Poe Poe*. Garden City: Doubleday & Company, Inc., 1973.

Horowitz, David. "Black Murder Inc." *Heterodoxy*, Vol.I, No. 10, March, 1993.

Hotchner, A.E. *Papa Hemingway*. New York: Random House, 1966.

Huie, William Bradford. *He Slew the Dreamer*. New York: Delacorte Press, 1970.

Hyde, H. Montgomery. *Stalin: The History of a Dictator*. New York: Farrar, Straus & Giroux, 1971.

Iacocca, Lee with Novak, William. *Iacocca: An Autobiography*. New York: Bantam Books, 1984.

Ireland, W.M., M.D. *The Blot Upon the Brain, Studies in History and Psychology*. London: 1893.

Israel, Lee. *Miss Tallulah Bankhead*. New York: G.P. Putnam's Sons, 1972.

-------------------- *Kilgallen*. New York: Delacorte Press, 1979.

Jackson, Joan. "The Adjustment of the Family to the Crisis of Alcoholism." *Quarterly Journal of Studies on Alcohol*, June, 1954.

Jellinek, E.M., D.Sc. *The Disease Concept of Alcoholism*. New Haven: Hill House Press, 1960.

Kamm, Henry. "Swiss Are Shaken by Spy Case Involving General and Wife." *The New York Times*, November 25, 1976.

Katkov, George. *The Trial of Bukharin*. New York: Stein and Day, 1969.

Keats, John. *You Might As Well Live: The Life and Times of Dorothy Parker*. New York: Simon and Schuster, 1970.

Kellerman, Joseph. *Alcoholism: A Merry-Go-Round Named Denial*. Charleston Council on Alcoholism, 1969.

Kent, Patricia. *An American Woman and Alcohol*. New York: Holt, Rinehart and Winston, 1967.

Kessel, Neil and Walton, Henry. *Alcoholism*. London: Penguin Books, Inc., 1965.

Kessler, Ronald. *Moscow Station: How The KGB Penetrated the*

American Embassy. New York: Charles Scribner's Sons, 1989.
----------------------- *The Spy in the Russian Club: How Glenn Souther Stole America's Nuclear War Plans and Escaped to Moscow.* New York: Charles Scribner's Sons, 1990.

Kilduff, Marshall, and Javers, Ron. *The Suicide Cult: The Inside Story of the People's Temple Sect and the Massacre in Guyana.* New York: Bantam Books, 1978.

Knightley, Phillip. *The Master Spy: The Story of Kim Philby.* New York: Alfred A. Knopf, 1989.

Khrushchev, Nikita. *Khrushchev Remembers.* Boston: Little, Brown and Company, 1970.

Koslow, Jules. *Ivan the Terrible.* New York: Hill & Wang, 1961.

Kurtz, Ernest. *A.A.: The Story.* San Francisco: Harper & Row, 1979.

Landis, Mark. *Joseph McCarthy: The Politics of Chaos.* Selingrove: Susquehanna University Press, 1987.

Langer, Walter C. *The Mind of Adolf Hitler: The Secret Wartime Report.* New York: Basic Books Inc., 1972.

Lasky, Victor. *Never Complain, Never Explain: The Story of Henry Ford II.* New York: Richard Marek Publishers, 1981.

Latham, Aaron. *Crazy Sundays: F. Scott Fitzgerald in Hollywood.* New York: The Viking Press, 1971.

L'Etang, Hugh. *The Pathology of Leadership.* New York: Hawthorn Books, Inc., 1970.

Levant, Oscar. *Memoirs of an Amnesiac.* New York: G.P. Putnam's Sons, 1965.

Levine, Isaac Don. *Stalin's Great Secret.* New York: Coward McCann, 1956.

Leyton, Elliot. *Compulsive Killers: The Story of Modern Multiple Murder.* New York: New York University Press, 1986.

Lincoln, Victoria. *A Private Disgrace.* New York: G.P. Putnam's Sons, 1967.

Lindsey, Robert. *The Falcon and the Snowman.* New York: Pocket Books, 1979.

Logan, Andy. *Against the Evidence: The Becker-Rosenthal Affair.* New York: The McCall Publishing Company, 1970.

Lomask, Milton. *Andrew Johnson: President on Trial.* New York: Farrar, Straus & Giroux, 1960.

Lukas, J. Anthony. "One Too Many for the Muse." *The New York Times Book Review,* December 1, 1985.

Ludwig, Arnold M., M.D. *Understanding the Alcoholic's Mind*. New York: Oxford University Press, 1988.

Ludwig, Emil. *Stalin*. New York: G.P. Putnam's Sons, 1942.

Lustgarten, Edgar. *Verdict in Dispute*. New York: Charles Scribner's Sons, 1950.

Maas, Peter. *Manhunt: The Incredible Story of a C.I.A. Agent Turned Terrorist*. New York: Random House, 1987.

MacNalty, Arthur. *Henry VIII, A Difficult Patient*. London: Christopher Johnson, 1952.

MacDonald, John M. M.D. *The Murderer and His Victim* (Second Edition). Springfield: Charles C. Thomas, 1986.

Mangold, Tom. *Cold Warrior: James Jesus Angleton: The CIA's Master Spy Hunter*. New York: Simon & Schuster, 1991.

Mann, Marty. *Marty Mann's New Primer on Alcoholism*. New York: Holt, Rinehart and Winston, 1958.

Marek, George R. *Beethoven*. New York: Funk & Wagnalls, 1969.

Mark, Vernon H., M.D. and Ervin, Frank R., M.D. *Violence and the Brain*. New York: Harper & Row, 1970.

Marshall-Corwall, James. *Grant As Military Commander*. New York: Van Nostrand Reinhold Company, 1970.

Massie, Robert K. *Peter the Great: His Life and World*. New York: Alfred A. Knopf, 1986.

Mc Ginniss, Joe. *Heroes*. New York: Viking, 1976.

Medvedev, Roy A. *Let History Judge: The Origins and Consequences of Stalinism*. New York: Alfred A. Knopf, 1971.

-------------------------- *On Stalin and Stalinism*. Oxford: Oxford University Press, 1979.

-------------------------- *Let History Judge: The Origins and Consequences of Stalinism*. (Revised and expanded edition.) New York: Columbia University Press, 1989.

Merrill, Boynton, Jr. *Jefferson's Nephews*. Princeton: Princeton University Press, 1976.

Methvin, Eugene H. "The Unquiet Ghosts of Stalin's Victims." *National Review*, September 1, 1989.

Michaud, Stephen G. and Aynesworth, Hugh. *The Only Living Witness: A True Account of Homicidal Insanity*. New York: Simon & Schuster, 1983.

Milford, Nancy. *Zelda: A Biography*. New York: Harper & Row, 1970.

Mitchell, Dave, Mitchell, Cathy, and Ofshe, Richard. *The Light On*

Synanon. New York: Seaview Books, 1980.

Montague, Richard. *Oceans, Poles and Airmen*. New York: Random House, 1971.

Newell, Nancy. "Alcoholism and the Father Image." *Quarterly Journal of Studies on Alcohol*, September, 1950.

Newton, Verne W. *The Cambridge Spies: The Untold Story of Maclean, Philby, and Burgess in America*. Lanham: Madison Books, 1991.

The New York Times. "Anderson, Ex-Treasury Secretary, Faces Sentencing in Bank Fraud Case." June 16, 1987.

-------------------------- Article on Manson. December 7, 1969.

-------------------------- "Notes on People." (Edwin E. Aldrin, Jr.) August 3, 1976.

-------------------------- Article on harm by alcoholic parents. August 20, 1975.

-------------------------- "Inmate Survey Finds Heavy Alcohol Use By Many Criminals." January 31, 1983.

-------------------------- "High Tech Boom is Said to Turn Some Into Spies." October 23, 1983.

-------------------------- Article on Montague's claim of Byrd's deceit. December 19, 1971.

-------------------------- "Admiral Byrd's Son Found Dead." October 9, 1988.

-------------------------- Various stories about Jeffrey L. Dahmer. July 26, 1991, *et seq*.

Nichols, Beverley. *Father Figure: An Uncensored Autobiography*. New York: Simon and Schuster, 1972.

Nichols, Roy Franklin. *Franklin Pierce*. Philadelphia: University of Pennsylvania Press, 1959.

Norris, Joel. *Serial Killers: The Growing Menace*. New York: Doubleday, 1988.

Olsen, Jack. *The Man With The Candy: The Story of The Houston Mass Murders*. New York: Simon and Schuster, 1974.

Orlov, Alexander. *The Secret History of Stalin's Crimes*. New York: Random House, 1953.

Pace, Eric. "Robert B. Anderson, Ex-Treasury Chief, Dies at 79." *The New York Times*, August 16, 1989.

Page, Bruce: Leitch, David, Knightley, Phillip. *The Philby Conspiracy*. New York: Doubleday & Company, Inc., 1968.

Payne, Robert. *The Life and Death of Adolf Hitler*. New York:

Praeger Publishers, 1973.

Penrose, Barrie and Freeman, Simon. *Conspiracy of Silence: The Secret Life of Anthony Blunt*. New York: Farrar, Straus & Giroux, 1987.

Perry, Hamilton Darby. *Libby Holman: Body and Soul*. Boston: Little, Brown and Company, 1983.

Pincher, Chapman. *Traitors*. New York: Viking Penguin Inc., 1987.

Pittman, David, ed. *Alcoholism: An Inter-Disciplinary Approach*. New York: Harper & Row, 1959.

Pollack, Jack Harrison. *Dr. Sam, An American Tragedy*. New York: Henry Regnery Company, 1972.

Prang, Gordon W., Goldstein, Donald M., Dillon, Katherine V. *Target Tokyo: The Story of the Sorge Spy Ring*. New York: McGraw-Hill Book Company, 1984.

Pritchett, V.S. Review of *James Thurber* by Burton Burnstein (Dodd, Mead, 1975). *The New Yorker*, June 23, 1975.

Rada, R.T. "Alcoholism and Child Molesters." *Annals of the New York Academy of Science*, 1976.

Rancour-Laferriere, Daniel. *The Mind of Stalin: A Psychoanalytic Study*. Ann Arbor: Ardis Publishers, 1988.

Ressler, Robert K., Burgess, Ann W., Douglas, John E. *Sexual Homicide: Patterns and Motives*. Lexington: Lexington Books, 1988.

Rice, Julius. *Ups and Downs: Drugging and Doping*. New York: The Macmillan Company, 1972.

Ridley, Jasper. *Henry VIII*. New York: Viking Penguin Inc., 1985.

Roach, Mary K. Ph.D., McIsaac, William M., M.D., Ph.D., D.Sc., Creaven, Patrick J., M.D., Ph.D., eds. *Biological Aspects of Alcohol*. Austin: University of Texas, 1971.

Robe, Lucy Barry. *Co-starring Famous Women and Alcohol*. Minneapolis: CompCare Publications, 1986.

Roberts, Steven V. "Charles Manson, Nomadic Guru, Flirted With Crime in a Turbulent Childhood." *The New York Times*, December 7, 1969.

Robertson, Nan. *Getting Better: Inside Alcoholics Anonymous*. New York: William Morrow and Company, 1988.

Roscoe, Theodore. *The Web of Conspiracy*. Englewood Cliffs: Prentice-Hall, 1956.

Roth, Lillian. *I'll Cry Tomorrow*. New York: Frederick Fell, Inc., 1954.

Rouse, A.L. "The Tudor Stalin." Review of *Henry VIII* by Jasper Ridley (Constable, 1984). *Sunday Times*(London), November 4, 1984.

Rovere, Richard H. *Senator Joe McCarthy.* London: Methuen & Co., Ltd., 1960.

Rudorff, Raymond. *Studies in Ferocity: A Book of Human Monsters.* New York: The Citadel Press, 1969.

Ruggles, Eleanor. *Prince of Players: Edwin Booth.* New York: W.W. Norton & Co., 1953.

Rule, Ann. *The Stranger Beside Me.* New York: W.W. Norton & Company, 1980.

Salisbury, Harrison E. Review of *Let History Judge* by Roy A. Medvedev. *The New York Times Book Review*, December 26, 1971.

------------------------- Review of *Codeword Barbarossa* by Barton Whaley (MIT Press, 1973). *The New York Times*, May 6, 1973.

Scarisbrick, J.J. *Henry VIII.* Los Angeles: University of California Press, 1969.

Schorer, Mark. *Sinclair Lewis: An American Life.* New York: McGraw Hill Book Company, Inc., 1961.

Schuyler, Eugene. *Peter The Great.* New York: Charles Scribner's Sons, 1890.

Sheaffer, Louis. *O'Neill: Son and Playwright.* Boston: Little, Brown and Company, 1968.

Sheppard, Stephen. *My Brother's Keeper.* New York: Van Rees Press, 1964.

Sinclair, Upton. *The Cup of Fury.* New York: Hawthorn Books, Inc., 1956.

Smith, Frank. *Tom Paine, Liberator.* New York: Frederick A. Stokes Company, 1938.

Smith, Lacey Baldwin. *Henry VIII: The Mask of Royalty.* London: Jonathan Cape, 1971.

Souvarine, Boris. *Stalin: A Critical Survey of Bolshevism.* New York: Longmans, Green & Co., 1939.

Steiner, Claude. *Games Alcoholics Play: The Analysis of Life Scripts.* New York: Grove Press, Inc., 1971.

Stern, Phillip Van Doren. *The Man Who Killed Lincoln.* New York: The Literary Guild of America, Inc., 1939.

Stringfellow, William, and Towne, Anthony. *The Death and Life of Bishop Pike.* Garden City: Doubleday & Company, Inc., 1976.

Sullivan, Allanna. "Former Ship's Officer Says He Reported Exxon Captain's Drinking, To No Avail." *The Wall Street Journal*, April 11, 1989.

Sullivan, Terry with Maiken, Peter T. *Killer Clown*. New York: Grosset & Dunlap, 1983.

Tarn, W.W. *Alexander The Great*. Boston: Beacon Press, 1948.

Thomsen, Robert. *Bill W.* New York: Harper & Row, 1975.

Time. Obituary: Audie Murphy. June 14, 1971,

Tompkins, Calvin. *Living Well is the Best Revenge*. New York: The Viking Press, 1962.

Tolstoy, Nikolai. *Stalin's Secret War*. London: Jonathan Cape, 1981.

Trice, Michael. *Alcoholism in America*. New York: McGraw Hill, 1966.

Troyat, Henri. *Ivan the Terrible*. New York: Berkley Books, 1986.
------------------ *Peter the Great*. New York: E.P. Dutton, 1987.

Trotsky, Leon. *Stalin: An Appraisal of the Man and His Influence*. New York: Grosset & Dunlap, 1941.

Tucker, Robert C. *Stalin As Revolutionary*. New York: W. W. Norton and Company, 1973.

Turnbull, Andrew. *Thomas Wolfe: A Biography*. New York: Charles Scribner's Sons, 1947.

Ulam, Adam B. *Stalin: The Man and His Era*. New York: The Viking Press, 1973.

Ullman, Albert D. *To Know The Difference*. New York: St. Martin's Press, 1960.

Vaillant, George E., M.D. *The Natural History of Alcoholism*. Cambridge: Harvard University Press, 1983.

van Dorn, Theodore. *Drunk's Diary*. New York: Philosophical Library, 1966.

The Wall Street Journal. "Life in Prison." August 20, 1981.

Wagenknecht, Edward. *Edgar Allan Poe*. New York: Oxford University Press, 1963.

Waite, Robert G.L. *Adolf Hitler: The Psychopathic God*. New York: Basic Books, 1977.

Watkins, Arthur V. *Enough Rope*. Englewood Cliffs: Prentice-Hall, Inc. 1969.

West, Rebecca. *The New Meaning of Treason*. New York: The Viking Press, 1964.

West, Nigel. *Mole-hunt: The Full Story of the Soviet Spy in MI5*. London: Coronet Books, 1987.

Wholey, Dennis. *The Courage To Change*. Boston: Houghton Mifflin Company, 1984.

Wiegall, Arthur. *Alexander The Great*. New York: G.P. Putnam's Sons, 1933.

Williams, Harry T. *Huey Long*. New York: Alfred A. Knopf, 1969.

Williams, Tennessee. *Memoirs*. Garden City: Doubleday & Company, Inc., 1975.

Wilson, William Griffith. *Alcoholism: The Illness*. New York: Alcoholics Anonymous World Services, Inc., (undated).

---------------------------- *The A.A. Way of Life*. New York: Alcoholics Anonymous World Services, Inc., 1967.

Winn, Steven, and Merrill, Davis. *Ted Bundy: The Killer Next Door*. New York: Bantam Books, 1980.

Wise, David. *The Spy Who Got Away: The Inside Story of Edward Lee Harvey, the CIA Agent Who Betrayed His Country's Secrets and Escaped to Moscow*. New York: Random House, 1988.

Witten, Thaddeus. *Commissar*. New York: MacMillan, 1972.

Wright, Peter. *Spy Catcher*. New York: Dell Publishing, 1987.

Wright, William. *Lillian Hellman: The Image, The Woman*. New York: Ballantine Books, 1986.

Yee, Min S., and Layton, Thomas N. *In My Father's House: The Inside Story of the Layton Family and the Reverend Jim Jones*. New York: Holt Rinehart and Winston, 1981.

Index

Don Juanism
(See Sexual aggressiveness)
Donovan, William 142
Dooley, Mr. 83
"Doormatting"
Bankhead, Tallulah 66
symptom 66
Dos Passos, John 94
Dreiser, Theodore 83
"Dry" versus "sober"
AA terminology 7
Berryman, John (on) 91
Crosby, Gary 91
Dederich, Charles E. 125
Ludwig, Arnold M. M.D. (on) 91
O'Neill, Eugene 91-92
Dunne, Peter Finley 83
Eden, Anthony 192
Ego deflation
emphasized by AA 10, 70-72
essential to recovery 122
Fitzgerald, F. Scott 92
role in treatment 70-72
supports inflation idea 10
Ego inflation
caused by alcoholism 13
early start 13
Egomania
caused by alcoholism 9
Eisenhower, Dwight D. 32
Eitner, Horst 49
Eliot, T.S. 93
Elizabeth (daughter of Peter the
Great) 167
Emerson, Ralph Waldo 147
Ervin, Frank 130
Ethical deterioration
Anderson, Robert B. 32, 63
Deaver, Michael 63
symptom 63
Executive alcoholics
Ford, Henry II 148-150
general 148
Extraordinary consumption
(See Tolerance for alcohol)
examples 74-75

Exxon Valdez 63-64
False accusations
Angleton, James Jesus 55
Beethoven, Ludwig von 18, 19
Fickert, Charles M. 28
Ford, Henry II 149
four despots, by 168
Hellman, Lillian 99
Hemingway, Ernest 93-95
Henry VIII 159
Houston, Sam 151
Kilgallen, Dorothy 100, 107n (?)
Long, Huey 21-22
marital infidelity, of 65-66
McCarthy, Joseph 6, 65
Nichols, John 17
O'Neill, Eugene 89
Paine, Thomas 85
Parker, Dorothy 88
Peter the Great 166
Poe, Edgar Allan 86
Stalin, Joseph (See)
symptom explained 23, 65-66
Whitman, Charles 28-30
why used by alcoholics 23
Wolfe, Thomas 87
Family abuse
general 15-17, 136-138
Farley, James 22, 193
Faulkner, John 96
Faulkner, William 11, 83, 94, 95-96
FBI study of serial killers 114-115
Fickert, Charles M. 27-28, 55
Fields, W.C. 80, 84n
First drink
as start of alcoholism 7
Roth, Lillian 4-5
significance 4-5
Fitzgerald, F. Scott 63, 74, 83, 92-
93, 94-95, 105, 113, 199
FitzGerald, Kathleen Whalen,
Ph.D. 9
inherited vulnerability concept 5
Fitzgerald, Zelda 92, 105
Ford, Ford Maddox 93
Ford, Henry II 8, 148-150, 202

PERMISSIONS AND ACKNOWLEDGMENTS

ORDER FORM

Additional copies of VESSELS OF RAGE, ENGINES OF POWER: The
Secret History of Alcoholism may be obtained from your bookseller or directly from the publisher:

Aculeus Press Inc.
P.O. Box 142
Lexington VA 24450

Telephone: 1-800-345-6665 or

1-703-464-4554

Fax: 1-603-357-2073

—— Copies Cloth: $21.95   ISBN-0-9630242-2-1   S&H: $3.50

—— Copies Paper: $12.95   ISBN-0-9630242-4-8   S&H: $2.50

Payment method:

—— Check or money order.   —— Visa or Master Charge.

Name: _____

Address: _____

_____

_____

Credit Card Number: _____

Name on Card: _____

Expiration Date: _____

Virginia residents please add 4.5%.

Volume buyers: contact Aculeus Press for discount schedule.

(This page may be photocopied.)

A SPECIAL REQUEST FROM ACULEUS PRESS

Lexington, Virginia

Dear Reader,

When librarians decide to add new books to their collections they try to select titles that their patrons will read and appreciate. In order to do this they rely, to a large extent, on published reviews to inform them of new and interesting books. Unfortunately, because of the enormous number of books that are now published, reviewers that specialize in screening books for librarians frequently ignore titles published by small independent publishers like Aculeus Press. As a result, librarians do not acquire certain worthwhile books for the simple reason that they are not aware of their existence.

We ask you to help us overcome this serious, and we think unfair, obstacle to dissemination of worthwhile books published by America's small presses.

If you think that others in your community would like to read James Graham's *Vessels of Rage, Engines of Power* why not let your librarian know this? You could telephone your librarian or simply send her or him a photocopy of the following page.

With thanks,

John Allison
Vice President

READER'S LIBRARY RECOMMENDATION

To: _____
    _____
    _____

I strongly recommend that you add James Graham's book
VESSELS OF RAGE, ENGINES OF POWER: The Secret History of
Alcoholism to your collection.

As pointed out by alcoholism specialist Conway Hunter, M.D.,
this is a book that will appeal to "everyone," including
recovered alcoholics, their families, professionals and anyone
else seeking knowledge of this wide-spread disorder.

Psychiatrist Scott C. Guth, M.D., calls it "extremely important... fascinating and chilling."

Former US Senator Harold E. Hughes says it is "a book that
will hold your attention from beginning to end."

I too was fascinated by this highly readable and important
book and think that many of your patrons would benefit from its
availability on your shelves.

Sincerely,

_____

****
ORDERING INFORMATION

Cloth: ISBN-0-9630242-2-1 $21.95

Paper: ISBN-0-9630242-4-8 $12.95

236 pages + xx. Bibliography.   Index.   Publisher's CIP.

Publisher: Aculeus Press Inc.

Available from major library wholesalers.

(This page may be photocopied.)

ANOTHER FASCINATING BOOK
BY THE SAME AUTHOR

If you were intrigued by James Graham's analysis of alcoholism's role in human history, you should also learn about his highly original idea that cancer played a central role in evolution. This proposal, which radically revises neo-Darwinism, was originally published in *Journal of Theoretical Biology*, an influential science journal. Graham thoroughly explains this idea, and argues for its acceptance, in his book *Cancer Selection: The New Theory of Evolution*.

According to Graham's theory, all animals, including humans, owe their very existence to cancer. Although this seems startling and counter-intuitive, the powerful arguments that Graham has included in his book have attracted favorable scientific attention.

Dr. John W. Galloway of Britain's Nuffield Foundation, reviewing the book for *Nature,* the most widely read science journal, said "I agree with him. Evolution by natural selection does not explicitly explain complexity (notwithstanding the eloquence of people such as Richard Dawkins)... I like [the] idea."

Dr. Lotte R. Geller, who teaches biology at the Roeper School for Gifted Students in Bloomfield, Michigan, reviewed Graham's book in *The American Biology Teacher*. She found it "thought provoking... a wonderful challenge in logic and scientific thinking," and recommended that high school and college librarians acquire it.

Another enthusiastic review appeared in *Rapport: The West Coast Review of Books* which awarded it four stars. The reviewer, Brian W. Firth, said Graham was a "master of logical reasoning." He found the book "fascinating for its sheer intellectual virtuosity." Firth noted that Graham had already met the requirement of a peer-reviewed journal but said his book is nonetheless "for the ordinary educated person."

If you are interested in new ideas and would like to read Graham's fascinating new theory of evolution we suggest you order *Cancer Selection: The New Theory of Evolution* from your bookseller or directly from Aculeus Press. For your convenience, we enclose an order form on the next page.

ORDER FORM

Copies of James Graham's CANCER SELECTION: The New Theory of Evolution may be obtained from your bookseller or directly by telephone, fax or mail from the publisher:

Aculeus Press Inc.
P.O. Box 142
Lexington VA 24450

Telephone: 1-800-345-6665 or

1-703-464-4554

Fax: 1-603-357-2073

——— Copies Cloth: $20.00   ISBN-0-9630242-0-5   S&H:$3.50

Payment method:

——— Check or money order.   ——— Visa or Master Charge.

Name: _____

Address: _____

_____

_____

Credit Card Number: _____

Name on Card: _____

Expiration Date: _____

Virginia residents please add 4.5%.

Volume buyers: contact Aculeus Press for discount schedule.

(This page may be photocopied.)